# Children Making Meaning

This ground-breaking text highlights the value of drawing as a meaningful way for children to communicate, demonstrating how it is inextricably linked with children's everyday experiences, thinking processes, imagination, emotions, and learning.

By exploring what intrigues and concerns children, *Children Making Meaning: Exploring Drawings, Narratives, and Identities* demonstrates how drawing is so much more than an insignificant pastime. Illustrated throughout, this book includes examples of children's drawings to explore and explain the processes, relationships, and modes they use, as well as the themes and meanings that emerge from them. Practical case study material illuminates the complexity of children's thinking, intentions, and knowledge as they find creative and individual ways to convey their thoughts, fears, excitements, contentments, and fascinations. This book also explores the relationship between drawing and talk and how children's ongoing drawing-narratives help them to develop and change their meanings as they draw.

Accessibly combining relevant theories with numerous original examples, this essential resource is a must-read for educators and other professionals who use children's drawings in their work. It will also be useful for parents who wish to support their children's drawing activities and extend such opportunities at home.

**Josephine Deguara** is Senior Lecturer in Early Childhood and Primary Education at the University of Malta, Malta.

**Cathy Nutbrown** is Professor of Education at the University of Sheffield, UK.

# Children Making Meaning
Exploring Drawings, Narratives, and Identities

Josephine Deguara and Cathy Nutbrown

LONDON AND NEW YORK

Designed cover image: "Erika and mum before I was born" - by Thea

First published 2025
by Routledge
4 Park Square, Milton Park, Abingdon, Oxon OX14 4RN

and by Routledge
605 Third Avenue, New York, NY 10158

*Routledge is an imprint of the Taylor & Francis Group, an informa business*

© 2025 Josephine Deguara and Cathy Nutbrown

The right of Josephine Deguara and Cathy Nutbrown to be identified as authors of this work has been asserted in accordance with sections 77 and 78 of the Copyright, Designs and Patents Act 1988.

All rights reserved. No part of this book may be reprinted or reproduced or utilised in any form or by any electronic, mechanical, or other means, now known or hereafter invented, including photocopying and recording, or in any information storage or retrieval system, without permission in writing from the publishers.

*Trademark notice:* Product or corporate names may be trademarks or registered trademarks, and are used only for identification and explanation without intent to infringe.

*British Library Cataloguing-in-Publication Data*
A catalogue record for this book is available from the British Library

ISBN: 9781032548050 (hbk)
ISBN: 9781032548043 (pbk)
ISBN: 9781003427582 (ebk)

DOI: 10.4324/9781003427582

Typeset in Galliard
by codeMantra

For our families for their support.
For Luke, Thea, and Bertly for being part of this journey.
For all young children who deserve to be listened to.

# Contents

*List of figures* ix
*List of tables* xiii
*Acknowledgments* xiv
*About this book* xv
*Companion website* xvii
*About the authors* xviii

1 Young children's meaning-making 1

2 Interpreting children's drawings from a social semiotics perspective 9

3 Children drawing meanings 18

4 Researching children's drawings 31

5 Luke's story 44

6 Thea's story 70

7 Bertly's story 94

8 Form and content in children's drawings 115

9 Drawing identities 128

10 Love, power, good and evil 155

11 Drawing, talk, narrative, and collaboration 174

viii  *Contents*

12  Children's funds of knowledge: pedagogical considerations    191

13  Listening to children drawing    208

*References*    217
*Index of authors*    237
*Index of subjects*    241

# Figures

| | | |
|---|---|---|
| 1.1 | *Only Me (LH11)* – by Luke | 1 |
| 2.1 | *A Fighter Aeroplane (LS23)* – by Luke | 9 |
| 3.1 | *The Mushrooms (LS4)* – by Luke | 18 |
| 4.1 | *Ben Ten Fight (LS18)* – by Luke | 31 |
| 5.1 | *Me Carrying a Bag Full of Candy (LH49)* – by Luke | 44 |
| 5.2 | Luke's *Data Cross-grid* represents his home (blue) and school (black) drawings | 46 |
| 5.3 | A summary of Luke's *Data Cross-grid* with his preferred drawing pattern marked with a red circle | 47 |
| 5.4 | A sample of Luke's drawings in *simple-to-complex modes* and corresponding themes | 49 |
| 5.5 | Luke during the process and narration of the drawing *Ben Ten fight (LS18)* | 51 |
| 5.6 | *Cutting the Bad Guy Out 1 (LH21)* full drawing [1], and with the "bad guy" cut out [2] | 53 |
| 5.7 | *A Worm (LS16)* – by Luke | 55 |
| 5.8 | Sample of Luke's drawings illustrating *People* | 57 |
| 5.9 | Static drawings of *Family* members – by Luke | 58 |
| 5.10 | *My Family with Matthias Playing Football (LH1)* [1], *Mum, Dad and I Eating Ice-cream (LH15)* [2] the family in action – by Luke | 59 |
| 5.11 | *My Mum and I Walking in the Dark (LH18)* [1], *My Mum and I Playing with the Ball (LH38)* [2], *Luke and Mum Fighting on a Picnic (LH54)* [3] – by Luke | 60 |
| 5.12 | *My Mother Tied Up (LS8)* – by Luke | 61 |
| 5.13 | *Luke and Matthias Playing Swordfight with Wii (LH53)* – by Luke | 62 |
| 5.14 | *Throwing Pink Goo at Jacob (LH26)* – by Luke | 63 |
| 5.15 | *Matthias in a Cage (LH20)* – by Luke | 64 |
| 5.16 | *Two of Me (LH28)* – by Luke | 65 |
| 5.17 | *Me Stretching (LH25)* – by Luke | 65 |
| 5.18 | *Nicholai and I (LH39)* – by Luke | 66 |
| 5.19 | Examples of drawings illustrating different *Weather and Sky* – by Luke | 67 |
| 6.1 | *A Man Dressed as a Koala Bear (TS1)* – by Thea | 70 |

x  Figures

| | | |
|---|---|---|
| 6.2 | Thea's *Data Cross-grid* represents her home (orange) and school (purple) drawings | 73 |
| 6.3 | Thea's *Data Cross-grid* with her preferred drawing pattern marked with a red circle | 74 |
| 6.4 | Examples of Thea's drawings in *simple-to-complex modes* and *themes* corresponding to each section of the grid | 75 |
| 6.5 | *Travelling in a Car and Aeroplane (TS40)* in *simple mode* and *complex* theme [1], with Neil's similar drawing [2] | 78 |
| 6.6 | Snapshots of playful interactions between Thea and Neil in *TS40* | 79 |
| 6.7 | *Erica and Mum before I was Born (TH8)* – by Thea | 81 |
| 6.8 | *An Aeroplane that Flies (TS23)* – by Thea | 83 |
| 6.9 | Examples of Thea's drawings on the theme of *Animals* | 85 |
| 6.10 | *Animals Hide and Seek (TH27)* – by Thea | 86 |
| 6.11 | *Myself (TH13)* – by Thea | 87 |
| 6.12 | *Fish in an Aquarium (TH24)* – by Thea | 88 |
| 6.13 | *The Crab (TS5)* [1] and *Me as a Crab (TS9)* [2] – by Thea | 89 |
| 6.14 | Examples of Thea's drawings on the theme of *People* | 91 |
| 6.15 | *Dad Waking Up (TH36)* – by Thea | 92 |
| 7.1 | *Fireworks (BS16)* – by Bertly | 94 |
| 7.2 | Bertly's *Data Cross-grid* represents his home (orange) and school (green) drawings | 96 |
| 7.3 | A summary of Bertly's *Data Cross-grid* with his preferred drawing pattern marked with a red circle | 97 |
| 7.4 | Examples of Bertly's drawings in *simple-to-complex modes* and *themes* correspond to each section of the grid | 99 |
| 7.5 | *The Choo-choo Train (BH23)* – by Bertly | 101 |
| 7.6 | *A Party at Sea (BS11)* – by Bertly | 105 |
| 7.7 | *An Octopus (BS7)* – by Bertly | 107 |
| 7.8 | Examples of Bertly's drawings illustrate the theme of *People* | 108 |
| 7.9 | *Pink Panther for my Birthday (BH32)* – by Bertly | 109 |
| 7.10 | *A Portrait of Myself with a Moustache (BS13)* – by Bertly | 110 |
| 7.11 | *Bertly dressed as Father Christmas and Jael as Queen of Hearts (BH24)* – by Bertly | 111 |
| 7.12 | Examples of Bertly's drawings of *Animals* | 112 |
| 7.13 | *A Shark in the Sea (BH14)* – by Bertly | 113 |
| 7.14 | *A Whale at the Beach (BH18)* – by Bertly | 114 |
| 8.1 | *The Reindeer (TH10)* – by Thea | 115 |
| 8.2 | A summarised representation of the three children's drawing preferences | 116 |
| 8.3 | *The Lobster Story (LS11)* – by Luke | 120 |
| 8.4 | *Our House (TH7)* [1] and *Dad Coming Home (TH20)* [2] – by Thea | 122 |
| 8.5 | *My Family (TH22)* [1] and *(TH32)* [2] – by Thea | 123 |

*Figures* xi

| | | |
|---|---|---|
| 8.6 | The interplay between *semiotic style*, *configuration style*, *types of drawing*, and *drawer patterns* to form the drawer's identity | 125 |
| 9.1 | *Only Me (LH11)* – by Luke | 128 |
| 9.2 | *My Face (TS8)* – by Thea | 130 |
| 9.3 | *Things Falling in my Dream (TS16)* – by Thea | 130 |
| 9.4 | *Myself (LS12)* – by Luke | 133 |
| 9.5 | *A Ship (TS38)* – by Thea | 134 |
| 9.6 | Luke, Bertly, and Thea in fantasy roles. *I am Ben Ten (LH23)* [1], *Cutting Out the Bad Guy 2 (LH22)* [2], *Killing a Dragon (BS4)* [3], *Father Christmas and Jael the Queen of Hearts (BH24)* [4], *Me as a Crab (TS9)* [5] and *The Fairy Princess (TS10)* [6] | 135 |
| 9.7 | *My Family and I Shooting the Bad Guys (LH17)* – by Luke | 136 |
| 9.8 | Drawings communicating Thea's fears. *A Monster Story (TH35)* [1], *The Monster (TS32)* [2], *The Interactive Whiteboard Activity (TS31)* [3], *The Wicked Witch (TS21)* [4] | 138 |
| 9.9 | *A Shark in the Sea (BH21)* – by Bertly | 139 |
| 9.10 | *A Nice Scribbled Rainbow (BH12)* – by Bertly | 140 |
| 9.11 | Drawings reflecting Luke's happiness *Mum and I (LH39)* [1], *An Ice-cream in the Sun (LH40)* [2] | 141 |
| 9.12 | Wishes for pets. Luke's *Cousin James Jumping in the Pool with a Dog (LH51)* [1], Bertly's *A Dog in a Box (BH11)* [2] and Thea's *Animals Not Allowed (TH37)* [3] | 142 |
| 9.13 | *Jacob in a Volcano (LH31)* – by Luke | 143 |
| 9.14 | Bertly's *(BS20)* [1] and Thea's wishes *(TS30)* [2] *(TS18)* [3], *(TH3)* [4], *(TS18)* [5], *(TS39)* [6], and *(TS44)* [7] | 144 |
| 9.15 | *Happy Birthday Grandma (BH34)* [1], *Balloons for Grandma's Birthday (BH33)* [2] and *More Balloons for Grandma's Birthday (BH35)* [3] – by Bertly | 146 |
| 9.16 | *A Birthday Card for Eman (TH5)*, outside [1] and inside [2]; *A Birthday Card for Belle (TH28)*, outside [3] and inside [4] – by Thea | 147 |
| 9.17 | *A Butterfly-monster Story (TS28)* – by Thea | 149 |
| 9.18 | *The Aquarium Shop (TH23)* – by Thea | 149 |
| 9.19 | *An Octopus for You (BH28)* – by Bertly | 150 |
| 9.20 | *The Storm (BH16)* – by Bertly | 151 |
| 9.21 | *Daddy's Aeroplane (TS26)* – by Thea | 153 |
| 10.1 | *A car with a heart (TH4)* – by Thea | 155 |
| 10.2 | *A Heart (BH15)* – by Bertly | 156 |
| 10.3 | *Grass, Sea, Sky and a Mountain (TS24)* [1], *Frogs in the Sea (TH19)* [2], *A Snail (TH12)* [3], *A Flower (TH21)* [4], *Flying Hearts (TS22)* [5] - by Thea | 157 |
| 10.4 | *Kisses (BH4)* – by Bertly | 158 |

| | | |
|---|---|---|
| 10.5 | *Mummy and I (LH6)* [1], *You and I (LH37)* [2], *A Cake for Mama (LS19)* [3] – by Luke | 160 |
| 10.6 | *My Loveable Grandpa (TH9)* – by Thea | 161 |
| 10.7 | *Me in a Muddy Puddle and Lots of Birds (TH14)* – by Thea | 161 |
| 10.8 | *Mum and Dad* (BH5) – by Bertly | 162 |
| 10.9 | *Rings, Hearts and Flowers for Daniel (TH16)* – by Thea | 163 |
| 10.10 | *Matthias, Mum and I (LH14)* – by Luke | 164 |
| 10.11 | *Killing a Dragon (BS4)* [1] and *When a Dragon Came to School (BS17)* [2] – by Bertly | 166 |
| 10.12 | *The Good and the Evil (LS1)* [1], *A Fight between Good and Evil (LS14)* [2], *The Good Guy and the Bad Guy (LS1)* [3] – by Luke | 167 |
| 10.13 | *Tying the Blue Lady (LH24)* – by Luke | 170 |
| 10.14 | *I am Ben Ten (LH23)* – by Luke | 172 |
| 11.1 | *In the Garden 2 – Talking Animals (LH30)* – by Luke | 174 |
| 11.2 | *Two Diamonds in the Sky (LH36)* – by Luke | 179 |
| 11.3 | *The Snail (LS10)* [1] – by Luke; *The Snail (TS12)* [2] – by Thea | 180 |
| 11.4 | *A Fan (TS20)* [1] – by Thea, *An Octopus (BS7)* [2] – by Bertly, *A Hanger for Presents for my Friends* [3] – by Sandra | 186 |
| 11.5 | *A Party at Sea (BS11)* [1] – by Bertly, *People Flying in the Sky* [2] – by Sandra | 188 |
| 12.1 | *A MacDonald's Box (TH26)* – by Thea | 191 |
| 12.2 | *A Wine Bottle and an Ice-cream (TH17)* – by Thea | 194 |
| 12.3 | *Grass in our Field (BH30)* [1], *Pizza (BH1)* [2], *My Mum Driving (BH37)* [3] – by Bertly | 195 |
| 12.4 | *The Holy Mary (TH2)* – by Thea | 198 |
| 12.5 | *On the Gozo Ship (LH2)* – by Luke | 199 |
| 12.6 | *Me in the Rain (TH15)* [1] – by Thea; *Heavy Rain (BS12)* [2], *Tank in the Wind (BH9)* [3] – by Bertly | 201 |
| 12.7 | *A tunnel to the farm (TS29)* [1]; *Two churches, a roundabout and a swimming pool (TH33)* [2] – by Thea | 202 |
| 12.8 | *Presents and Fruit (TS19)* [1] – by Thea; *Jael the Witch (BH19)* [2]; *An Easter Egg (BH31)* [3] – by Bertly; *An Easter Egg for Me, Sausage Rolls for Mama (LH32)* [4] – by Luke | 204 |
| 12.9 | *Jack and the Beanstalk (BH7)* [1]; *Pinocchio (BH26)* [2]; *Pink Panther (BH27)* [3] – by Bertly | 205 |
| 13.1 | *Me (LS25)* – by Luke | 208 |

# Tables

| | | |
|---|---|---|
| 4.1 | A summary of the three children's number of drawings by duration and context | 40 |
| 4.2 | The *Data Cross-grid* indicates the integration of *Simple* and *Complex Modes* and *Themes* | 41 |
| 4.3 | The *Inventory of Content* identifies themes and sub-themes in the drawings of the three children | 42 |
| 8.1 | Summary of the children's semiotic and configuration styles, indicating drawer profiles | 116 |
| 8.2 | Drawer identities of Luke, Bertly, and Thea | 125 |
| 8.3 | The *Inventory of Content* shows the number of occurrences by each theme for each child | 127 |

# Acknowledgments

We extend our sincere gratitude to the three participant children, Luke, Thea, and Bertly along with their families for their unwavering commitment, enthusiasm, and trust in the study.

Our thanks also extend to the Head of School and Kindergarten Educator who supported the study.

We are also grateful to all the children who attended Luke's, Thea's, and Bertly's class, for their eagerness and interest to engage with the study.

We would also like to thank Ms Nicole Pace, of the University of Malta for her invaluable work on the images. Thanks to Mr Gabriel Spiteri, of the University of Malta for his work on the companion website to the book.

We express our sincere appreciation to the University of Malta for their financial support, towards the data collection process of this study, and to the Early Childhood Education Research Group at The University of Sheffield, UK.

# About this book

This book focuses on the value of drawing as an important meaning-making tool, and mode of communication for young children.

Taking a social semiotics perspective, we investigate children's representations around their social and cultural interests. Using 223 drawings from an original study, we examine and explain the ordinariness and the extraordinariness in children's everyday drawings. We explore how young children use drawings to make and communicate meaning, their drawing processes, the modes they use to create their drawings, and the themes and meanings that emerge from those drawings. Original case study material illuminates the complexity of children's thought, design, and determination as they find creative and individual ways to convey their thoughts, fears, excitements, contentments and fascinations. We also explore the relationship between drawing and talk, and how children's ongoing drawing-narratives help them to develop and adapt their meanings as they draw.

From a children's rights standpoint, the book promotes the use and value of drawing as a mode for children to meaningfully communicate what intrigues and concerns them, and shows how drawing can lead to a valuable pedagogical approach. Uniquely, the book presents an original tool to analyse children's drawings, which can also be adapted to understand how children make use of other media (such as construction play) to communicate what they know and understand as well as how they feel and what they imagine. The book also contributes to international research and practice focusing on young children as participants in their own learning. It provides an example of how research can be conducted with young participants, how their opinions and voices can be respected in research processes, and how ethical issues can be identified and positively navigated.

Providing an authentic, in-depth account of the form and content in young children's drawings at home and in their early years setting, the book opens up an understanding of children's funds of knowledge, and how such knowledge can be used by parents and early years educators to validate and extend children's learning. In linking research and practice the book provides educational professionals with a deeper understanding of how understanding of children's experiences and thinking can be used to inform curriculum planning, pedagogical practice and assessment of children's knowledge and understanding of their worlds. It further demonstrates how, provided with more information about the importance of drawing, parents support children's drawing activity and extend the drawing opportunities they offer their children at home.

The book shows how insights gained from understanding children as they draw, can be used to enhance children's lives and learning, as adults sensitively interpret what young children are trying to say, and use those insights to facilitate young children's holistic living, development and learning. Combining accessible and relevant theories with numerous original examples, the book provides readers with an insightful approach to understanding children's drawings and shows how drawing is inextricably linked with children's everyday experiences, their thinking processes, their emotions, their rights, and their learning; in other words, who they are.

# Companion website

A website supporting this book provides further information and resources related to each chapter. Dedicated pages for each chapter include:

- Chapter overview
- Drawings
- Film clips
- Additional resources
- Links to downloadable information
- Further reading.

These are available at: https://sites.google.com/view/childrenmakingmeaning

# About the authors

**Josephine Deguara** is Senior Lecturer in Early Childhood and Primary Education within the Faculty of Education at the University of Malta. Her research over the last 16 years has focused on curriculum philosophy and pedagogy, play and learning, children's rights and children's voices, policy and practice, as well as language use in diverse early childhood and primary education settings. She also has a long-held research interest in children's drawings, identity as well as children's rights and participatory approaches to research. She currently serves on the Faculty of Research Ethics Committee (FREC), at the University of Malta, ensuring the ethics and integrity of research. Josephine has worked on several funded projects. She has presented several papers at international conferences and is the author of several journal articles, book chapters, research reports, and book reviews. She is a co-editor of two book chapters: *Innovations in Pedagogical Practice and Curriculum Development in Higher Education: Contemporary Global Perspectives*, Emerald (2025) and *Innovations in Assessment, Student Experiences and Professional Development in Higher Education: Contemporary Global Perspectives*, Emerald (2025).

**Cathy Nutbrown** is Professor of Education in the School of Education at The University of Sheffield and President of Early Education, UK. Her research over the last 30 years has focused on working with parents to support young children's literacy development and on young children's voices, their learning, their inclusion, and their rights. Cathy chaired the *Nutbrown Review of the Early Years Workforce in England* in 2012, which aimed to influence a government policy change to improve educators' qualifications. She has won an ESRC Award for *Research with Outstanding Impact on Society* and a Nursery World *Lifetime Achievement Award*. She is the author of over 150 publications, including *Threads of Thinking*, Sage (2011); *Early Literacy Work with Families* (with Hannon & Morgan), Sage, (2005); and *Early Childhood Educational Research*, Sage, (2019), and editor of *Early Childhood Education: Current Realities and Future Possibilities*, Sage, (2023). In 2023, she was awarded a Damehood for *Services to Early Childhood Education*.

# 1 Young children's meaning-making

Figure 1.1 *Only Me (LH11)* – by Luke.

## Introduction

Most children begin to draw from a very young age – often making their earliest marks within their first year. Drawing comes naturally to most children (Farokhi & Hashemi, 2011; Lyon, 2020), with many enjoying

DOI: 10.4324/9781003427582-1

some form of drawing daily (Kim & Han, 2022). Yet, many adults consider drawing a superficial activity, useful merely to occupy children. So, children's meanings can remain obscure to adults who do not know how to understand their drawings (Zlateva, 2019). This book explores how children use drawings to communicate, explore concepts, and construct their identities (Goodman, 2018). They can communicate their wishes, emotions, concerns, and interests as they draw themselves in the present (Figure 1.1), the past, or in imagined identities in the future. This book shows how children's drawings reflect the connections they make between their thinking, social contexts, knowledge, and experiences. We explore how children use drawings as play, to interact and develop social relationships (Capurso et al., 2021), and as a key communication tool (Türkcan, 2013).

Adults in young children's lives – parents, family members, and early childhood educators[1] – should provide young children with opportunities to communicate through different modes, as in Malaguzzi's metaphor of "the hundred languages of children" (Edwards et al., 1998, p. 12). These multiple "languages" of expression include play, model-making, painting, drawing, talking, and writing. Children's drawings have, for decades, been of interest to a wide range of professionals, including researchers, psychologists, art therapists, teachers and play specialists. Throughout this book, we respect and value the remarkableness of children's drawings and their right to have their voices heard as we seek to understand more of children's worlds (Zlateva, 2019) and appreciate something of their unique ways of being.

Recognising drawing as a semiotic activity, we consider children's drawings as expressions of their meaning-making (see Ahn & Filipenko, 2007; Hall, 2008, 2010b; Hopperstad, 2008a, 2010; Wright, 2010a; Coates & Coates, 2011). We explore the meanings children develop and communicate through their every day, free drawings. Drawing is seen as a tool that children use to create meaning (Vygotsky, 1978), whereby they convey their thoughts, knowledge, experiences, and imaginations. In drawing, children interact with others: family and friends, at home, school, and in their community, as their socio-cultural contexts influence their interactions, creations, and communications.

This book explores how three, four-year-old, Maltese children, Luke, Thea, and Bertly,[2] who attended the same kindergarten classroom[3,4] used different modes to draw. In-depth analyses of their drawings and drawing interactions have illuminated the children's interests and concerns. This uncovers some unique meanings they attributed to their drawings, how they communicated those meanings to others, and the socio-cultural influences of drawings. Based on a four-month study[5] yielding 223 free drawings, 98 hours of video-recorded observations, the children's own drawing-related narratives, and drawing-related conversations with the children, we offer our analysis of the children's drawing meanings and processes.

This chapter discusses the theoretical underpinnings of this book, including theoretical tools used to interpret children's meanings. Here we discuss:

- A definition of drawing
- Drawing as communication
- Drawing as meaning-making
- Theoretical perspectives on children's drawings

## What is drawing?

Drawing has been defined as a creative activity that is "deeply resonant with the expressive side of personality and feeling and therefore having the potential for interaction" (Paine, 1997, p. 147). It is considered an "elementary form of expression" (Eisner, 2013, p. 13) that allows children to creatively develop their imaginations, emotional responses, and personalities. Machón (2013, p. 77) defined drawings as "graphic representations ... the depiction of an object, situation or event which may or may not be preset." Drawing has variously been described as a product, a process, and an expression of emotions and relationships, represented by making meaningful marks (Kress, 2000b; Albers, 2007; Hall, 2008; Coates & Coates, 2011; Adams, 2012). Children's drawings are multimodal artefacts, through which they interpret and reinterpret the meanings in their drawings to shape and translate their thoughts; a visual language that helps children to communicate what they might not easily express otherwise (Clark, 2005).

Our conceptualisation of drawing adopts a theory of social semiotics (Kress, 1997, 2010; Kress & Jewitt, 2003), and our understanding of drawing involves children's construction, interpretation, and communication of meanings. Thus, we consider drawing as a spontaneous and complex mode of communication that children intertwine with other modes, such as talking, writing, cutting, and glueing, to create a "rich mêlée of meaning-making" (Anning & Ring, 2004, p. 117). A social semiotics discourse considers both the product and process of drawing to be significant in uncovering children's multiple layers of meaning-making (Frisch, 2006; Hope, 2008). We consider each drawing as a triad of *form*, *content*, and *meaning*. In our description of the physical aspect of drawing (*form*), we define young children's drawings as two-dimensional "texts" that represent images, graphics, or mark-makings (*content*) that they create on paper using one or more media. Children's drawings are a form of social communication, so drawing is a means of knowing, understanding, thinking, and feeling to communicate the self (*meaning*). Children engage in an often unconventional "constructive process of thinking in action, rather than a developing ability to make visual reference to objects in the world" (Cox, 2005a, p. 123) which frequently have elements of invention and challenge the accepted.

Our exploration of children's drawings takes the form of a "contextual drawing analysis" (Frisch, 2006, p. 76), focusing on the ordinary and extraordinary made freely as they are inspired to do. During their processes of drawing, children develop continuous and interchanging dialogue with themselves, the image they create, the modes and materials they use, the context, their experiences, and the people who interact with them. Drawing here is a language for symbolising and meaningfully communicating children's world to others (Cox, 2005a; Leigh & Heid, 2008; Wright, 2011).

## Drawing as a visual language of communication

When children are free to draw, they can communicate whatever is important or of interest to them (Walker, 2007; Farokhi & Hashemi, 2011). Drawing, unlike verbal and written modes of communication – allows children to express graphically what might otherwise be difficult to express. Thus, drawing is a communication tool through which children can voice their thoughts (Bland, 2018) and express their worlds to others (Farokhi & Hashemi, 2011; Wang & Brown, 2019). Young children take drawing seriously, so their drawings can expose children's insights as they identify, process, synthesise, and represent their perceptions of themselves, others, and the world (Sunday, 2017). Drawings can offer adults a deeper understanding of what children know and experience and sometimes, how they think or feel (Lamm et al., 2019), and they are useful to child psychologists and counsellors seeking to understand children's fears and difficulties and for understanding children's perspectives (see Blagdanic et al., 2019; Lamm et al., 2019; Kim & Han, 2022).

Drawing, combined with children's narratives, takes the forms of play and storytelling, as children meaningfully express their thoughts and perspectives (Bruner, 1986; Einarsdottir et al., 2009). Drawings sometimes portray imaginings as children try to create alternative scenarios. Drawing can be useful for children who are reluctant to speak or have yet to develop the language they need, making drawing an important tool for representation and a rich means of communication (Capurso et al., 2022).

From a social semiotics perspective, drawing is an essential component of multimodal meaning-making, conveying meaning to the drawer and others (Wright, 2011; Türkcan, 2013; Soundy, 2015). Children's "multisemiotic" drawings (Kress, 1997, p. 79) include two or more semiotic resources (for example, drawing and sticking) to create and communicate a meaningful representation. In terms of social semiotics, children's drawings are valued as a complex process of symbolisation as well as a product. When they draw, children use multiple signs to *internalise* their concepts and *externalise* their representations (see Kress, 1997; Davis, 2005; Hall, 2010b) in a "tangible and permanent form" (Thompson, 1995, p. 11). Children often combine talk and drawing to convey their ideas and interests (Wright, 2011); thus, drawing is a complex process with thought, body, and emotions in interplay (Wright, 2003, 2007), as children's ideas become integral to their interactions. This takes drawing from "art" to thinking and meaning-making, which informs how we approach understanding children's drawings, what children say, and truly "hear" their voices.

## Drawing as a mode of meaning-making

Within a social semiotics framework, drawing is seen as a form of meaning-making, linking visual literacy to oracy and other modalities (Kress & Van Leeuwen, 2001). Children's drawings can be foundational to alternative ways of representing and communicating knowledge and understanding (Dyson, 1993a). When children draw for meaning, they are situating themselves in the world, using drawing to express themselves as they creatively respond to their encounters (Souzandehfar & Soozandehfar, 2020).

Children make meaning in their drawings by including modalities of talk, gesture, and play, thus extending and embellishing their drawings (Kress, 2010; Soundy, 2015). As children apply a multiplicity of modes to their drawings, "meanings are made, distributed, received, interpreted and remade through many representational communicative modes – not just through language – whether as speech or writing" (Jewitt, 2009a, p. 14). Within multimodal ensembles, drawings, narratives, vocalisations, gestures, and facial expressions are intertwined as children communicate their meanings. If children can choose the modes that best fit their meaning-making, they can better express themselves. At times, children explore the "semiotic potentialities" (Mavers, 2011, p. 37) of their drawing: attributing changed and alternative meanings to the same sign, they change interpretations of the same drawing, altering their intent and narrative accordingly. Within this social semiotic approach, children are influenced by the signs and messages that are immediately available within their social and cultural contexts; they are *sign-makers* and *meaning-makers* who use the resources at hand. Thus, a child's drawing goes beyond a created image to become a purposeful mode invested with signs and layers of meaning. Embedded within a social semiotic approach, the aim here is to "investigate meaningfulness" in a "cohesive orchestration of meaning" (Mavers, 2011, pp. 38 & 45).

## Using theories to interpret children's drawings

Any understanding of children's drawings must be informed by the sociocultural contexts in which they live. Thus, in addition to a theory of social semiotics, we draw and build on theories that stem from sociocultural theory (Vygotsky, 2012), the neo-Vygotskian concept of *perezhivanie* (Vygotsky, 1994), and funds of knowledge (Moll et al., 1992) to interpret children's drawings as meaningful signs.

### Socio-cultural theory and children's drawings

From a socio-cultural theoretical perspective (Bruner, 1996; Vygotsky, 2012), learning, development, and meaning are intertwined with children's social and cultural worlds (Vygotsky, 1978; Kozulin et al., 2003). Children create their drawings based on their knowledge, experiences, imagination, and environment. Vygotsky (1978) posits that through their drawings, children process their reality as they construct new meanings deeply situated in, and reflective of, their socio-cultural contexts. The interconnections between children, their social environments, other people, and the drawings they are creating are critical to this socio-cultural view (Brooks, 2009b; Malin, 2013). A socio-cultural perspective holds that amalgamating social structures, cultural mediation, modes of participation, and continuous deliberation between individuals helps to create meaning that is inextricably intertwined with and dependent upon the contexts in which they occur (Rose et al., 2006; Berthelsen, 2009).

For socio-cultural theorists, the interaction between children, their cultures, and geo-contexts influences children's thinking processes, helping them to acquire new insights about themselves and new knowledge of the world (Vygotsky, 1997). Thus, children repeat or reflect on their cultural worlds; they process, reinterpret, and construct new meanings and understandings of familiar cultural constructs and signify them by drawing (Lähdesmäki et al., 2022). This theoretical positioning is mirrored on two levels in this book. First, we show how children can be *offered opportunities to create and express* their thoughts and meanings through their drawings (Hall, 2008; Einarsdóttir et al., 2009; Coates & Coates, 2011). Second, we explore the *influences of the interactions and contexts* on the children's drawings to emphasise how meaning-making is influenced and processed from a socio-cultural perspective (Lähdesmäki et al., 2022). If we want to interpret children's drawings, we must have some understanding of children's socio-cultural contexts and their intentions (Podobnik et al., 2021).

Our observations of children's drawings show the value of socio-cultural theory. We stress the importance of getting to know children, their families, friends, and the everyday contexts of home and school. As well as watching children draw, it is important to *listen* to them drawing, because their narrations add meaning to their drawings. Drawing-narrations include whatever children want to say to accompany and extend their drawings. Meaning-making is a dynamic process that occurs in interaction with socio-cultural contexts, where children's drawings are influenced by their everyday experiences, relationships (Smith, 2007), and imaginations. Drawing can be considered a *portal* to children's minds and lived experiences; if we know how to look and learn from them, children's drawings can offer insights into their thinking and their knowing. The neo-Vygotskian concept of *Perezhivanie* as an "intensely-emotional-lived-through-experience" (Ferholt, 2010, p. 164) closely relates to socio-cultural theory (Blunden, 2016; Christodoulakis et al., 2021). Vygotsky (1994) explained *Perezhivanie*[6] as grounded in emotion, where the self, "I" is represented in connection with emotional experience. When children interconnect with each other and within their environments (people, objects, and events), they develop as socially connected individuals (Blunden, 2014).

### Funds of knowledge and children's drawing

Informed by a sociocultural perspective, a theory of funds of knowledge refers to the value of "historically accumulated and culturally developed bodies of knowledge and skills essential for household or individual functioning and well-being" (Moll, 2019, p. 133). This includes knowledge of the social history of families, their work skills and strategies, routines, rituals, and leisure activities that occur within a child's home and community (Riojas-Cortez, 2001; González et al., 2005a). It also includes daily household practices and domestic chores, cultural and cognitive resources, cultural traits, languages, beliefs, and cultural values (Moll et al., 1992; Hedges et al., 2011), ways of doing things, thinking and learning, and attitudes and approaches to learning (Moll, 2000). Children's engagement with popular culture, social media, digital technologies, and games at home and within their communities also contributes to their funds of knowledge (Hedges, 2011; Chesworth, 2021). In short, funds of knowledge are children's personal store cupboards of wisdom, stocked with what they have garnered from all they have experienced. Some children's store cupboards are packed full, others less so, depending on the richness of their socio-cultural lives, but every store cupboard holds rich resources for future use, which families and educators should understand and respect as part of children's unique development.

Through their social relationships and connections with people, places, and events in their lives, children build their funds of knowledge. Acquired within the social and cultural context of their homes, schools, and communities, funds of knowledge are drawn upon by children to actively participate in their families and communities and contribute to their identities and sense of belonging (Riojas-Cortez, 2001; Chesworth, 2021). Adopting a positive view of children's diverse home backgrounds and cultures, a funds of knowledge perspective acknowledges that households are "repositories of knowledge" (González et al., 2005, p. 26) rich in cultural capital (Moll et al., 1992). Children are competent and knowledgeable; their individual lived experiences are personal repositories of knowledge. Through inter-generational home and community experiences, children interpret and make meaning of their world, which they then bring to their play, drawings, and other experiences in school. Thus, the concept of funds of knowledge respects children's understanding of their cultural contexts (Hedges et al., 2011). Through engagement in shared experiences and opportunities, children continually extend their thinking. As children acquire new knowledge and develop social relationships, they use their funds of knowledge to generate their own "working theories" (Hedges & Jones, 2012, p. 32). Their ideas are often used in drawing to re-interpret information and evolve their thinking and understanding (Hedges & Jones, 2012; Chesworth, 2016).

Adults who appreciate the thinking underpinning children's funds of knowledge and the resources, norms, and rituals in families, can better understand the children's meaningful connections in their drawings (D'warte & Woodrow, 2023). This book offers an original interpretation of how children's funds of knowledge illuminate how children make sense of their "culturally situated social understandings" (Chesworth, 2016, p. 303) within their homes and communities. Taking a funds of knowledge approach positions us to value children's socially and culturally diverse experiences.

### Sociocultural theory and funds of knowledge connections

From a socio-cultural theoretical perspective, children's drawings arise from the socio-cultural contexts of their lived experiences and imaginations. The theory of funds of knowledge values all that children learn from their socio-cultural contexts.

The relationship between socio-cultural theory, funds of knowledge, and social semiotics, in combination, come together in children's meaning-making through drawings. Inspired by the work of Cope and Kalantzis (2000), Einarsdottir et al., (2009), and The New London Group (1996, 2000), our thinking in this book is positioned within what Unsworth (2001, p. 15) calls the "socio-cultural construct of literacy." As such, we merge socio-cultural and social semiotics theories (Chapter 2), which recognise the importance of children's interactions with their social and cultural worlds and their meaningful understandings and representations of them (Lähdesmäki et al., 2022)

### Notes

1. In both our countries (Malta and England), people who are responsible for young children and their care have different roles. For the sake of clarity, we use the terms "educator" and "teacher" (unless otherwise specified) to embrace all the different roles of those who work with young children, including psychologists, therapists, and other professionals.
2. These are the children's real names – see Chapter 4 for justification.
3. Children aged three to five years old attend Kindergarten classes in Malta, which are grouped by age. The children of this study attended Kindergarten Class II, for four- to five-year-old children.
4. Kindergarten settings are, in the main, situated within primary schools in Malta. Thus, we will be using the terms Kindergarten (KG) setting or school interchangeably.
5. Conducted by Deguara (2015).
6. For further exploration of *Perezhivanie*, refer to the Companion website. https://sites.google.com/view/childrenmakingmeaning

# 2 Interpreting children's drawings from a social semiotics perspective

*Figure 2.1* A Fighter Aeroplane (LS23) – by Luke.

## Interpreting children's drawings

This chapter explains how we use the theory of social semiotics to interpret children's drawings. Considering children's drawings as sign-making, we first define multimodality and then discuss how children use multiple modes to create meaningful signs. Elaborating on the *form* and *content* of sign-making and how such signs are interpreted, we argue that sign-making in children's drawings is a social process influenced by and reflecting a child's socio-cultural contexts. We next consider how young children portray their experiences in drawings that hold multiple layers of meaning. Regarding drawing as a visual language (Hall,

DOI: 10.4324/9781003427582-2

2009) which children use to communicate their meanings, we conclude this chapter by describing meaning-making from a social semiotics perspective and how children's drawings are often considered to be visual metaphors.

## What is multimodality?

Modes are simply those things that are used for meaning-making, for example, a pencil and paper for drawing.[1] Multimodal approaches use and coordinate several modes of representing and communicating a unified meaning (Kessler, 2022). A social semiotic approach to multimodality perceives children's drawings as signs, made using different modes to create meaning (Kress et al., 2001; Bezemer et al., 2012)[2]. Stein (2008, p. 1) suggests that multimodality is a "communicational ensemble"; for example, a child may add stickers and feathers to a crayon drawing to make a single meaning of a bird; their ensemble (the bird) is a combination of their choice of modes (crayon, stickers, and feathers) in a unique unit of meaning (Graham & Benson, 2010). Examples of semiotic modes include speaking, gesture, facial expression, drawing, and other visual modes where, for example, an image might be used with verbal or written text, vocalisation, and gestures. If we think of multimodality as interaction (Norris, 2004; Seizov et al., 2017), we can say that children use a variety of modes to create representations, as they generate and communicate meaning to others in a cohesive, multi-layered way. Multimodal meaning is created when several modes (movement, gesture, and written text) and modalities (the body for movement and gestures, the pen for writing) are used and integrated (Jewitt, 2008; Vasudevan, 2011; Hibbert, 2013). If we accept that a mode is for making meaning, multimodality is the amalgamation of modes to create, represent, and communicate meaning (Bateman et al., 2017; Dressman, 2020). In the context of this book, we consider that children bring together different modes in their drawings (such as narratives, vocalisation, and gestures) to create and communicate meaning.

Most human communication – by children or adults – is multimodal; speech, for example, is often accompanied by hand gestures. Unbounded by convention, children may use many different tools and resources to make meaning, employing many modes and materials in different ways. Modes have been defined as "a socially and culturally shaped resource for making meaning" (Kress, 2010, p. 10). Later, we show how children, as sign-makers, shape, re-shape, edit, and re-edit, and how they use modes to make and convey meanings at home and school. Kress (1997, p. 92) suggested that children "act multi-modally, both in the things they use, the objects they make, and in the engagement of their bodies; there is no separation of body and mind." Many examples in this book show children's "means and processes for making meaning" (Bezemer & Kress, 2016, p. 7) as they combine several modes to create meaningful representations.

Of course, some modes are better suited to communicating certain meanings than others; what can be communicated in one mode might not be communicable in another or by using a combination of modes. For example, pictures and words together convey a different message than pictures or words in isolation.

Kress and Jewitt (2003) argue that new ways of thinking, theorising, and discussing meaning-making are needed for contemplating multimodal representations.

## A basis for multimodal communication

Three theoretical principles create a basis for multimodal communication (Kress & Van Leeuwen, 2001):

i *Media are intertwined with modes to make meanings*, where the medium (markers or crayons, picture books, storyboards, emojis, and modelling clay) becomes the message.
ii *Modes have equal importance* (drawing, speech, reading, writing, dancing, movement, cutting, attaching, and sculpting).
iii *Modes are always in a fluid state of transformation in interplay with each other* as children move between different modes: drawing, writing, tracing, glueing, narrative, sound/speech, and gestures. The use of each mode changes or elaborates meaning (for example, if a child glues glitter to their drawing of a house and accompanies it with a narrative about a "castle of fairies," they change the original meaning of "house" to a "castle of fairies").

We briefly discuss these three principles and their interconnections.

### *Using modes to make meaning*

Multimodality focuses on what signs are made of. Children use modes fluidly and dynamically; a young meaning-maker (or sign-maker) transforms existing modes to suit their interests and needs. From a social semiotic approach, sign-making is always subject to the aptness of the available modes (Jewitt et al., 2016), and children gradually extend and refine their expertise in using modes and in combining and switching between modes as they create new meanings. Modes hold the potential for meaning-making, with each mode offering different potential (Bezemer & Kress, 2016). So, for example, a sign made in one mode (mark-making) using a single medium (felt tip pen) is different from a sign made in another mode (e.g. sculpting using modelling clay). Modal affordances thus contribute to the decisions made by the sign-maker about which mode to use to convey their meaning and which media to use within that mode. What a mode offers influences the meanings that can be created. Different properties of each mode provide different meaning-making potentials and limitations. For example, words convey a different meaning from an image. Narration (while drawing or dancing) can articulate a different connotation from an image. Children can be given the choice of media and modes to best convey their meanings; the limited availability of modes (and their affordances) might restrict children's capacity to richly represent their meanings.

### *The equal importance of all modes for meaning-making*

Claims that all modes are equally important for communication and meaning-making (Kress & Van Leeuwen, 2001) conflict with generally held views that privilege certain modes over others (Bezemer & Cowan, 2021). For example, traditional literacy skills tend to be favoured as the main means of expression. This risks the relegation of other modes (drawing, sculpting, dancing, and movement) to secondary value (Danielsson & Selander, 2021). Talk is clearly important in children's development generally, yet the spoken word might not always be the best mode for some meaning-making (Bourne & Jewitt, 2003). Language and literacy are often the preferred ways to communicate (certainly in formal education systems), yet most people also communicate through non-verbal modes such as gaze, gestures, pictures, or diagrams, which can sometimes more effectively convey meaning (Norris, 2004). Increasingly, multimodality is used to support children's communications (Bezemer & Cowan, 2021). Modes of communication should not be regarded hierarchically, with traditional forms of reading, writing, and speech preferred to other digital modes and media. Taking a multimodal, social semiotics perspective means valuing all modes equally, concerning what modes can contribute to a dynamic and continuous fusion (Vasquez, 2005; Kress, 2008; Mills, 2009).

A sign-maker juxtaposes different modes to create their meaning (Bearne, 2009) in a semiotic arrangement of genre, layout, and designs to create a multi-layered sign (Kress, 2005). Similarly, a sign-reader can interpret it according to their interests because the interpretation depends on individual perspectives.

### *Modes in interplay: transformation and translation*

Modes can be continually transformed (Kress et al., 2001) as the sign-maker changes or reuses materials and makes new meanings from existing ideas. Using multiple modes, children make new meanings as they continuously transform their signs (drawings, objects, stories, texts, or play episodes). In this process of transformation, meaning is re-made by changes within the same mode (Jewitt et al., 2016); for example, an image of an object (a drawing of a car) can take a different meaning from a 3D construction of that car, and if accompanied by words that embellish or change meaning (by calling the car a racing car). Pahl (1999, p. 23) highlights the "fluid quality" of multimodality as children move between the different modes of drawing, writing, and playing to transform their drawings into props that they incorporate into play. We see multimodality as a fluid and fluent intertwining of modes that are interpreted and combined to create unique meanings according to each child's interests.

## Social semiotics and understanding children's drawings

Social semiotics refers to the way humans present and represent aspects of their lives to themselves and others (Mehawesh, 2014). Focusing on making new signs to convey meaning rather than using and conforming to ready-made sign systems (Kress, 2010), semiotics form an integral part of social relations in society, contributing to shaping and changing such relations and cultures

(Aiello, 2020). Children make signs as part of their social relations, cultural contexts, and the societies they live in (Mavers, 2011; Djonov & Zhao, 2017). They are also influenced by the signs they see around them. Thus, a social semiotic perspective sees meanings as fluid: children, being agents of their meaning-making processes, use the modes available to design, sign-making resources and create new meanings.

Multimodality is an inherent part of social semiotics where all forms of sign-making are equally valued (Siegel, 2006, p. 68). Anything that signifies or stands for something is a sign that can be used to convey meaning (Bezemer & Cowan, 2021). The focus in this book is on how children organise, represent, communicate, and interpret the signs they make as they combine modes and modalities. Through this process, children convey their understanding of cultural and community-specific practices, including how people create, understand, and communicate experiences (Long & He, 2021). Children are *sign-makers*, who each create their own individually meaningful signs, and adults and peers are *sign-readers* who interpret those signs.

The interdisciplinary field of *social semiotics* has a focus on people as social beings, and the signs they make. The focus here is on the agency of a child as a sign-maker, where children create and convey their meanings by creating tangible signs. How that meaning changes depends on and makes sense in a particular context, because while some signs and meanings are globalised and similar for all humans, they can also be culture-specific (Fulková & Tipton, 2011; Jewitt et al., 2016). Deriving from the Greek word semeion, meaning sign, semiotics is the study of signs and symbols and their use or interpretation.

Halliday (1994, p. 23) purported a model of social semiotics with three overarching components necessary for producing and representing a text for communication: *ideational* (the subject matter); *interpersonal* (the construction of social relations); and *textual* (the creation of coherence). According to Halliday, these three principles are always used together and concern "who does what to whom, where and when" (Stein, 2008, p. 20), with meaning being central to the interests of both the sign-maker and sign-reader. Thus, Halliday transformed social semiotics from an interpretation of a fixed, monomodal sign system within a language to the interpretation of socially and culturally situated multimodal sign systems of communication.

## The making of signs

Signs convey meaning by representing what they symbolise (Danesi, 2007; Wright, 2011). Signs are everywhere, both *complex* and *simple*, and include everyday signs in public places (fast food chain logos and perfume brands) and individually made signs such as drawings. Kress (2010) argues that social interaction with a sign creates a new meaning; what, as individuals, we "see" in a sign makes our meaning.

Combining a socio-cultural perspective with the neo-Vygotskian theory of *perezhivanie*, we consider that signs are socially and culturally influenced tools.

They are representations that reflect socially shaped experiences that can bring about change as cultural meanings are conveyed (Bezemer & Kress, 2016; Ngwenya et al., 2022, p. 118). Children's drawings are often infused with layers of meaning, which can have two levels of interpretation (Wright, 2010b, p. 15):

- Content: the message at the surface level
- Meaning: a deeper "symbolic message"

*Sign-making as meaning-making*

Meaning-making is fundamental to human interaction. Personal and social experiences are merged into what a sign-maker communicates. Thought and feeling combined shape the sign-maker's meaning (Kress, 2000a). Anything can become a sign when it is given meaning by a sign-maker or sign-reader (Kress, 2003a; Chandler, 2007). Sign-making ranges from representation to interpretation. We need to distinguish between *making the sign* by a sign-maker and the *meaning the sign-maker wants to communicate*, alongside its active interpretation *by the sign-reader*. In this process, the sign-maker and sign-reader are engaged in dynamic processes of meaning-making: the sign-maker creates the sign to communicate their meaning, and the sign-reader interprets the sign according to the meaning they bring to it. Both sign-makers and sign-readers are influenced by their life experiences, interests, and cultural context. So, the same sign can offer different meanings to the sign-maker and sign-reader, as they each create individual and intersubjective meanings. Social semiotics involves the sign-maker communicating, through the use of semiotic modes, to make meaning, which is then conveyed to others in a social act.

## Sign-making as a social process

Sign-making and sign-reading are human, social processes. Combining socio-cultural theory (Vygotsky, 2012), the neo-Vygotskian perspective of *perezhivanie* (Vygotsky, 1994), and the theory of funds of knowledge (Moll et al., 1992), social semiotics focuses on how people communicate to create meaning in social contexts (Kress, 2013). Environment, materials, culture, events, interactions, and relationships are essential elements of sign-making (Kress, 1997, 2010; Frish, 2006). Thus, sign-making involves multiple culturally specific processes of meaning-making between people as they interpret their meanings (Bakhtin, 1981). Through the social process of sign-making in interaction with other people, a sign-maker creates their sign, which is interpreted by the sign-reader according to personal social, cultural, and historical discourses and practices (Stein, 2008; Mavers, 2011). A social semiotics perspective can be used to appreciate how meanings are understood from social and cultural perspectives (Long & He, 2021). Thus, when children draw to create meaning, their social and cultural environment is influential.

## Meaning-making

Human beings are predisposed meaning-makers, whose meanings are stimulated by everyday experiences (Krauss, 2005; Hartle & Jaruszewicz, 2009; Tang et al., 2022). The meanings in children's drawings can be fluid and hypothetical (Timonen, 2023) – as they emerge from interactions between the child (sign-maker) and the sign-reader, who may interpret a drawing differently and change that interpretation in the process. The meaning a child first gives to their drawing may later be changed as their context and evolving thinking and interactions influence it. Every mode and medium offers children different semiotic applicability, which can influence the meanings they create (Mavers, 2011).

Different modes and media combine in a process of *intertextuality*, whereby children transfer content and knowledge from different sources (books, artwork, songs, TV programmes, films, stories, and life experiences) to make their original drawings according to their individuality and agency (Kress, 2013). In their drawings, children may transfer culturally mediated material (including content, genres, and symbols) in ways that make sense to them (Bezemer & Kress, 2008). When a sign-reader interprets a drawing, they relate it to what they know, to bring meaning to what they are "reading" (Short et al., 2000; Semali, 2002; Han, 2011). These "intertextual threads" (Dyson, 2001b, p. 9) offer children ways of relating their drawing to personal, social, cultural, and communicative practices at home and school. Thus, meaning-making in children's drawings is a social practice (Stein, 2008).

### *Signs as a metaphor for meaning-making*

Besides being physical artefacts, symbolic meaning can be attributed to a sign, transforming it into a metaphor (Bezemer & Kress, 2016). Children's playful drawing experiences are often full of metaphors, which frequently combine children's societies, cultures, and stories (Nielsen, 2009). Hope (2008, p. 11) considers children's drawings "as a bridge between the inner world of the imagination and reason, and the outer world of communication and sharing of ideas." From a social semiotics perspective, children are active sign-makers and meaning-makers, whose signs and meanings are limited only by the span of their social environment and the availability of resources.

## Children as sign-makers and meaning-makers

As expert sign-makers, children create different signs and use a range of modes in experimental and spontaneous ways to ascribe their signs to their intended meaning (Mavers, 2007b). Young children often use vocalisations, movement, facial expressions, and gestures alongside 3D and 2D materials in complex, multimodal meaning-making. They are "meaning-makers *par excellence*" (Wright, 2008, p. 1), creative and resourceful sign-makers, and "designers of meaning" who skilfully make "semiotic choice" (Archer & Newfield, 2013, p. 6), selecting the most suitable modes for their communication. The rich and detailed drawings children create are laden with multiple layers of meaning. The many examples in this book show the children's ability to make meaning spontaneously, often engaging in a process of "self-reflexivity" (Archer & Newfield, 2013, p. 6) and interpretation as they communicate their identity in their drawings.

For young children, "meaning is an act" (Eisner, 2013, p. 14), where meaning lies in what is made and the process of making it. Children use anything at hand to create a drawing that communicates their meaning, moving from one form of depiction to another, shifting between modes to represent something that communicates their meaning and to connect with others (Ormerod & Ivanic, 2002; Mavers, 2009, 2011; Wright, 2011). When they create multi-modal drawings, children seem to make conscious decisions about how they can make meaning. The drawings (and accompanying drawing-narratives) in this book show how the children decided which meanings to create and how to create them as they drew. Children's choices of modes and media depend on their availability and suitability for what they want to make (Mavers, 2011). Sometimes, children's meanings are intentional – pre-planned to convey something in particular (an event, a place, or a person); on other occasions, meanings spontaneously unfold moment by moment as their ideas develop. Meanings conveyed in children's drawings might sometimes be regarded as somewhat ordinary and consequently disregarded (Mavers, 2011). However, something remarkable might be found in the unremarkable because children's graphic representations contain thoughtful, deliberate semiotic processes and meaning-making as they play with familiar ideas and meanings to create new ones (Mavers, 2009). A social semiotics perspective values children's representations and considers them worthy of attention, with the concept of *perezhivanie* (Vygotsky, 1994) adding a further dimension of meaning and allowing adults insights into children's emotions and ways of thinking (Bezemer & Cowan, 2021). Children's agency is given more prominence when their semiotic work is valued. When children make cutouts from available craft materials (cardboard, fabric, and magazines) and stick them to their drawings, they mix different modes to create multi-layered meanings (Anning & Ring, 2004). As they select and use available resources, children merge their personal, conventional, and societal knowledge to create unique motifs with distinct meanings. For example, Luke drew two rectangular shapes to represent *A Fighter Aeroplane* (*LS23*, Figure 2.1), which he said differed from a passenger aeroplane as it had "combat equipment on the outside," marked by wooden sticks. His knowledge of fighter jets led Luke to insist that his aeroplane was firing bombs on a mission. Thus, he engaged in a process of complex sign-making and narrative to convey his understanding of fighter jets and how they work.

When they use multiple resources in their drawings, children learn the characteristics of each semiotic resource and how to manipulate them to make different signs and meanings. Children often change their drawings through a sophisticated process of adding, deleting, cutting, and covering; they are active and informed sign-makers and meaning-makers. As agents in their social lives and cultures, children intentionally invest time and purpose to effectively and seriously make and convey their meanings – for themselves and others. The challenge for parents and educators is to understand children's signs and meanings.

Kress (1997) suggests that before formal schooling, young children may not have learned to bind their meaning-making to socially and culturally facilitated norms, forms, and media. Beginning formal education, Kress argues, is the point when children learn that their semiotic disposition, ways of communication, and meaning-making are not necessarily appreciated in schools. When children are directed to use adults' ways of communication, they are frequently restricted to using language and literacy as the most used and valued modes by educators, or those given greater value and emphasis in formal curriculum policy and adult-dominated pedagogic approaches. Children's individuality can be stifled if adults in educational settings decide that everyone should, for example, use the same template to make a card for Mother's Day, resulting in a "monomodal" (O'Halloran, 2009, p. 98) product with little meaning. Children's creativity and communication can be stifled if educators miss the opportunity to learn more about children's potential and abilities (Kress, 2000a).

To understand children's drawings and the complex and intriguing ways they create, translate, and transform their ideas into meaning-making representations, we must observe children as they draw and listen to their drawing narratives, which add meaning to what they are making. Frequently, an object is "always more than one thing" for a child (Kress, 1997, p. 141); the real challenge for adults is to be able to value, recognise, and understand the many forms and modes children use and the meanings they try to convey. Kress (2003b) argues that adults and children use similar processes to make and change meaning, though the two processes are different. Adults may opt for conventional ways of meaning-making based on the "correct use of culturally ready-made resources" (Kress, 2003b, p. 154); contrastingly, children's ways of meaning-making may not be confined by conventional ways, being influenced instead by their need to produce a drawing stimulated by their present interest. Developing skills in interpreting children's drawings is a process adults need to develop and refine to better understand their representations by becoming sensitive to the children's ways of drawing and their meaningful intent. To do this, adults must consider children's social and cultural contexts and their funds of knowledge (Chesworth, 2016). This demands space for adults and children to co-construct meanings in shared conversations, narratives, and sustained "shared understanding" (Bezemer, 2021, p. 9). This can be achieved when children's drawings are valued and interpreted in discussions between children, families, and educators.

## Notes

1 A list of the relationship between modes and media is provided on the companion website. https://sites.google.com/view/childrenmakingmeaning
2 A list of studies of multimodality in children's meaning-making is provided on the companion website. https://sites.googlecom/view/childrenmakingmeaning

# 3 Children drawing meanings

*Figure 3.1* The Mushrooms (LS4) – by Luke.

## Valuing children's drawings

The status of children's drawings has changed over time, from a developmental perspective focusing on the final product to a more post-modernist stance, which values the process of drawing as contextualised meaning-making (Anning, 2003; Ivashkevich, 2009). In this chapter, we discuss how some theories have influenced the way adults have perceived children's drawings.

### Developmental stage theories of drawing

George-Henri Luquet (2001/1927) deemed children's first drawings to be unintentional scribble, with drawings becoming more realistic and sophisticated

DOI: 10.4324/9781003427582-3

(therefore more valued) as children grow older. Lowenfeld and Brittain (1947) based their interpretation of children's artistic development on stage theory, considering children's drawings inferior to adults' representations. Their stage categorisation implied that two- to four-year-olds were only capable of uncontrolled scribble, thus adopting a deficit approach to early drawings in a study that ignored contextual, social, and cultural influences (Frisch, 2006). Kellogg (1959, 1969, 1979), also claimed that children's drawings followed developmental stages. Intentionally eschewing social and cultural differences, Kellogg (1969) argued that children began to draw basic scribbles and eventually made pictorial representations of humans, animals, and objects. During this transition, Kellogg suggested that children learned to transform symbols into images to intentionally represent their perceptions (Kellogg, 1969).

Focusing on children's inexperience, a developmental and sequential stance emphasises realistic, "representational accuracy" (Thompson & Schulte, 2019, p. 135), predictability, and reproduction (Golomb, 2002, 2004). Interpreting children's drawings through a developmental lens rather than focusing on the content a child is communicating, the intent in their drawings is ignored (Anning & Ring, 2004; Cox, 2005a; Thompson & Schulte, 2019). Matthews (1999, p. 93) argues that children do not begin to represent their perceptions when their drawings are a "correct form of representation," but their very first marks are made with intention and meaning. Deficit models that privilege visual realism and accurate representations risk missing the meanings young children create and see the early stages of drawing as immature or inaccurate (Anning & Ring, 2004; Cox, 2005a). More recently, Machón (2013) developed a view of children's graphic development that considered drawing as a language and representation of space.

For several decades, developmental stage theories[1] were used to analyse children's drawings, but new perspectives illuminate the inadequacy of theories that ignore a child's personal meaning in a drawing and the relationships between drawing, thinking, and other modes of communication (Pariser, 1995; Atkison, 2009; Thompson & Schulte, 2019). Pablo Picasso summarised the value of children's drawings: "It took me four years to paint like Raphael, but a lifetime to paint like a child. Painting with an open heart, an innocent eye, seeing the essence of a subject, took a lifetime."

### Contextualised meaning in drawing

The emergence of a sociology of childhood (James & Prout, 2015) and recent studies of children's culture (Dyson, 2003; Sunday, 2015; Thompson, 2017), together with Malaguzzi's (1995, p. 52) "image of the child," have prompted us to view children's drawings as a social practice, increasingly emphasising intention, meaning and attunement to children's cultural contexts. Dyson (1993a) perceived drawing as a vehicle for meaning-making, first as exploratory behaviour and later as a tool for representing objects and actions. Drawings may be used as play props to make meaning, and children's accompanying narratives further communicate their meanings to others (Dyson, 2002; Anning & Ring,

2004; Wohlwend, 2008; Coates & Coates, 2011; Bock, 2016). Initially, children do not distinguish between drawing and writing, using these two modes interchangeably (Dyson, 1993a) unfettered by adult definitions of marks which are writing, and marks which are drawing.

Studies of children's drawings show that their multidirectional marks (straight, zig-zag, and circular lines, shades, and patches) can contain meaningful detail, intention, and purpose (Cox, 2005b; Mavers, 2011; Adams, 2012). Lancaster and Roberts (2006) and Longobardi et al. (2015) showed that children under three years old showed their intent before making marks on paper and attributed meaning to their drawings. Similarly, Lancaster (2007) concluded that children under three can intentionally explore and use symbolic systems and mark-making. The simplest marks can be important to children, who often draw with intent and are in control of the drawing process (Hall, 2009); they need the freedom to experiment with mark-making without encumberment of intent.

Coates and Coates (2011) acknowledge that early marks could be an accidental outcome of their explorations of mark-making materials and suggest a set of broad descriptions in drawing for meaning. They defined children's first drawings as composed of intentional lines that they use to draw figures and objects. While the first mark may be an unintentional surprise, subsequent marks are probably intentional repetitions of actions that result in a mark. Later, children go on to draw what they know while mixing plans and front elevations (Coates & Coates, 2011). Drawing within a baseline and a skyline is another important characteristic of children's drawings, as they bring knowledge of their world to their drawings. Emergent writing is also regarded as a responsive, supporting mode for children's drawings (Dyson, 1993a; Matthews, 2003; Coates & Coates, 2011).

As children draw, they include their perceptions and interpretations of objects, creating possibilities for meaning-making (Matthews, 1997; Coates & Coates, 2011). A circle signifies a car (Kress, 1997), a dot becomes a duck (Cox, 2005b), and lines, arcs, and dots are combined to represent a thunderstorm (Mavers, 2011); the same lines, arcs, and dots, differently combined, make letter-like forms in emergent conventional writing (Bissex, 1980; Ferrerio & Teberosky, 1983). Children's action, combined with drawing, represent their meanings; all young children's drawings are modes of meaning-making (Dyson, 1993a; Matthews, 1999; Coates & Coates, 2011), and narration with drawing opens up an intentional meaning-making mode. Kress (1997) claimed that the children's use of multiple modes in drawing complements their ways of creating meaning, and the children's flexible transition between drawing modes frequently helps them to create multiple transformations and interpretations.

Young children are citizens with rightful entitlements as enshrined in the *United Nations Convention on the Rights of the Child* (United Nations, 1989), attesting their rights to individual identities, citizenship, education, health, homes, play, protection, and place in society, to be heard. Even before they begin to talk, children are on an explorative journey of shape, pattern, location, and movement to create "a visual language of great eloquence and meaning" (Matthews, 2003, p. 34). Young children's mark-making systematically evolves to reflect their purposes, processes of perception, relevance, technique, and thought, in relation to their interests at the time (Dyson, 1993a; Lancaster, 2003). If children's mark-making is seen by some to fall short of ideals of representation (Atkinson, 2009), this should not reduce their marks to meaningless activity (Paine, 1981). Dismissal of young children's drawings, because they do not conform to adult expectations and perceptions of what drawing should be, is naive. Some might not understand Pablo Picasso's cubist works, yet as Picasso himself said, "The fact that for a long time, Cubism has not been understood and that even today there are people who cannot see anything in it, means nothing."

## The content in children's drawings

Children draw many different subjects; personal, real-life episodes are often merged with fictional popular culture (Jolley, 2009; Wright, 2010b), reflecting their social, historical, and cultural contexts (Senzaki et al., 2014), where the ordinary takes centre stage. Children draw for several reasons: to represent objects or ideas that intrigue them; to share affections for people; to communicate personal values, concerns, emotions, and wishes (Ahmad, 2018; Talu, 2019; Lähdesmäki et al., 2022); to document special occasions and places; to plan and solve problems (Thompson, 1995; Jolley, 2009; Mavers, 2011; Adams, 2012). In drawing, children capture the ordinary and extraordinary – their real and imagined worlds – reflecting aspects of their unique socio-cultural contexts (Albers, 2007; Coates & Coates, 2006, 2011).

Attempts to categorise content themes in children's drawings[2] do not sufficiently acknowledge the meanings in their drawings, which require more nuanced lenses of actions, events, time sequences, narratives (Atkinson, 2009), and children's perspectives on what they know and question (Coates & Coates, 2006). Coates (2002) identified progression in children's drawings, from drawing figures, houses, and vegetation to including more culturally specific objects such as school buildings, motorways, and characters from popular culture such as Superman, Batman, and Pokémon (see also Anning & Ring, 2004; Coates & Coates, 2006; Jolley, 2009; Kress, 2010). This evolution is well documented (Marsh, 2003; Hall, 2010b), and influences include storybooks, fantasy worlds, cartoon characters, television programmes, digital games, and associated play artefacts (Coates & Coates, 2011). Popular culture, where "commercial culture often does become semiotic material for making sense of social experience" (Dyson, 1997, p. 15), seems to have brought changes in children's graphic creations and concocted storylines, including the drawing of animated superheroes and scenes rooted in mythical legends.

Taking a socio-cultural perspective, we show in subsequent chapters, how the content of children's drawings is frequently influenced by and reflects their immediate social and cultural contexts across time.

## Drawing as meaning-making

Adopting a theory of social semiotics, we consider drawing as a semiotic meaning-making tool that foregrounds young children's meaning-making

(Brooks, 2004; Wright, 2011), helping children convey what they cannot otherwise easily express. Drawing is a *portal* to children's inner and social words, an important language for children who often convey their thoughts, understandings, and emotions in a visual-graphic form. Children draw to explore and share their ideas with others, to record experiences, convey knowledge, and develop their imagination (Kress, 1997, 2010; Mavers, 2011). Adams (2003) suggested that children's drawings have three main functions of meaning-making: "*perception*" (p. 222), where children follow their interests, explore, and organise their thinking and understandings of the world; "*communication*," where children communicate their ideas to others; and "*manipulation*," where children explore and refine their thoughts to create alternative possibilities. Ahn and Filipenko (2007, p. 279) suggested three taxonomies of communication in children's drawings: "*engendering*" – construction of the self as a social and cultural being; "*re-configuration*" – perceiving themselves in relation to others; and "*reconstruction/re-imagination*" – drawings as a dramatic and imaginative narrative to process abstract concepts and knowledge.

Children's drawings can be a powerfully rich potpourri of their perspectives, thinking processes, and cognitive and emotional growth, as children use them to articulate their ideas and shape their understandings (Pinto et al., 2021). They are dynamic expressions of meaning generation, where children make sense of their ideas and emotions as they construct their theories. While many see drawing as a way of *making meaning*, for us, drawing *is* meaning; in the *act of drawing*, children *are* the meanings they create. Constructive processes of drawing allow children to be active participants and agents of their learning (Cox, 2005a). Thus, when children accompany their drawings with talk, vocalisation, and gestures, they are embellishing their understanding. From an interpretive and constructivist position, using children's drawings to understand what children know, and seeing their "structures of meaning" (Nicolopoulou et al., 1994, p. 106) is fundamental.

## Fluidity in meaning-making

Children's drawings are not fixed; their meanings can be unpredictable, dynamic, and fluid, where new meanings are continuously created (Kress, 1997; Davis, 2005). Meanings can be complex and selective, as children decide what to include and omit; thus, an adult may think important details are missing. Using symbols to manipulate images and concepts and moving between modes to bring new possibilities and alterations to their drawings, children design and redesign their drawings, making new interpretations, reinterpreting original features, and creating new meanings in the process. The examples in this book show how children's interactions within their drawings are elaborated as they unfold their drawings.

The semiotic process of drawing is a *transformation* of meaning; children begin their drawing by representing an initial idea, which they change as new ideas emerge (Hope, 2008; Hopperstad, 2008a; Kress, 2010; Mavers, 2011).

When Luke drew *The Mushrooms* (Figure 3.1), he began with two circular shapes while showing his friend Shaun how to draw balls. Later, he returned to the drawing, adding two eyes, a mouth, a pair of moustaches, and a nose to the circles, transforming the balls into two talking mushrooms. After talking to Shaun, Luke decided that his mushrooms were close together, so they were married. Children's drawings change in the moment, as transformations bring new thinking and semiotic meanings (Wright, 2005; Flewitt, 2006; Jewitt, 2009b). We shall see later how children's accompanying drawing narratives demonstrate intentional and coherent change. As agents of their drawings, children purposefully change their minds in response to the complexity and fluidity of the semiotic process and context.

Drawings can be "polysemic" (Christmann, 2008, p. 3), with multiple related meanings to be construed. Adults often interpret children's drawings differently from children's intended meanings, but they should not limit their interpretations to an adult perspective of identifying what is immediately recognisable. To appreciate children's meanings requires our intersubjective understanding and knowledge of children's interests and socio-cultural practices (Atkinson, 2002; Wright, 2011).

*Copying*

Children often include features from their lives and popular culture in their drawings, sometimes copying ideas from other children. Copying has been considered undesirable, unethical, or a form of cheating, but copying is an intrinsic part of the semiotic process and not mere unthinking replication (Dyson, 2010; Mavers, 2011). Later examples show that drawings frequently involve a "remix" of selectively borrowing and transforming existing material, ideas, images, and techniques, which are then reconfigured. Copying is not an effortless or elicit act but an active, creative process of reselecting, redesigning, and reproducing meanings. In copying, children uniquely shape their drawings to create personal meanings (Hopperstad, 2010; Ring, 2010), "There is no such thing as a copy because copying is an agentive process of remaking afresh" (Mavers, 2011, p. 16). Copying from each other "mediates relationships" (Dyson, 2010, p. 26), displaying collegial interest, shared talk, and thinking, thus enabling children to connect, experiment, and co-construct meanings (Sunday, 2017).

## Talk and narrative during drawing

A drawing can be an effective mode of communication, yet it may be different from what was intended. Kress (2003b) and Hopperstad (2008a) suggest that children are aware of this limitation and may try to overcome it by combining talk and other modes such as gestures and vocalisations to enhance and inform the mode of drawing. Children's telling enhances adults' understanding of what they are communicating (Nutbrown, 2011).

Talk during and about a drawing is often an established practice in early childhood education (Wright, 2008; Tay-Lim & Lim, 2013), providing insights into the children's thinking processes (Podobnik et al., 2021). This allows the *form* and *content* of the drawing to emerge together, and subsequently, it uncovers children's ways of making associations and generating their understandings. Talk and drawing become integral during the drawing process (Cox, 2005a), and listening adults can find children's drawing-telling illuminating. When talking as they draw, children sometimes explore complex notions and concepts, providing a more comprehensive account of their thinking. However, talking while drawing and post-drawing talk frequently vary and convey different meanings, confirming the fluidity of children's sense-making (Coates & Coates, 2006; Wright, 2008). Such talk is valuable because talking and drawing together form an integrated creative process, giving deeper insights into children's meaning-making than drawing alone.

Coates and Coates (2006) found that children used to talk about drawing in three different ways: they talk about subject matter; they interact with their peers in seemingly unrelated conversations; and they communicate drawing-related ideas with an adult. Children's talk influences their drawings, irrespective of whether they are engaged in self-absorbed conversations or dialogue with others. The following section briefly discusses these three variants of talk and Wood and Hall's (2011) forms of playing while drawing, which only become "visible when the drawings [were] are shared through talk" (Hall, 2010b, p. 368).

### Talking about drawing content

Narratives can be a meaning-making tool (Ahn, 2006, p. 198), helping children to think and make sense of their worlds. Through their narratives, children communicate their knowledge (Sunday, 2017) or re-experience themselves, other people, and things that matter to them (Nicolopoulou et al., 1994; Coates & Coates, 2020). Drawing-talk can be a dynamic platform of mediation where children use metaphors to convey their ideas (Egan, 1998; Nielsen, 2009; Jewitt & Forceville, 2021). These visual narratives also allow children to explore abstract, scientific, and moral concepts as they construct the world as they know it or wish it to be where "The central concern is not how a narrative text is constructed, but rather how it operates as an instrument of mind in the construction of reality" (Bruner, 1992, p. 233).

### Social talk in drawing narratives

Children's drawings can have a social value where shared drawing becomes part of children's social relationships (Frisch, 2006; Coates & Coates, 2020). Children often talk together as they draw (Mavers, 2011), with drawing and talking being a social, playful experience (Fulková & Tipton, 2011), and their talk is sometimes disassociated from their drawing (Coates & Coates, 2006).

As children draw together, they often talk, joke, and share stories (Cox, 2005a; Sunday, 2017; Kaplun, 2019), thus developing their social skills and maintaining their relationships (Ahn & Filipenko, 2007; Kangas et al., 2011). Drawing can be a conversation aid – an intermediate object that stimulates thinking while supporting the development of friendships (Hopperstad, 2008a; Coates & Coates, 2020).

### Talking with an adult

Interaction between a child and an adult is a type of drawing-telling that can be crucial to the meaning-making process (Coates & Coates, 2006), where a child declares their intentions, seeks support, plays with ideas, and exchanges perspectives about their subject matter. Contextualised talk often centres around a finished drawing (Sunday, 2017), as children and adults co-construct a shared understanding and meaning-making. This social constructivist view involves an adult using knowledge about a child's interests, and experiences, to support their exploration and articulation of ideas and thoughts (Tay-Lim & Lim, 2013). Adult-child drawing-focused talk can help to focus attention and thinking, thus mediating a child's perception of their drawing (Brooks, 2009a). This helps to link a child's subjective level of communication, meaning-making processes, and inter-subjective level of social interaction (Hall, 2008; Jordan, 2004). Drawing without accompanying talk may not provide the adult with enough information about its attributed meaning (Ring, 2010; Hall, 2011). Therefore, talk often becomes part of the multimodal process that complements visual representation, as "the talk feeds into the drawing ... [and] sometimes the drawing feeds into talk" (Cox, 2005a, p. 123). In the drawing-related talk, adults must value the process, respecting each child's intent through sensitive-attuned awareness of their in-depth and spontaneous sense-making. Adult-child drawing conversations should maintain a child's intent as central to the dialogue without imposing an adult agenda.

Open-ended dialogue between child and adult can be reciprocal; with materials, actions, and dialogue in the play, the adult must follow the child's thinking processes, ways of meaning-making, and perspectives to sensitively tune in to their drawings (Anning & Ring, 2004). This process allows a child to make sense of their thinking processes and to voice such processes to others (Wright, 2010b) while providing adults with a lens on children's perspectives (Sunday, 2017).

### Drawing patterns and styles

Accounts of children's drawing tendencies can contribute to our understanding of children's drawing approaches, though individual children should not be categorised as having one particular drawing pattern; they may have a miscellany of categories in their repertoire (Dyson, 1986; Egan, 1995; Watson & Schwartz, 2000); patterns and styles are fluid, not absolute.

Many children engage in individual and/or group talk, which enriches their drawing experience; some prefer solitary immersion in their drawings, where talk is secondary. Children who make extensive narratives, dramatisations, and vocalisations while drawing have been described as "inveterate verbalisers" or "dramatists" (Gardner, 1980, p. 47). Such drawers are considered "socializers" (Dyson, 1989, p. 68), who depict actions, events, relationships, and imaginary tales and stories full of adventure, magic, and fantasy. Contrastingly, "committed visualisers" (Gardner, 1982, p. 118) or "patterners" (Gardner, 1980, p. 47) focus on the detail of their drawings, emphasising form, pattern, commonalities, and consistencies.

Some children need no encouragement to draw, being "self-starters" (Gardner, 1982, p. 117) and "subject matter generalists" (Thompson, 1999, p. 155), who engage effortlessly in drawing. Those who draw mostly people tend to be "person-centred ... emphasising communication over creation" (Gardner, 1982, p. 118); more object-focused drawings feature "physical elements and machines" (Gardner, 1982, p. 118).

## *Drawing identity construction*

As children bring together their preferred patterns, styles, and interests with available semiotic resources and modes, they explore and construct their identities (Brockmeier, 2001; Jewitt & Oyama, 2001; Hall, 2008). Identity construction occurs when children's drawings become symbolic and semiotic spaces, allowing them to explore their sense of self (Hall, 2010b). Children may reference their past and future actions and relationships, intentionally representing their worlds, as they author themselves in their drawings (Bleiker, 1999). Children's drawings can include continuous social, cultural, and individual dynamics (Brockmeier, 2001), which act as "tools of identity" (Holland et al., 1998, p. 43) for the exploration of different aspects of self (Edmiston, 2008). As they shift modes, children explore their self-identity, creating multiple identities in their drawings (Norris, 2004; Wright, 2007), and "the self is seen as a product of the texts that write the individual into being" (Hawkins, 2002, p. 211), as identities intertwine to bring out each child's unique personhood.

Children draw their imagined selves (Kendrick & McKay, 2004), amalgamating real- and pretend-world identities, to communicate who they are or wish to be (Ahn & Filipenko, 2007; Wright, 2011). Drawing becomes a playful space where fantasy and reality merge as children explore personal, social, and moral issues and notions of integrity (Edmiston, 2010). Hall (2011) suggests that children's drawings frequently involve self-transformation, where they can do or be anything and anyone at any time or in any situation where they amalgamate fiction with reality.

In drawing, children show what they know, unbound by power structures or hierarchies of relationships, as they affirm their social place and personal identities within their families and other social structures in their lives. Children's interactions with others around drawing can significantly impact the portrayal and formation of their identities. When peers or adults join children's drawing narratives, they participate in a co-construction of meanings where personal, social, and cultural identities interrelate (Hagood, 2008).

### Drawing as a play process

Educational settings can facilitate children's drawing-talk (Hopperstad, 2008b) by encouraging free drawing, opening up a "space for intellectual play" (Wood & Hall, 2011, p. 267) when their conversations include processes of, and subjects in, their imaginary and playful drawings. Wood and Hall (2011, pp. 274–276) suggest drawing as play takes three distinct forms: playing *at*, *in*, and *with* drawings. Playfulness in children's drawings is a space for visual meaning-making where play emerges through action, talk, and imagination.

Playing *at* drawing involves physical and social play where children use their drawing as a play prop with narratives and whole-body actions, gestures, and sound effects to enhance their drawing narrative. Playing *at* drawing at the *social* level, involves children in playful social interactions while they draw, as their influential interactions with others extend their drawing. Children plan together, copy each other, and discuss their drawing decisions. They dramatise, narrate, question, and appraise; they seek and offer help in how to draw something. Children often influence each other as social drawers, engaged in detailed explanations, complex discussions, and solitary or shared narrations about their drawings (Ahn, 2006; Coates & Coates, 2006).

When "playing *in* drawings" (Wood & Hall, 2011, p. 275), children engage in *physical* and *imaginative* play that captures the essence of their drawings. Children make "action representations" (Matthews, 1999, p. 31) during physical play *in* drawings as they depict the movement of figures running, jumping, fighting, and so on, talking about and describing the action in their drawings to interest others. Their imaginative playing *in* drawings often develops like dramatic role-play on paper as children imagine, draw, and describe people as assumed real or fictional selves, often taking the role of the main character of their drawing, sometimes changing protagonists, mid-drawing.

Children sometimes play *with* drawings (Wood & Hall, 2011), a *physical* form of play and *storytelling*. Children merge gesticulation, movement, and talk to demonstrate and extend action that a drawing alone cannot communicate. Drawing-storying involves children playing with their drawing (Hopperstad, 2008a), thus creating a visual narrative (Golomb, 2004), where children combine fantasy-based characters, plots, and scenery, using drawing to manipulate and invent ideas and events (Adams, 2004) with embedded layers of action, character development, and running narrative. In drawing-talk, children develop imaginary and "possible worlds" (Bruner, 1986, p. 13) on paper to organise and communicate fictional experiences to others. This involves making authorial decisions around when and how to develop the plot, change scenery, and conjure up fictional characters or objects, often with magical superpowers. Moving from the roles of author to director to artist, scriptwriter, performer, or narrator of their original text, children create spontaneous, complex stories filled with personal thoughts and feelings and universal moral qualities of bravery, proficiency, and audacity. In so doing, they may engage with immortal emotional opposites such as good, evil, power, weakness, life, and death, all of which confront children with ethical issues as they variously resolve or ignore while drawing (Edmiston, 2008; Wood & Hall, 2011; Jones, n.d.). Graphic-based stories frequently portray struggles between the "good guys and the bad guys" that end in victory and righteousness for the good vanquishers (Golomb, 2004; Wright, 2006; Edmiston, 2010). Such narratives can be appealing because they enable children to assume control and power in an adult-dominated environment, while they confront human truths of life and death (Marsh, 2000; Jones & Ponton, 2002; Edmiston, 2008).

## Children's funds of knowledge in drawing

From a socio-cultural construct of multimodality, children use contextually situated signs that are embedded in the social interactions of everyday routines to create their drawings. The contexts of children's drawings are important for understanding the intentions and purposes children attribute to their drawings. Drawing as meaning-making acknowledges the influence of socio-cultural contexts on children's representations (MacNaughton, 2004; Ahmad, 2018). This includes children's daily lives, routines, stories, images, events, and the range of experiences and accumulated knowledge that make up children's funds of knowledge (González et al., 2005). Funds of knowledge profoundly shape children's intentions, imagination, and sense-making, reflecting constantly changing ordinary and familiar everyday routines, practices, and objects (Amanti, 2005; Mavers, 2011). Children bring their unique funds of knowledge to all aspects of their lives, including their drawings. They draw what they know about, whether that knowledge is derived from life or their unique repositories of stories and imagination. A socio-cultural paradigm also acknowledges the importance of the attitudes and practices of significant others: peers, friends, parents, teachers, and pets, as they too contribute to a child's drawing experience.

Several scholars whose work we have referred to in this chapter have suggested that children's home and school contexts, daily events, cultural lives, and experiences form an essential part of the children's semiotic process and influence what and how they draw. The interconnection between home and school contexts, together with children's interactions with others, influence meaning-making processes in their drawings.[3]

### Home drawing contexts

Children's homes are all different, with varying influences of art, music, talk, ceremony, and traditions, so children bring unique funds of knowledge to drawing. Where homes are imbued with rites, routines, and family heritage that impact the daily patterns, these may emerge – as realistic or manipulated – representations in the children's drawings. Home environments, family structures, relationships, practices, and lifestyles shape children's drawings differently from the influences of early years settings and schools (Ring & Anning, 2004). Children's home cultures include ornaments, visual media, photographs, toys, experiences, and relationships with people and pets (Lancaster, 2007). Their home drawings are likely to reflect individual home cultures, including conversations and experiences (Ring, 2006; Rose et al., 2006; Hall, 2010b; Ahmad, 2018). Home drawings may differ from drawings done in educational settings, especially where there is less freedom. For some children, drawing at home is a socio-cultural activity (Anning, 2002), involving interaction with significant others who suggest, question, prompt, celebrate, or draw with them.

From a socio-cultural perspective, children's home and school drawings are influenced by and connected with globalised, contemporary popular culture (Marsh & Millard, 2000; Marsh, 2006; Hall, 2010b; Coates & Coates, 2011; Wright, 2011). Disney cartoons and films, television programmes, storybooks, playing cards, digital games, and artefacts linked to media can influence what and how children draw, as children import ideas from popular culture into their drawings. Children's drawing lives often intermingle everyday happenings and themes from popular culture organised and displayed in elaborate scenes (Anning & Ring, 2004). Their drawings often uniquely combine scientific and historical facts, media-mediated elements, personal experiences, narratives, fantasy, home experiences, and wishes. Anything is possible in young children's drawings.

### *School and setting contexts*

Most young children already have some drawing skills and experience an open attitude towards drawing before they attend an educational setting. They may have enjoyed drawing freely at home. However, if early years settings emphasise educator-centred pedagogy, confining drawing to a low-value, low-priority activity where there is a "correct" way to draw, the meaning-making potential of drawing is restricted (Anning, 2002; Einarsdottir et al., 2009). Early childhood educators can effectively enhance children's drawing experiences by supporting children's confidence and building positive attitudes towards free drawing and associated meaning-making in a setting. Teachers have been found to communicate positive opinions towards drawing, encouraging children, and providing space and choice to decide on the modes and content of their drawings (Rose et al., 2006; Hall, 2008). However, teachers in Anning's (2002) study tended to prioritise teaching reading and writing, using drawing to occupy children after such activities; thus, children were less interested in drawing at school when their teachers were hesitant to engage with them while they drew.

Where time and space are given to free drawing in school, children variously influence each other's drawings (Boyatzis & Albertini, 2000), co-constructing content and meaning as they draw. They share and evaluate each other's drawings, exchanging ideas, challenging, comparing, supporting, and inspiring each other about what to draw and how to draw it. They model, observe, compare, borrow, and appraise techniques as they import each other's ideas in their efforts to improve their drawing content and skills, alongside their knowledge of what they draw (Cox, 1997; Frisch, 2006; Hall, 2008). Influenced by their peers, children tend willingly to change the content of their drawings to meet their friends' thematic preferences, drawing styles, and techniques as they seek peer approval and acceptance (Gee, 2000). Studies of children's teacher-initiated drawings suggest that such drawings were primarily influenced by texts read and topics discussed in class, with out-of-school experiences regarded as of secondary importance (Hall, 2010b; Hopperstad, 2010).

Often considered separately, in reality, children's home and school contexts are mutually influential and intertwine in their drawings. Meanings and influences cross boundaries and are recontextualised and transformed by children, who create intertextual meanings between these two most important and influential parts of their worlds.

### Notes

1 The companion website provides supporting material for this chapter, with further information about developmental stage theories and analyses in more depth the perspectives of Luquet (2001), Lowenfeld and Brittain (1947) and Kellogg (1959, 1969, 1979). https://sites.google.com/view/childrenmakingmeaning
2 The companion website provides a summary of how theorists have classified the content of children's drawings. https://sites.google.com/view/children makingmeaning
3 The companion website provides further detail on how form, content, and meaning are integral parts of children's drawing, and how these are influenced by the children's socio-cultural context. https://sites.google.com/view/childrenmakingmeaning

# 4  Researching children's drawings

*Figure 4.1* Ben Ten Fight (LS18) – by Luke.

## Participatory research with children

This book focuses on a study of three, four-year-old children: Luke, Thea, and Bertly. All lived in the same area of Malta, attended the same kindergarten class, and had similar socio-economic backgrounds. We use their real names here because the children frequently wrote their names and letters from their names in their drawings, which are integral to the drawings and our analysis of them. Full permission has been obtained for the replication of their drawings, names, words, and identities, and we discuss related ethical issues later in the chapter.

DOI: 10.4324/9781003427582-4

We adopted a participatory approach, ensuring that children's unique voices are heard throughout the research process. Gallacher and Gallagher (2008, p. 502) define children's voices as "the most authentic source of knowledge about themselves and their lives." Throughout the study, we followed the children's cues, listened to them, and tried respectfully to understand their ways of thinking and how they made meaning through their drawings. The children's voices dominated drawing discussions and processes; it was important to ensure that they were free to speak or stay silent while they fluidly unfolded their experiences and understandings. We learned more of their perspectives in drawing-related conversations as and after they drew. Such shared meaning-making was instrumental in the learning of the children's unique understandings. This process took time to establish as children became accustomed to power-sharing with an adult – something unusual in the traditional approach in their kindergarten class. At times, it was necessary to be silent and restrained to avoid interrupting what the children did or said; on other occasions, shared conversations included questioning and prompting as children articulated their ideas and constructed their meanings. The children became confident in drawing in adult company and were keen to talk about their drawings.

Adoption of a participatory framework includes a process of dialogue, reflection, and change (Eckhoff, 2019; Rodríguez-Carrillo et al., 2020). The children were involved at different levels of the research, including sharing information, producing knowledge, evaluating everyday events, and taking some responsibility for data collection. Our commitment to involve children as much as possible is rooted in personal values and the belief that children have the right to be fully considered and included, especially when they are essential to the research process. Of course, the major share of research labour was ours, leaving the children free to draw and contribute to other parts of the process as they chose.

The children were involved in the data collection process if they chose (MacNaughton & Smith, 2005) and had space to voice their unique understandings and interpretations (Kjørholt et al., 2005; Nyland, 2009). Recognising and trusting the children as important collaborators, we offered them the choice to participate at each point of the study (Bucknall, 2014); this at times seemed to give additional importance and value to the drawings, which the children regarded as artefacts of interest to others. To facilitate the process, we used video cameras and the drawings themselves, making the research process tangible and meaningful for the children.

This positionality informed our way of doing research *with* children. As we studied their drawings and drawing processes, we tried to truly listen to their voices to better understand their choices, interpretations, and narrations without imposition. In an ethos of respect towards children's feelings, wishes, and rights, children were free to decide the *form* and *content* of their drawings and how much time they spent on a drawing. They were encouraged to act as data collectors by collating their drawings, and video-recording themselves if they wished. With adult help as needed, children contributed valuably to this process, helping to interpret their drawings and making decisions about consent and ownership each time they offered a drawing to the study collection.

Sometimes children decided to make several consecutive drawings, while sometimes they chose not to draw. Children's interpretations varied in length and detail, at their choice. These approaches to participation and decision-making facilitated the data collection process through child-appropriate methods and helped children voice their perspectives in genuine and unfiltered ways (Clark & Moss, 2001; Mukherji & Albon, 2010). Thus, relationships with children grew into partnerships (Smith, 2011), where they were respected as key contributors of authentic data about themselves and their meanings.

## Drawing as child-appropriate data collection

Drawing can be an inclusive and familiar data collection tool for use with children (Fargas-Malet et al., 2010; Loizos, 2000). Children can draw and make drawing-talk at their own pace (Punch, 2005); for most, drawing is a non-threatening, often pleasurable, process that children control. The three children understood that nothing they drew would be "wrong," and all their drawings and stories about those drawings were of interest. Providing children with opportunities to draw what was relevant to them without quality or time pressures, puts the children at ease.

## Research context and participants

In this section, we set out the context for our drawing case studies and introduce the children.

### The classroom context

In the kindergarten class of the study, there were a total of 17 children, 6 girls, and 11 boys, aged between 4 and 4:6 years. All children were Caucasian; most were from middle-class Maltese families who lived locally. Maltese was their home language, and they all practised the same religion.

The drawing table was basic, containing a stack of paper, some pencil colours, and crayons. To motivate the children to draw freely, during the study, the kindergarten educator[1] agreed to the development of a drawing area that intrigued the children. A variety of materials to facilitate multi-modal representations were added, with a range of media including crayons, markers, and gel pens; craft, recycled, and natural materials; and a range of paper, sticky tape, and scissors.

### The study children and their families

The three participant children, Luke, Thea, and Bertly, were aged between 4:2 and 4:6 at the beginning of the study.

### Luke

Luke (4:6) was the oldest child in the study. He was a vociferous, assertive, and extrovert character; attributes helped by his fluency in Maltese and English languages. He seemed popular with his friends and very caring and sensitive towards others. Luke liked playing Wii Nintendo games with his family and watching superhero films, mainly *Iron Man* – a fictional superhero character with a powered suit of armour to fight evil and make the world a safer place (Marvel Comics, 2015), and *Ben Ten* – an animated television series about a ten-year-old boy whose watch held superpowers, allowing him to transform into ten different alien heroes with the strength and power to fight evil aliens (TV Tropes Foundation, n.d.). Perhaps this interest was inspired by Luke's love for play-fighting and his passion for adventure, action, destruction, power, and victory, as reflected in his dramatic play.

*Thea*

Thea (4:3) was the youngest child in the study. She seemed very caring, affectionate, and sensitive, with a sense of humour. She was independent and determined to follow her ideas. She was also very creative, and drawing was one of her pastimes. Like her mother, Thea appeared skilled in using craft materials, often spending considerable time drawing and adding detailed decoration. In common with her father, Thea seemed interested in how things worked. At school, she seemed very confident and liked leading, guiding, and sharing what she knew with friends, who often followed her suggestions.

*Bertly*

Bertly (4:5) seemed sensitive and introverted, with few friends at school. Initially, he did not enjoy drawing, and his drawings were dominated by mark-making, but during the study, his experimentation with different media seemed to enhance his enjoyment. Bertly's favourite pastimes included playing computer games and watching cartoons, mainly *Pink Panther* (Metro-Goldwyn Mayer Studios, 1969–1979) and *Fireman Sam* (Mattel Television, 1987). He enjoyed the outdoors, playing in his father's field at weekends, and was particularly interested in nature, animals, and flowers. He was also knowledgeable about the weather, which seemed to influence his mood.

We will be looking at Luke, Thea, and Bertly as individual children with unique characteristics and interests, not defined by gender and gender-based norms. Resisting conventional and stereotypical expectations of children, we interpret their drawings outside a gender-biased lens, instead adopting an inclusive approach and valuing individual differences unconditionally (Tembo & Benham, 2023, p. 117). Luke, Thea, and Bertly are unique children, and the content and meanings in their drawings do not need to be defined according to limiting gender stereotypes but rather reflect interests and their immediate socio-cultural contexts.

## Research methods

The study data comprised:

- children's drawings made in their kindergarten and home settings

- films of each child's drawing processes
- informal drawing-conversations with the children and their parents

These three sources of data meant that each drawing episode, each drawing, and each case were "entirely unique, personal, and incapable of replication" (Coates & Coates, 2006, p. 226).

### Home and kindergarten visits

Drawings were collected over four months, with regular parallel visits to the kindergarten and the children's homes. With the parents' agreement, children were provided with a range of drawing materials for home use, similar to those provided in the kindergarten drawing area. It was important to get to know the children, their families, and their contexts to develop research relationships and best understand their drawings. Seven preliminary visits[2] were made to the kindergarten and one to each child's home to become familiar with the families in their homes. This helped the children and their families become fully informed about the research process and well prepared for the study. The preliminary home visits also helped Jo[3] to begin relationships with the children, acquire their trust, and familiarise herself with their home cultures, conventions, preferred language, routines, and circumstances as she collected the data throughout the study.

By the third preliminary kindergarten visit, the children seemed comfortable in Jo's presence, knowledgeable, and sufficiently empowered to make informed decisions about their involvement in the study. They indicated that they were happy to participate and to be filmed while drawing and talking about their drawings. Children were shown how to start and stop recording, charge the batteries on the small digital camera, recognise when the memory was full, and where best to position the camera to film themselves drawing. The cameras initially stirred excitement, but children soon became accustomed to them, and they quickly became part of the drawing process.

Following the sixth preliminary visit to the kindergarten setting, Jo visited each child's home to further explain the study to them and their parents and provide drawing materials and recording equipment. She demonstrated how to use the camera, agreed on the frequency of the visits, discussed the duration of the study, and reviewed with parents their responsibilities and commitment towards the study. The preliminary visits provided a foundation for the study and led to positive research relationships, resulting in few errors in the research process and yielding more authentic data.

### Drawing-oriented kindergarten visits

After preliminary kindergarten visits, nine weeks of intensive observations began, during which Jo visited the school three or four times a week. Each school visit began with preparing the drawing area. Once all the children were settled for small group activities with the educator, Jo invited four children from the class to the drawing area. Adopting an inclusive approach, all

17 children could use the drawing area if they were available, but only drawings by case study children were used as data.

Twenty-seven drawing sessions were held in the kindergarten setting, each averaging three hours, totalling 80 hours of drawing time during the study. All children were free to draw as they wished, without coercion, choosing what, when, and how to draw, and using the same available material while engaging with Jo as the three case study children; non-study children were not filmed. During drawing sessions, there was a continuous flow of children into the drawing area. Children's freedom to draw as much or as little per session aligns with our participatory approach, emphasising children's agency. Sometimes no case study children drew during school sessions; on other occasions, two or all three of them drew simultaneously. Their role as active participants and decision-makers empowered them to decide when to draw, which modes and media to use, the subject, and the time spent drawing. This approach fostered personally driven, voluntary drawings, where the children made the process open-ended.

### *Drawing-oriented home visits*

Home visits were conducted in the same timeframe as school visits; each child was visited once a week for five weeks, making 15 visits (totalling 18 hours). Visit times fitted families' preferences and usually began with the child and parents talking about the drawings done at school and home that week. Children drew as much and for as long as they wished during a visit, and drawing materials for home use were replenished. It was important to respect family homes as private sanctuaries, avoiding intrusion into personal lives. Jo was conscious not to intrude too much on family time and stayed for about an hour. Children were invited to elaborate while drawing or when they had finished, and frequently, parents contributed to interpretations.

Between Jo's visits, the children were encouraged to draw whenever they wished at home; they quickly learned to operate the small digital cameras to film themselves; parents helped if needed. Parents welcomed the drawing-oriented visits, which provided unique insights about the children and contextual information that contributed to the interpretation of drawings.

A final home visit for each child celebrated the study; initial findings were shared with the children and families, and the children received a small thank-you gift.

### Filming children drawing

During home and school drawing visits, observations were conducted informally, without formal or written records; instead, Jo wrote as many details as possible immediately after each visit. Filming captured children's drawing processes and voices. After each visit, the films were saved in the respective child's digital folders and watched closely and repeatedly to enable close interpretation of the multi-layered processes of each drawing.

## Ethical considerations

This study was conducted according to specific institutional research ethics guidelines and the Ethical Guidelines for Educational Research (British Educational Research Association [BERA], 2018) and informed by scholarship on research with young children and a children's rights agenda (United Nations, 1989). While protocols can offer some guidance, they do not solve complex ethical dilemmas. It is for researchers to engage in and struggle with ethical predicaments to ensure the protection of participants and, in so doing, adopt an "ethic of care" (Schulz et al., 1997, p. 475) throughout the whole process from conception to final report and beyond.

### *Informed consent and assent*

Having given consent for the study, the Head of School identified a kindergarten educator, Ms Anna,[4] who was willing to participate in the study. The Head of School, in consultation with Ms Anna, chose three children from her class whose mothers were willing for their children to participate in the study. Valuing the need to establish a good relationship with parents (Nutbrown, 2011), once the three children were identified, a meeting for parents was held at the school (attended by the mothers only due to fathers' work commitments). This was to introduce the study and begin to establish a relationship with parents. After obtaining the parents' written consent, Jo sought the children's active agreement (Thomas & O'Kane, 1998) to obtain their personal, unprejudiced, informed free assent (Harcourt & Conroy, 2011). All three children were very eager to participate and share their drawings and ideas. In seeking children's assent, we wanted to ensure that their agreement was not an act of compliance with an authority figure. Had a child refused assent, their decision would have been respected, and another child would have been invited. Consent and assent were also sought from the other children in the class to ensure that they agreed to join in the kindergarten drawing sessions, but their drawings were not collected.

Children's continuous assent was obtained at the start of each visit and before drawings were photographed. Staying attuned to the children's ways of communicating and vigilant to their responses during each encounter was crucial. Verbal and non-verbal cues were interpreted to verify ongoing assent and ensure a positive disposition towards their participation. Occasionally, the children were reluctant to draw, perhaps because they preferred to play with their friends or drawing did not appeal, indicating how the children were gatekeepers of their involvement. They communicated their transient refusal to participate verbally or through signs such as shaking their heads, frowning, or simply ignoring the invitation. Children's refusal to participate shows their agency in conveying their preferences, their ability to understand the research process, and their right to non-participation. Remaining attuned to the children's wishes and staying watchful for changes in their levels of engagement ensured their participation was always voluntary.

## Publication, privacy, and authorship

Issues of confidentiality are key concerns when researching with young children (David et al., 2001). This study reported in this book presents two main privacy dilemmas:

i The use of the children's real names and
ii Showing children's faces in photographs and film footage

Early in the study, it became clear that default decisions to use pseudonyms and pixilated images would not do honest justice to the data and the children's accounts (Groundwater-Smith et al., 2015).

To maximise children's involvement in the study, they were initially invited to choose an assumed name they liked to make them unidentifiable. However, each child individually made it clear that they wanted their real names to be used (Harcourt, 2011; Wiles et al., 2008a). All three were unequivocal. Thea pointed out that she wrote her name on most of her drawings, "So that the people who see this picture, would know that I did the drawing ... that Thea drew this picture." Changing or obscuring her name to protect her identity would remove her sense of ownership. Luke wanted his real name used: "Because I drew all the pictures. It is all my work and I am proud of my work. I want people to know that; that it is my work." Bertly too said, "I only like Bertly as my name. I do not want any other name. I am Bertly."

Making their wishes clear and respecting children's views and the desire for true representation of their voices was a mainstay of the project. However, including young children's names is often contrary to the accepted default for ensuring anonymity by using pseudonyms. In the interests of protecting the "vulnerable" – ensuring anonymity assumes that participants would not want to be identifiable (Allen, 2005; Harcourt & Sargeant, 2011). In questioning this *status quo,* we contend that insisting on anonymity can contradict the basis of a rights-based, participatory approach, which aims to recognise and give voice to children and value their views. Anonymity, in this case, goes against the spirit of a qualitative design, which aims to value the authenticity of individual experiences.

Genuinely listening to children entails respecting their voices, thus, using their real names. BERA (2018, p. 21) guidelines suggest that researchers should "recognize participants' rights to be identified with any publication of their original works or other inputs if they so wish." Having deliberated with the children and their parents about any potential risks from being identifiable, we agreed the children's and their siblings' names would be used, but other names would be fictitious. Families' surnames and other information about the location of their homes or the name and location of the school were withheld, thus maintaining elements of confidentiality and privacy.

Parents also concluded that disclosing the children's identity would not incur harm, and both the children and their parents provided additional, specific, and exclusive written consent to identify the children by name and in visual images. The use of visual methods in research particularly brings challenging ethical issues. We were clear from the outset that the drawings belonged to the children, and we asked their permission to use them in the study. Still images and films of children drawing, including their faces, raise issues of privacy. The films focused on drawing processes, not the children, though from time to time they came into frame. During analysis, it became clear that visual images conveyed unique and sometimes unexpectedly crucial information (Banks, 2001; Wiles et al., 2008b). It seemed important to use photographs and film, which offered a full, authentic representation of the drawing process, including emerging narratives, articulated thinking processes, and meanings. Using images that identified children posed new challenges and ethical and moral dilemmas around anonymity (Rose, 2012). The personalised and contextualised drawings helped to uncover children's unique meaning-making. Thus, we did not pixilate the children's faces in visual images because, while protecting the children's anonymity in research can be necessary, pixelation silences their "voices-in-image" (Nutbrown, 2011, p. 9). Thus, using visual methods that identify the participants can be more ethical and respectful towards the participants' dignity than anonymising them (Holliday, 2004). As Nutbrown (2011, p. 10) argues, "Hiding children's faces seems wrong somehow... not showing a photo could be equally problematic and may, in itself, be unethical – in that it omits part of a research story given by a participant."

The moral obligation and professional responsibility to safeguard the children rest with us and the parents – and we must always be mindful of the children's interests as a priority. Through detailed, honest conversations with the children and their parents, we explored potential risks, including the possibility that when the children are older, they might regret disclosing their identity (Alderson & Morrow, 2011; Flewitt, 2006). After weighing the arguments, parents agreed with their children and approved the non-pixelation of faces, mainly because they considered the study to be risk-free where the children did not reveal any potentially harmful information. Parents were key to these decisions which were specific to this study. All studies involving young children must be subject to careful ethical decision-making, especially to protect anyone who may be considered vulnerable to the impacts of research at any stage.

## Analysing and interpreting children's drawings

The study reported in this book is based on 223 children's drawings, related observations of drawing processes, and respective conversations with the children and their parents, captured through photographs and film. Table 4.1 provides a summary of the number of drawings drawn by each child and the hours they spent drawing.

*Table 4.1* A summary of the three children's number of drawings by duration and context

| Name of child | Home drawings | | School drawings | | Total home and school drawings | |
|---|---|---|---|---|---|---|
| | Quantity | Duration | Quantity | Duration | Quantity | Duration |
| Luke | 55 | 5 hrs 23 mins | 25 | 4 hrs 15 mins | 80 | 9 hrs 38 mins |
| Thea | 40 | 15 hrs 1 min | 44 | 16 hrs 8 mins | 84 | 31 hrs 9 mins |
| Bertly | 39 | 2 hrs 46 mins | 20 | 3 hrs 56 mins | 59 | 6 hrs 42 mins |

Being given these data is a privilege, and in this book, we have woven rich accounts of the children's drawing lives. We created "tailored modes of interpretation" (Nutbrown, 2021, p. 90) with four stages of analysis based on Penn's (2000) mode of semiological analysis: (1) configuration of data; (2) exploration of data; (3) compiling an inventory of content; (4) and examining higher levels of signification (meaning).

*Step 1: Configuration of data*

First, the data analysis process involved cataloguing the drawings in a database of drawings by each child. Home and school drawings were filed separately (for each child), each coded by the child's first initial (e.g. T for Thea), H or S (for Home or School), followed by a chronological number for each drawing. When fully indexed, a *Data Log* was made for each drawing, which included the title of the drawing and related transcripts of conversations. These datasets were used to consider aspects of the *form, content,* and *meaning* of each drawing and the funds of knowledge that seemed to influence each drawing. Scanned copies of drawings and video recordings of observations were securely stored electronically, enabling us to keep a digital copy of each drawing and return the originals to the children at the next visit.[5]

*Step 2: Exploration of data*

Next, the *form* and *content* of drawings were explored, that is, *how* (modes) and *what* (objects) children drew were plotted on a *Data Cross-grid* (Deguara, 2019). This instrument provides a novel way of examining and interpreting young children's drawings, analysing *modes* and themes on a *simple-complex* gradient. Plotting the drawings thus offers an immediate graphic impression of each child's preferred *form* (*simple-complex mode*) and *content* (*simple-complex theme*) styles, respectively. The vertical line in Table 4.2 represents the "*Mode*"; the horizontal line represents the "*Theme.*" Both lines signify a gradient from *Simple* (S) to *Complex* (C). Using the *Data Cross-grid* creates a graphic representation of a child's preferences for *simple-complex modes* and *themes.*

*Table 4.2* The *Data Cross-grid* indicates the integration of *Simple* and *Complex Modes* and *Themes*

|  | Mode |  |
|---|---|---|
| **A** Simple mode / Simple theme | | **B** Simple mode / Complex theme |
| **Theme** | | |
| **D** Complex mode / Simple theme | | **C** Complex mode / Complex theme |

Each drawing can be plotted in one of the following categories and areas in the *Data Cross-grid* (Table 4.2):

- *Simple mode, Simple theme* (top left – A)
- *Simple mode, Simple theme* (top right – B)
- *Complex mode, Complex theme* (bottom right – C)
- *Complex mode, Simple theme* (bottom left – D)

*Simple-complex mode*

Our notion of a *simple-to-complex mode* is based on the semiotic concept that children make and communicate meanings through a combination of a range of modes, means, and media (Flewitt, 2008; Stein, 2008; Kress, 2010). Modes rarely occur in isolation but are used by the drawer in constant interplay (Jewitt, 2008). Consequently, we define *simple mode* as the use of one or two related modes in drawing (such as drawing and mark-making or the combination of drawing with writing or cutting with glueing). *Complex mode* is defined as the use of a variety of modes together, including drawing, glueing, tracing, colouring, writing, and cutting.

*Simple – complex theme*

We define a *simple-to-complex theme* according to the number of objects in a drawing. Children rarely draw one object; often, a series of objects denotes one meaning. Thus, we define a *simple theme* as the drawing of one or two (related or unrelated) objects to denote one meaning but which do not involve a narration or a complex description. In a *simple theme*, one idea or concept (e.g. an animal or a person) dominates a drawing. A *complex theme* features more than two objects drawn to create an elaborate scene or visual narrative.

Luke's *Ben Ten Fight* (*LS18*, Figure 4.1) was analysed in terms of the related modes of drawing and mark-making, thus classifying the drawing form as a *simple mode*. Luke drew a *complex theme* with various characters and objects, explaining that his drawing featured two video cameras fighting two *Ben Ten* characters. The drawing includes a monster, guns, and gunfire. This classifies the drawing as *simple in mode* and *complex in theme*, which we plotted at the top-right corner of the *Data Cross-Grid*.

### Step 3: Inventory of content

To compile an *Inventory of Content*, we listened to the children's talk about their drawings, which is key to maintaining each child's voice in the analysis of each drawing. Emerging and common content themes were then grouped

*Table 4.3* The *Inventory of Content* identifies themes and sub-themes in the drawings of the three children

| Content themes | Sub-themes identified from each theme |
| --- | --- |
| People | Self, family, friends, fantasy, unknown people, and named others |
| Animals and other creatures | Mini-beasts, farm, pets, wild, sea creatures, sky creatures, and fantasy creatures |
| Weather and sky features | Sky, stars, sun, rainbow, and rain |
| Natural environmental features | Flowers, grass, leaves, trees, and mushrooms<br>Pond, river, and lake<br>Sea and beach<br>Stones, rocks, and mountain |
| Natural elements | Fire and water |
| Food | Fruits<br>Sweets, ice cream, candy, cake, Easter egg<br>Sausage roll, bread, and<br>Pasta |
| Toys and play equipment | Balls, Wii, trampoline, and pink goo |
| Vehicles | Aeroplanes, boats/ships, cars, cranes, motorbikes, rockets, and trains |
| Built environments | Pool and well<br>Road, roundabout, and tunnel |
| Buildings | Houses, castle, church, farm, and apertures |
| Abstract | Shapes and symbols |
| Writing | Letters, names, numbers, and words |
| Miscellaneous objects (objects that do not fall under any category listed above) | Digital equipment<br>Warfare equipment and trophies;<br>Everyday objects and other oddities (unrelated objects) |

into a list of 13 items from the 223 drawings (Table 4.3). Each broad content theme was subdivided into several subthemes, revealing the rich detail of content in the children's drawings and ensuring that nothing was lost throughout various stages of analysis.

### Step 4: The meaning in children's drawings

Building on the *Inventory of Content*, Step 4 identifies the subjective interpretation of the often multiple symbolic "structures of meaning" (Nicolopoulou et al., 1994, p. 106), represented in the drawings, which makes some drawings challenging to interpret. Moral and ethical responsibilities require us to do justice to children's processes of meaning-making, exposing the depth, detail, and significance of their meanings (Nutbrown, 2011). The children's descriptions and related talk, and their parents' insights about possible influences, meant that each drawing was considered as a whole. Involving children in the research process by encouraging them and their parents to talk about their drawings assured "quality of interpretation" (Nutbrown, 2021, p. 92). Children's interpretations, integrated with their parents' and our interpretations, help to identify what each drawing means to them (Nicolopoulou et al., 1994; Toren, 2007). The meaning attributed to a drawing is context-dependent; therefore, any analysis should be contextually situated, taking account of socio-cultural background to better understand children's meaning-making.

The next three chapters look at Luke's, Thea's, and Bertly's drawing case studies.

### Notes

1 In Malta, educators who teach at the kindergarten level (three to five-year-olds) are formally known as "kindergarten educators" (KGEs). However, occasionally, in this book, we use the term "teacher." This is because children in kindergarten and at times, their parents and the public, refer to kindergarten educators as "teachers."
2 Jo collected all drawings and organised and transcribed all data.
3 Jo is fluent in Maltese and English and fully versed in Maltese cultures and contexts; an affinity with the children's contexts was important to achieving a depth of understanding of the children and their drawings.
4 Pseudonyms are used for all names in this book to protect the identity of those involved, except for the three children of the study and their siblings.
5 A sample of a Data Log is available at https://sites.google.com/view/children makingmeaning.

# 5 Luke's story

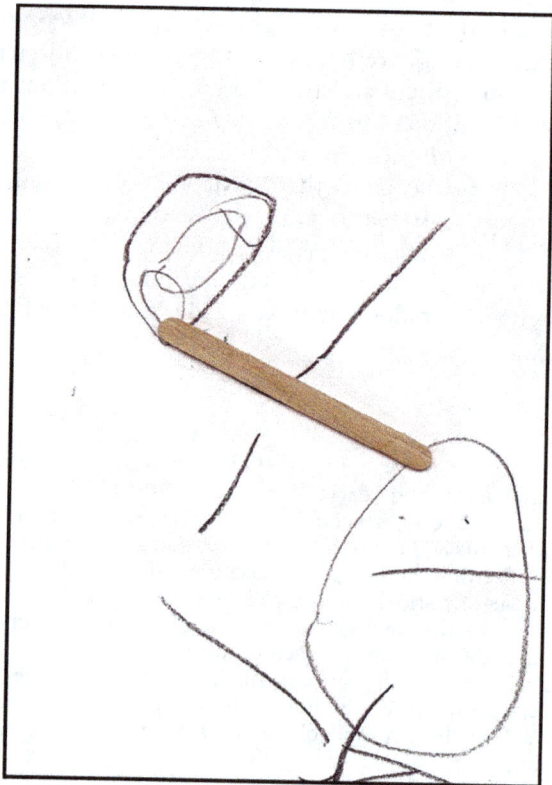

*Figure 5.1* Me Carrying a Bag Full of Candy (LH49) – by Luke.[1]

## Getting to know Luke

Luke (4:6) got along well with his brothers Matthias (9) and Jacob (3). Jacob and Luke attended the same school, and Matthias attended an all-boys school. The family lived in a relatively large, well-furnished, terraced house

DOI: 10.4324/9781003427582-5

near Luke's school. The house appeared child-friendly: the fridge was covered with the children's drawings and photographs; a tricycle and a pushchair were stored underneath the stairs; and the accessible playroom contained many toys. The living area was the children's space to entertain themselves: eat, read, watch television, or play with the Nintendo Wii. The television was often showing children's cartoons or a Wii game, which all the family enjoyed: tennis, sword fights, and basketball games being Luke's favourite games. Sometimes the boys brought toys from the playroom or spent time jumping on and off the sofa; they were free to use the living area as a play space.

Luke's parents were pharmacists. The mother seemed to take responsibility for daily household routines, school runs, and extra-curricular activities. Both parents regularly spent time helping and playing with their children. Luke was very close to his mother, frequently demonstrating his caring, tender self, protecting her, and regarding her as his role model. He also appeared to have a competitive rapport with his father, concurrently acting in complicity and reciprocity with him. At the time of the study, Luke's mother underwent surgery, which created tension and concern. During that period, Luke seemed worried and restless at home and school and uninterested in drawing. The family was well supported and had a close bond with their extended family.

Luke was described by both his mother and the kindergarten teacher as inquisitive, energetic, and dynamic, constantly moving from one thing to another and taking control of situations. His father described Luke as intelligent and witty, knowing how to manipulate a situation to his advantage. Luke seemed to be a good communicator, outspoken, assertive, and extrovert. His outgoing and humorous personality, where he cracked jokes, teased his friends, and narrated dramatic stories – in Maltese and English – helped him assume light-hearted "interactional control" (Dyson, 1993b, p. 72) over his peers, earning him popularity, respect, and friendship.

At home and school, Luke enjoyed playing with construction materials, toy guns, fast-moving toy cars, and motorcycles. He also enjoyed singing songs, and it was quite common to hear him humming or singing in an undertone. He loved exploring outdoor play spaces and engaging in physical play with his siblings. Once a week, he attended an extra-curricular sports programme, participating in different sports. His play and drawings reflected a passion for adventure, action, destruction, power, and victory, sword fight play on the Wii, and watching superhero films such as *Iron Man* and *Buzz Light Year* of *Toy Story*. Luke liked *Ben Ten*, experiencing an affinity for and identifying with *Ben Ten's* personality. Like *Ben Ten*, he enjoyed the attention of others and had a feisty character that sometimes verged on arrogance. This was balanced with positive qualities, manifested through his smartness, good-hearted character, and sincere wish to help others. Luke liked to be the leader, often describing and drawing himself as older, taller, bigger, stronger, and better than others, including his parents.

46  *Children making meaning*

## Analysing Luke's drawings: simple-complex modes and themes

Luke's home and school drawings and drawing time in each setting were summarised in Table 4.1 (Chapter 4). The difference in quantity and time spent drawing in the two settings could be because at school he sometimes preferred to play with his peers, whereas at home he spent time drawing with his mother. Luke spent anything from 25 seconds to over thirty minutes to complete a drawing.

We plotted Luke's 80 drawings on his *Data Cross-grid* (Figure 5.2). The school drawings, coded LS (Luke School) in black, are plotted in the top sections, while the home drawings, coded LH (Luke Home) in blue, are plotted

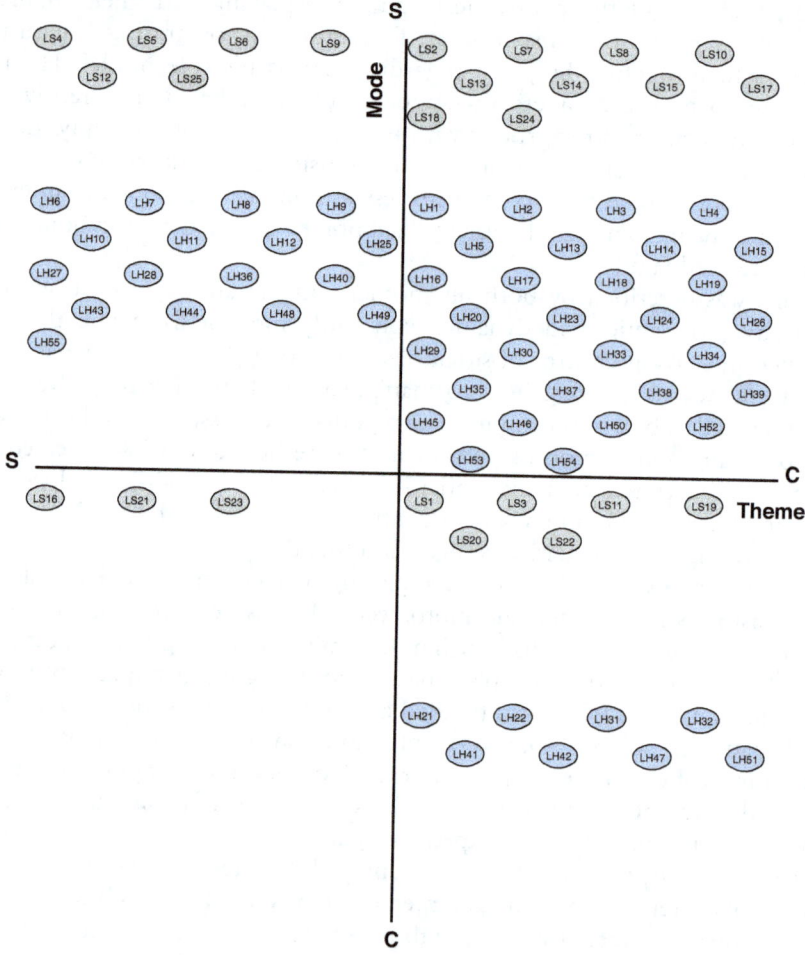

*Figure 5.2* Luke's *Data Cross-grid* represents his home (blue) and school (black) drawings.

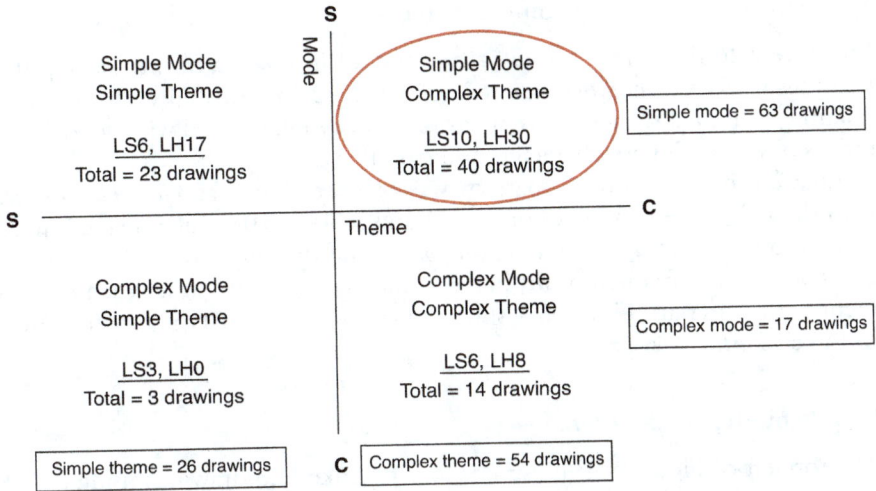

*Figure 5.3* A summary of Luke's *Data Cross-grid* with his preferred drawing pattern marked with a red circle.

in the bottom sections. Figure 5.3 summarises Luke's drawings, showing that with forty drawings (30 home and ten school), his drawings were mostly *simple in mode* and *complex in theme*. We next discuss Luke's drawings in that category.

## Luke's use of simple-complex modes

Sixty-three of Luke's 80 drawings were created using *a simple mode* (Figures 5.2 and 5.3), indicating that this was his favoured semiotic style. He preferred to use one or two related modes in his drawings. He exclusively drew in 27 drawings, frequently using crayons, gem markers, or both. Occasionally, Luke experimented with *complex modes* using several media, including sticky tape, glitter, glue, pens, corrugated and wrapping paper, and lollipop sticks.

At school, Luke frequently initiated using different modes as resources and also considered what his peers were doing; sometimes resulting in similarities between drawings. At home, Luke adopted a more dependent attitude, frequently asking his mother to help him use the various materials and modes available.

Prior to the study, at school, children used pencil colours or a set of crayons at the drawing table; other media, such as glue or glitter glue, sequins, or scissors, were regarded as too messy or dangerous to be used independently. Luke avoided some media because he had few opportunities to experiment, sometimes saying he did not know how to use particular media, such as "I do not know what I am going to do with the glitters." While his preferred use of simple modal choice could have reflected his lack of exposure, it is possible that Luke used the materials he found most convenient.

48  *Children making meaning*

### Luke's choice of simple-complex themes

Luke drew 26 drawings in *simple theme* and 44 in *complex theme*, making the latter his preferred *configuration style* (Figures 5.2 and 5.3). His drawings frequently combined scenes or events from his daily life merged with action narratives based on fantasy characters and storylines.

Luke's preferred drawing pattern was of *simple mode* and *complex theme*, with drawings spread across home (30) and school (10). Luke seemed more focused on the *content* rather than the *form* of his drawing, preferring to create a *complex theme* (frequently with an accompanying story) rather than experiment with materials. Figure 5.4 shows four drawings that typify each section of Luke's *Data Cross-grid*.

### Simple mode, simple theme

The top left of Figure 5.4[2] illustrates four of Luke's 23 drawings using a *simple mode* and *simple theme*. Common characteristics include sketch-type style and restricted use of *modes*, media, and colour. The theme in each drawing was also *simple*, where each picture included an object or person (*LS4, LS12, LH49, LH44*).

#### *Me Carrying a Bag Full of Candy*

Luke drew himself carrying a bag of sweets, which he is holding by a rod, on his shoulder (*LH49*, Figure 5.1)[3]. He took about four minutes; using a black crayon, he drew a circular shape with a protruding stem, 'a lollipop'. Adding a line on each side, he relabelled it: "A bag full of sweets with two handles." Declaring: "Now there is going to be me," Luke added an outlined image of himself with a huge head, a small stick body, and a bag on his shoulder. He stopped drawing and stood on the chair, exclaiming: "And it goes like this. March like this! Ta-ra! Psht! Psht! It goes like this. Bum. Bum. Vooom. Voom," while rhythmically marching across the room, miming while holding a bag on one shoulder. Accompanying his representation with vocalisation and active telling, Luke integrated a "graphic-verbal telling of events" (Wright, 2008, p. 39), extending his drawing and demonstrating his meaning. Luke's "playing *with* drawing" (Wood & Hall, 2011, p. 275) included gesticulation, movement, and action, beyond the paper that images alone could not communicate. Gestures and actions are two modes that children use in their "drawing-telling" (Wright, 2008, p. 1) to explain the meaning of their drawings.

Luke concluded his drawing by glueing a lollipop stick "to hold the bag," representing the rod holding the bag. This reminded him of Father Christmas giving out presents, which led to his wish for a lot of candy. He finished his drawing by adding three circles in the bag, saying: "Let me put the candy in … a little bit [of sweets] will not do any harm."

Figure 5.4 A sample of Luke's drawings in *simple-to-complex modes* and corresponding themes.

50  *Children making meaning*

Luke used a *simple mode* – drawing and glueing the lollipop stick – and a *simple theme* – two objects (himself and a bag of candy) with no complex description. Each step in the drawing process informs the next, enabling him to decide on the meanings made and the resources used (Mavers, 2011). Drawing a lollipop inspired Luke to draw a bag of sweets, then himself marching with a bag. The affordance of the lollipop stick communicated "stickness." The choice of mode seemed informed by a combination of an experience (peers at school using lollipop sticks) and his dramatisation inspired by Father Christmas role-play at school. Visual forms can have fluidity (Hopperstad, 2008a), with the possibility of multiple, evolving meanings (Hopperstad, 2008b). Luke's playing *with* the drawing (Wood & Hall, 2011) goes beyond the text, extending the drawing to his Father Christmas role-play.

Luke seemed to use his drawing to communicate (Adams, 2003) a personal request (for sweets); a "form of personal externalization" (Ahn & Filipenko, 2007, p. 280) of his wish for more sweets.

## Simple mode, complex theme

Luke preferred to draw in a *simple mode* and a *complex theme*. Four drawings (Figure 5.4 top right) reflect this style: three in a sketchy, mono-colour form using gem markers. They include elements of mark-making, which represent action in his drawings. The drawings are *complex in theme* because they feature more than two objects, depicting a scene (*LH30*) or a narration (*LH24, LS17, LS18*).

### Ben Ten[4] Fight

*Ben Ten Fight* (*LS18*, Figure 4.1)[5] was drawn in *simple mode*: drawing and mark-making, accompanied by a graphic narrative. The *complex* scene included two video cameras, *Ben Ten*, a helicopter, and black gunshot lines all over the paper.

It can be difficult to understand the narration of such a drawing, which is dominated by mark-making. Figure 5.5 shows the process of drawing, which Luke began by sketching two video cameras. Adding hands to the cameras (Figure 5.5, Image 1), he transformed them into characters in a fantasy-based narrative. Drawing *Ben Ten* (Figure 5.5, Image 2, left), Luke explained that *Ben Ten* is firing gunshots at the video cameras represented by the dots and lines (Figure 5.5, Images 3–9).

In his narrative, Luke transformed his drawing into playful action (Kangas et al., 2011; Wood & Hall, 2011). He denoted gunshots by vigorously and forcefully drawing dots and lines all over his characters, augmenting the struggle between them (Figure 5.5, Images 8 & 9). Action lines can signify strength, justice, and courage (Wright, 2007); the quantity, speed, and pressure Luke used conveyed ferocity, power, and intense combat.

Luke's story 51

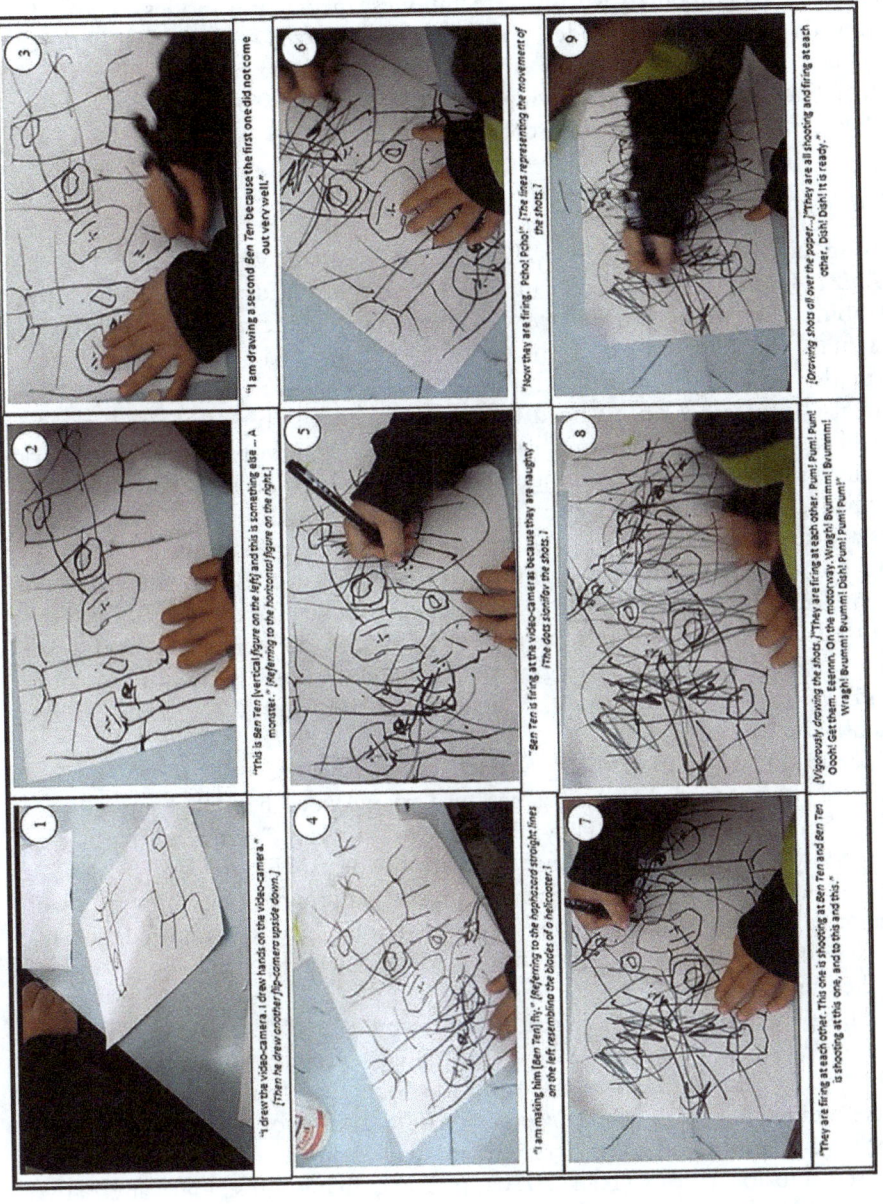

*Figure 5.5* Luke during the process and narration of the drawing *Ben Ten fight* (LS18).

## Complex mode, complex theme

Four examples of Luke's untypical drawings using a *complex mode* and *complex theme* (Figure 5.4; bottom right) show his shift from *simple* to *complex* modes, where he experimented with new techniques, media, and modes, repeatedly using an "ensemble of modes" (Kress, 2008, p. 92), as he moved between relatively unfamiliar modes of cutting, glueing, taping, and dabbing glitter glue. The themes in these drawings were *complex* too; *LS19* illustrates a scene, while *LS11*, *LH42*, and *LH21* represent a story.

### Cutting the Bad Guy Out 1

Using his usual sketchy style, Luke drew "*Cutting the Bad Guy Out 1*" (*LH21*, Figure 5.6, Image 1) in *complex mode* using drawing, cutting, and dabbing glitter glue. The *theme* was a *complex*, graphic narrative inspired by a fantasy character, which, at the content level, showed Luke as a superhero, armed with a knife, sword, gun, and two ropes "to tie someone with it." He also drew a hat on his head for protection. In each pocket, he sketched small figures of Matthias and his mother, "so that I would be able to carry them with me," and his younger brother, Jacob (blue line, top right), as a "bad guy." Casting himself as *Iron Man* (Marvel Comics, 2015), Luke's task was to protect Matthias and his mother from the "bad guy." The drawing incorporated a multi-meaning mythical narrative. Borrowing the text from *Iron Man* and integrating sound effects, Luke enacted a fight between himself, as a superhero, and Jacob: "The killer of the world: This is the bad guy ... and this one [pointing at the drawing of himself] is firing at him. Buff! He is dead. Buff ... and he died. Buff again. Buff! ... And this will be Jacob, the bad guy."

Jacob, unhappy about being a bad guy, complained: "I am not the bad guy... I do not die." Explaining his unswerving view that "Bad guys always die. They die with a gun. They die even with a sword." Luke used a pair of scissors to cut out the bad guy to signify his death (Figure 5.6, Image 2). "I will cut it out. I will cut his face... I am cutting him out ... So that he dies." Seemingly driven by a sense of justice and victory, Luke drew a medal on his chest and a trophy in each hand: his reward for defeating the bad guy, "I won. I killed him."

This play-infused drawing created a "space for intellectual play" (Wood & Hall, 2011, p. 267), where Luke appropriated "'pretend' identities" (Dyson, 1997, p. 14), emulating *Iron Man* and the "bad guy" to mediate his identity. Luke seemed keen to possess *Iron Man*'s traits and reposition himself in relation to his mother and brothers. He created an image of himself engaging in "self-transformation" (Hall, 2010a, p. 106), giving himself an "alternative identity" (Hall, 2010a, p. 108) as a strong, powerful, fearless hero like *Iron Man*, distinctively different from his real compassionate self. Luke enjoyed adopting *Iron Man*'s powers and identity to become central to the story,

*Luke's story* 53

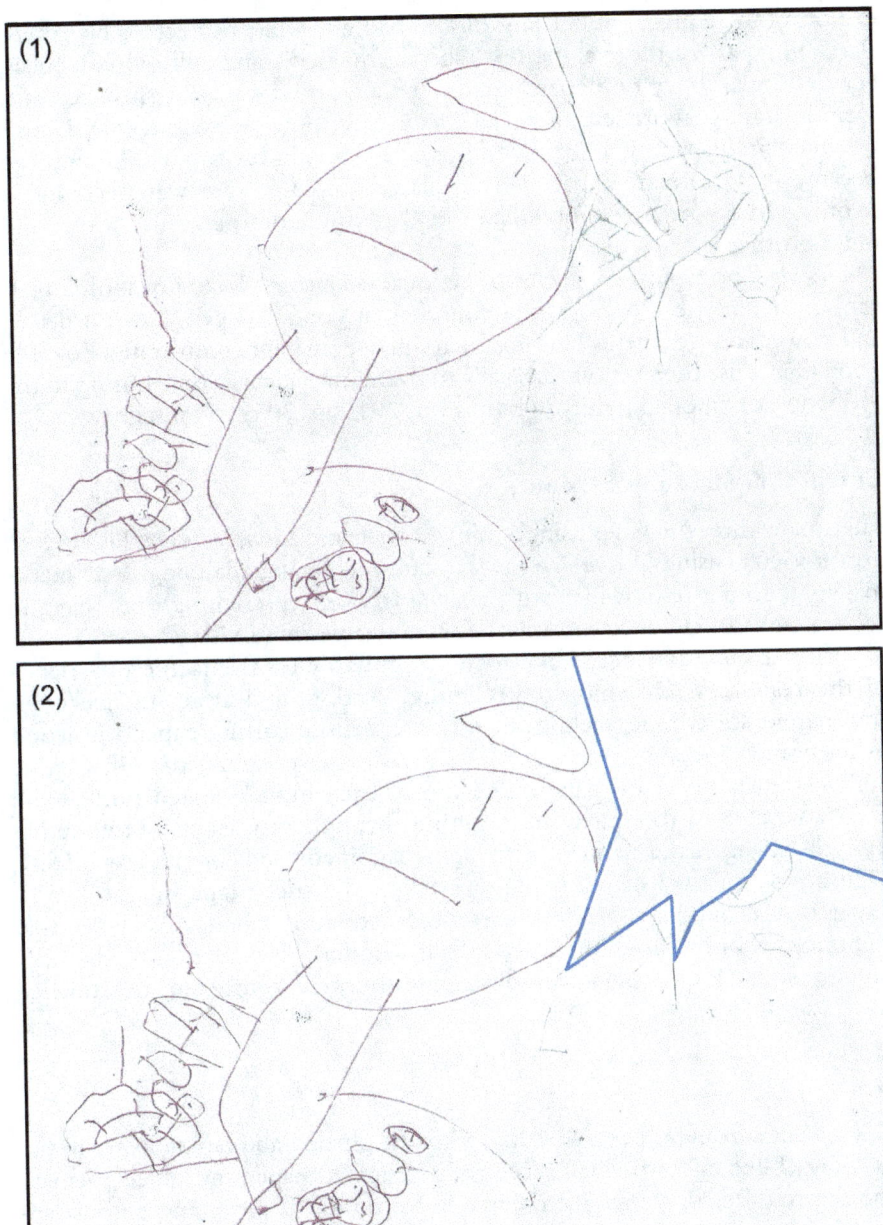

*Figure 5.6* **Cutting the Bad Guy Out 1 *(LH21)*** full drawing [1], and with the "bad guy" cut out [2].

exploring the dangers of fighting off the bad guy while protecting his family. Becoming part of the graphic text, shaped by media and cultural influences, enabled Luke to try on desired character traits and draw his desired persona. Demonstrating awareness of social hierarchies, power structures, and positions within his family, Luke reconfigured his role in his family. The drawing became a transformative space where Luke acquired more power, becoming a strong, smart superhero who killed the "bad guy" to protect his mother and older brother.

Drawing on typical narratives of fictional characters, Luke juxtaposed realism and fantasy, exploring moral concerns of good and evil, life and death, and power and weakness. This imaginary play-drawing demonstrated how the good might use their powers ethically to overcome villains, contributing to the formation of "moral identity" (Edmiston, 2010, p. 205) and integrity.

## Complex mode, simple theme

Luke made three drawings using a *complex mode* and a *simple theme* (Figure 5.4, bottom left), using a *complex mode* – cutting, taping, dabbing, and mark-making – to create drawings with a *simple theme*, representing one object in each: a cow (*LS21*), an aeroplane (*LS23*), and a worm (*LS16*).

Using a *complex mode*, Luke focused primarily on the tactile experience of the resources. He enjoyed stretching, cutting, and attaching pieces of transparent sticky tape, feeling the tacky sensation; cutting paper and wood using liquid glue and dealing with its messiness; spreading the glitter glue and seeing its effect on paper. The use of each mode seemed purposeful; each was selected to contribute meaning through affordance and materiality. For example, the dabbed glitter glue signified food for the cow (*LS21*, Figure 5.4) and worm (*LS16*, Figure 5.7). The sticky tape on the brown paper in the middle of *LS16* represented the worm's brain, used "so that the brain will not come out." The glued wooden sticks secured with sticky tape in *LS23* (Figure 5.4) symbolised the shooting equipment he attached to the aeroplane.

### A Worm

Taking a cue from his peer, Martina, who was glueing and taping paper to her drawing, Luke cut two small pieces of corrugated paper and glued them to the centre of his drawing. Sketching a line around the paper and enthusiastically intersecting the large enclosure mark with numerous lines, he said, "This is a worm. Those lines at the bottom are his legs, and the lines on top are its hair." The worm was the single, central object dominating the paper, making this drawing a *simple theme*.

Inspired by his peers to use the unfamiliar sticky tape, Luke used two pieces – one to secure the glued brown paper (left), and the other, rolled and

*Figure 5.7* A Worm *(LS16)* – by Luke.

crumbled into a sphere, attached to the middle of the brown paper (right). Playing with the sticky tape, Luke investigated its adhesive characteristics and explored how he could use it to create meaning in his drawing. Luke secured the worm's brain with the sticky-tape, knowing sticky-tape is used to join things together, which he did, literally and metaphorically.

Luke wanted to give the worm something to eat. Realising he had forgotten to draw its head, Luke drew a head using a pen on the left side, later dabbing and spreading glitter glue, a different medium from the paper, sticky tape, and a pen to signify, "Some food. I gave him some food."

Luke's mother suggested that drawing the brain could have been inspired by watching two children's television programmes about how the brain works. These perhaps sparked his interest in making his drawing work. Luke's narrative indicated his knowledge of worms, creating his realisation of a worm. Using his drawing to reconfigure what he knew, Luke communicated that worms have hair, legs, a brain, and eat food. In his drawings, one decision often leads to another in a fluid, dynamic process that transforms content and meaning (Siegel et al., 2008).

## Inventory of content: emerging themes in Luke's drawings

The two most frequently drawn themes across Luke's 80 drawings were *People* and *Weather and Sky*.

## People

Depictions of *People* occurred 82 times in Luke's 80 drawings. Several drawings featured his family members (35), self-portraits (19), and friends (9). He also drew unnamed people (8), fantasy (7), and named (4) people, defining him as a "person-centred" drawer (Gardner, 1982, p. 118).

While Luke sometimes drew static figures, his characters were frequently involved in action – playing, eating, or fighting. Figure 5.8 shows some drawings of Luke's *People*. In the following sections, we discuss some of these drawings from the most drawn sub-categories under *People*: family, self-portraits, and friends.

### Family

Luke drew family members in 35 drawings. Loosely classified into three groups: (i) members of his nuclear and extended family; (ii) himself with his mother; and (iii) his brothers. Like many young children's drawings, which convey emotional relationships and family dynamics (Malchiodi, 1998), Luke's suggests closeness to his family and the importance of family relationships. Reflecting the context of their content (Brooks, 2005), most family drawings were made at home, with three (of 35) made at school.

Some family drawings were static. Figure 5.9 shows Luke's dad and mum together (*LH7*, Image 1); Luke with his dad (*LH8*, Image 2); Luke's father (*LH10*, Image 3); Luke's mother, his brother Matthias, and himself (*LH14*, Image 4); Luke's mum, his dad, brother Matthias, and himself (*LH16*, Image 5); and the whole family (*LH19*, Image 6).

Other drawings of his family depicted action (Figure 5.10): playing, fighting, and enjoying time together. Luke drew his parents with himself in his mother's tummy while Matthias was playing football (*My Family: LH1*, Figure 5.10, Image 1), and Luke with his mum and dad eating ice cream (*Mum, Dad, and I Eating Ice-cream*, *LH15*, Figure 5.10, Image 2).

Omitting Matthias, "because we do not love him," and drawing an unborn Jacob in isolation, but being thought of (*LH15*, top left), the drawing conveyed Luke's plan to have his brothers out of the way so that he would have his parents' exclusive attention and ice-cream. Luke depicted himself (in the middle) with a moustache, taller than his parents, holding the biggest ice cream. Skattebol (2006) suggests that children find ways to change their size to gain more power; in what appears to be a simple family drawing, at the meaning level, the drawing addresses issues of power, family hierarchies, and dynamics, portraying Luke in a position of power in relation to his parents.

*Figure 5.8* Sample of Luke's drawings illustrating *People*.

58 *Children making meaning*

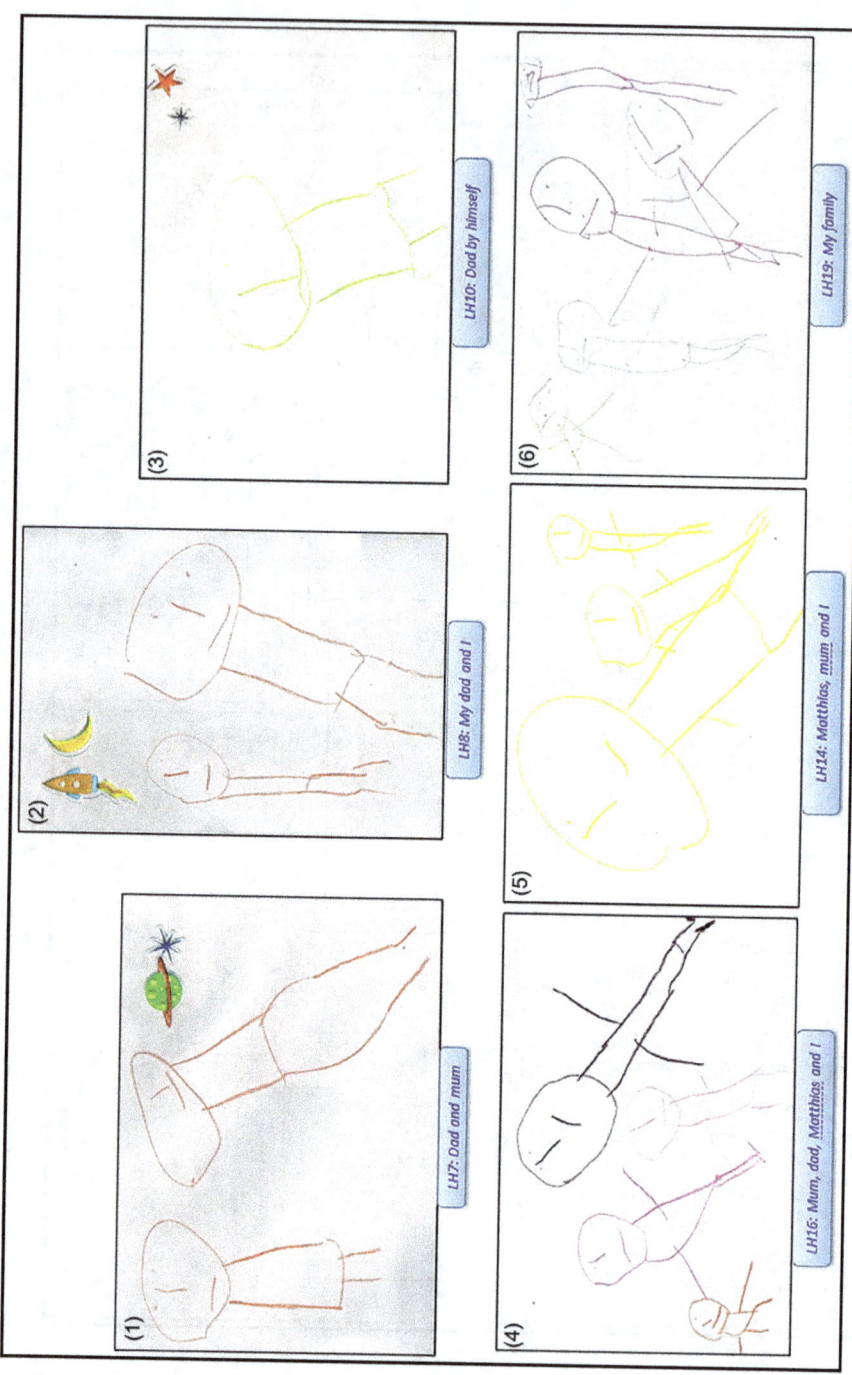

*Figure 5.9* Static drawings of *Family* members – by Luke.

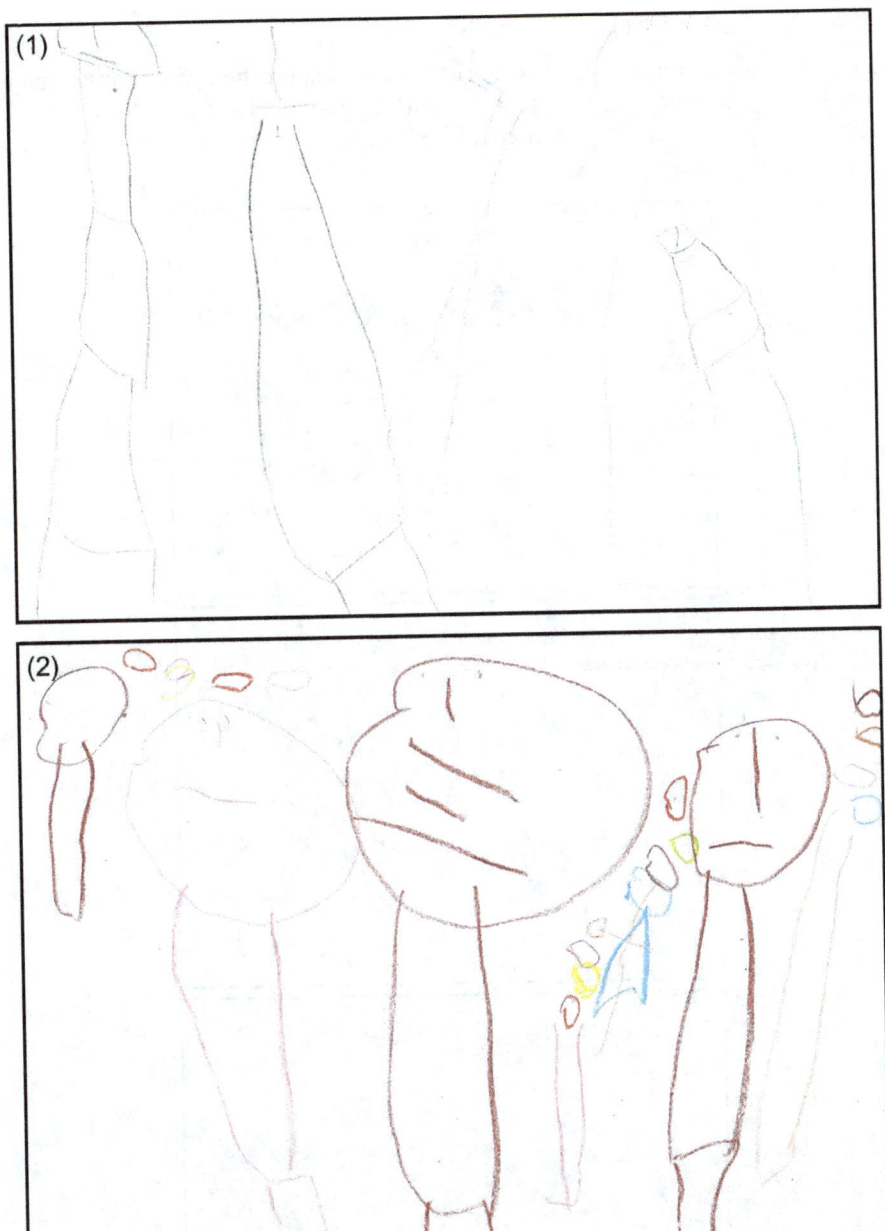

*Figure 5.10* My Family with Matthias Playing Football *(LH1)* [1], *Mum, Dad and I Eating Ice-cream (LH15)* [2] the family in action – by Luke.

60   Children making meaning

*Mother*

Luke's drawings mirrored his relationship with his mother, frequently depicting her alone or doing things with him (Figure 5.11). Luke drew himself and his mother walking together under a dark starry night (*My Mum and I*

*Figure 5.11* My Mum and I Walking in the Dark (LH18) [1], My Mum and I Playing with the Ball (LH38) [2], Luke and Mum Fighting on a Picnic (LH54) [3] – by Luke.

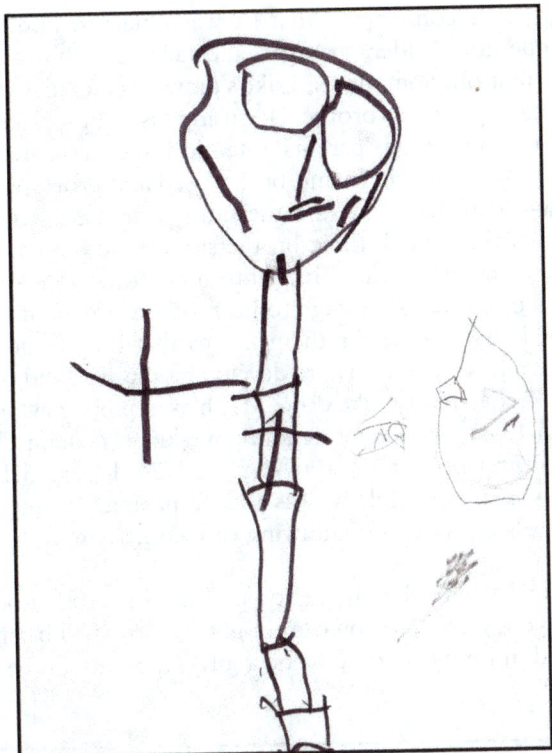

*Figure 5.12* My Mother Tied Up *(LS8)* – by Luke.

*Walking in the Dark: LH18*, Figure 5.11, Image 1), holding an Easter egg and his mother holding a sausage roll (*LH32*), something she regularly baked, and his mother taking him to school (*LH33*, Figure 5.8). In two drawings, his mother was playing with him: *My Mum and I Playing with the Ball* (*LH38*, Figure 5.11, Image 2), and *Luke and Mum Fighting on a Picnic* (*LH54*, Figure 5.11, Image 3), intermingling a real experience with his desire to play-fight with his mother (who disapproved).

In two school drawings of his mother, Luke conveyed his anger towards her. In *LS8*, Figure 5.12, Luke drew his mother tied up with a rope as his way of punishing her because she refused to give him sweets. Here Luke was using drawing to express his negative thoughts and to regulate his emotions (Drake, 2023).

Luke's drawings also communicate love for his mother. After drawing them both together (*LH6*), Luke hugged and kissed her, saying, "I will draw myself [next to you] because I love you. This is for you. And it is for me. It is yours and mine." Such drawings were a testimony to Luke's feelings.

## Siblings

Luke enjoyed a good, close relationship with his brothers; they played together, helped and cared for each other. Matthias (9) was a role model and partner in play, though Luke complained that he was unfair to him. He considered Matthias a competitor – older, stronger, and taller than him – with whom he competed for attention. Sometimes, Luke's drawings included elements of sibling rivalry: being angry at his brothers for using his things, waking him up, and sometimes having to share his parents' attention. Occasionally, he deliberately left Matthias out of his drawings, and both teased and protected Jacob (3).

Seven drawings depicted Luke's brothers: three featured Jacob, two featured Matthias, and two featured all three brothers; most were done at home, often when his brothers were there. Luke frequently used the drawings as a springboard to playfully tease or convey a message to his brothers. Luke's mother explained, "Drawing in pink and purple for them means that they want to spite someone." This use of pink enabled Luke to develop his drawing and connect with his brothers at an affective level. Luke drew Matthias in pink, playing Wii with him (*LH53*, Figure 5.13); pink perhaps denoting weakness, making Luke stronger.

Luke began *Throwing pink goo at Jacob* (*LH26*, Figure 5.14), explaining that Jacob had woken him while he was asleep, making him angry. With a pink marker, Luke drew lines over the drawing of Jacob, saying:

> Now I will make him [Jacob] pinky, pinky, with pinky goo... I make pink goo on you, Jacob. So you cannot get out. You will be stuck forever and ever. And mummy is going to be a girly ... She is always a girly. Let

*Figure 5.13* **Luke and Matthias Playing Swordfight with Wii (LH53)** – by Luke.

*Luke's story* 63

*Figure 5.14 Throwing Pink Goo at Jacob (LH26)* – by Luke.

me make you [to mummy]. You are angry and shouting. 'LUUKEE!' You are angry at Jacob because he woke me up. And I made some goo on him.

Luke included his mother, shouting angrily at Jacob for waking him. Having a strong aversion to pink and hearing Luke repeat that his brother will not be able to escape from the pink goo upset Jacob, who asked, "Why? I do not like pink. I do not want me pink." Realising that his brother was genuinely affected, Luke tried to console him, saying, "It is just a story … you are covered in sticky pink goo … just to tease you." Jacob calmed down, but Luke continued to tease him.

In some of his drawings, Luke vented his anger towards Matthias. *Matthias in a Cage* (*LH20*, Figure 5.15) has a stick figure on the right enclosed in a circle. Luke claimed that he put Mathias in a cage:

Because I always let him play with my toys, but he never lets me and I always let him… Because he never lets me play with his toys and I always let him … Because he never lets me play with his toys and I always let him … I let him play with everything … with the motorcycle.

64  *Children making meaning*

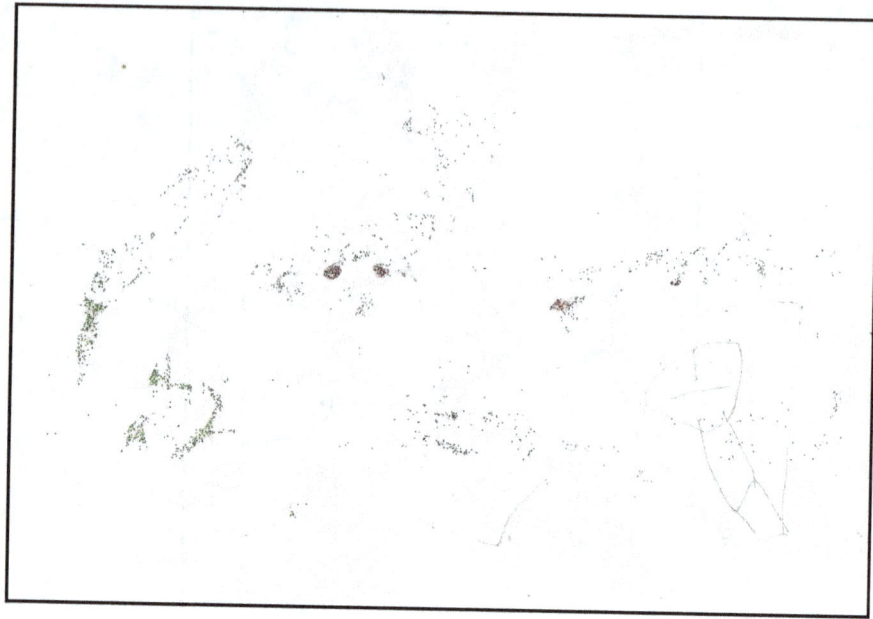

*Figure 5.15* Matthias in a Cage (LH20) – by Luke.

The repeated sentence emphasises Luke's anger, frustration, and sense of unfairness, as expressed in the drawing. Luke explained that the glitters were gunshots: "We are firing. All these, the good ones are firing at Matthias, the bad one. Jacob the good brother is firing at Matthias the bad one because he takes my toys."

Luke's drawing and comments provide insights into his feelings of frustration towards Matthias, indicating the importance of justice, perhaps expressing Luke's wish for some control over the situation. The mention of "gunshots" in the drawing and the explanation that "the good ones" are firing at "the bad one" indicate sibling rivalry, Luke's frustrations, and the importance of justice.

*Self-drawings*

Luke made 22 drawings of himself: seven solitary self-portraits and 15 including Luke with family members or friends (Figure 5.8). Luke drew himself in various roles and characters: as a child, as a grown-up man in an "ideal identity" (De Ruyter & Conroy, 2002, p. 510) in the future, and as a fantasy character in an "imagined identity" (Kendrick & McKay, 2004, p. 120). Two figures of himself appeared to be in conflict with himself (*LH28*, Figure 5.16); holding a dialogue with his "bad" self, enhancing his meaning through his narrative, while shooting and fighting the other self: "Me. Hahahaha. Wraaaghh. I am angry to the top. I want to kill you."

Luke's narrative indicated complex thinking and meaning-making as he communicated his feelings and self-conflicts. Another self-portrait (*LH25*,

Luke's story 65

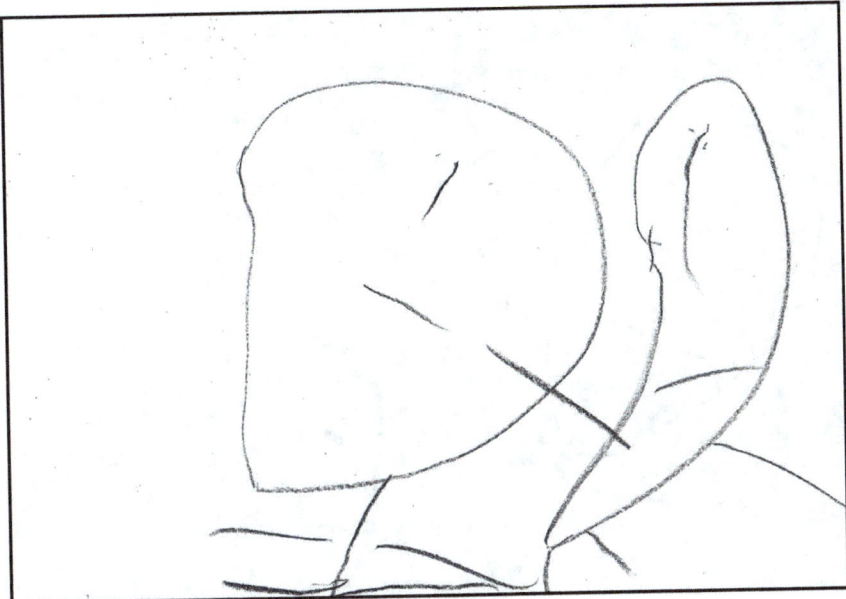

*Figure 5.16* Two of Me (LH28) – by Luke.

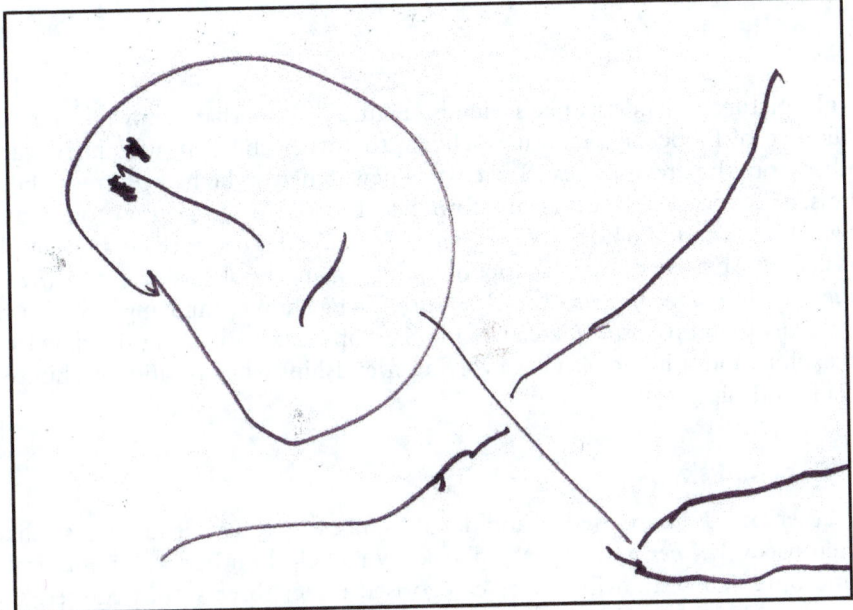

*Figure 5.17* Me Stretching (LH25) – by Luke.

Figure 5.17) reflected a real experience where he drew himself alone, furious at his brother for waking him up, saying, "I am stretching… Now I woke up and I am angry… Because Jacob woke me up. I shouted and I scared him."

66  *Children making meaning*

*Figure 5.18 Nicholai and I (LH39)* – by Luke.

*Friends*

Eight pictures included Luke's friends (Figure 5.8), perhaps showing the significance of friendships for Luke. Unlike the other children, who knew each other from the previous year, Luke was a newcomer, so he had yet to establish himself, be accepted by peers, and form new friendships. Luke drew four drawings of his friend, Nicholai. *Nicholai and I* (*LH39*, Figure 5.18) is an example of shared experiences with his friend, "jumping at school." Luke drew *Nicolai jumping on a Trampoline* (*LH43*, Figure 5.8) at home, implying his wish to invite his friend for a playdate at home. Perhaps Luke was using the drawings to explore and validate his new, evolving friendships while positioning himself in a friendship group.

## Weather and sky

Weather and sky were used to add detail to 52 of Luke's static drawings. Luke often used *Weather and Sky* metaphorically to help him better communicate a meaning. These drawings were categorised under three sub-categories: sky and sun (35), stars (13), and rain and rainbows (4). Figure 5.19 provides examples of Luke's drawings of *Weather and Sky*.

*Figure 5.19* Examples of drawings illustrating different *Weather and Sky* – by Luke.

### Sky and sun

Luke drew the sky in 20 drawings, 15, also included the sun, and in two the sky was black to denote the night. Weather often featured in his drawings of people, things, and events he liked, wished for, or which represented an enjoyable experience, such as the drawing of an ice cream melting in the sun (*LH40*, Figure 5.19), something Luke loved!

Luke was excited on the day he drew a family picnic (*LH50*, Figure 5.19). It was the week before his mother underwent surgery, and Luke was keen on the planned event. He used ready-made cut-outs of animals with the drawing of the bright, cloudless skies and the big yellow sun (seemingly to convey a sense of well-being, fun, and happiness, Egan, 1998). Metaphorically, the weather here reflected the feeling of the day (Nielsen, 2009, p. 90).

### Stars

Stars featured in 13 drawings, perhaps stimulated by real experiences, animated films featuring space scenes, space-related stickers, and a set of golden star-stickers (used as a reward system) in his phonics book. Luke's stars conveyed different meanings. On four occasions, he used space-themed stickers to draw interplanetary scenes; on seven occasions, he used stars to reward himself for hard work on his drawings. Two drawings (*LH36* & *LH18*, Figure 5.11, Image 1) featured night skies with stars. Metaphorically, "two diamonds in the sky" (*LH36*) seem to be an experiment with the effects of glitters, which he observed his peers using at school. The shimmering materiality of the glitter and sequins inspired him to epitomise the stars as diamonds. Through "successive transitions" (Kress, 1997, p. 29), Luke moved between modes, contexts, ideas, and meanings, exploring the modes of dabbing and spreading glitter and drawing stars to signify diamonds. Luke used "experiential metaphors" (Van Leeuwen, 2005, p. 29) to express ideas, perhaps fusing experiences of looking at a night sky with his physical interaction with the diamond-like qualities of glitters and sequins, where their affordances fit his intention. Luke also drew himself and his mother walking under a dark, starry night (*LH18*, Figure 5.11, Image 1). The main elements in this drawing are the star stickers that Luke attached and those his mother drew.

After attaching several coloured star stickers at the top of the page, Luke drew the night sky as a thick black line. Wanting to draw a star but not knowing how, he asked his mother to draw some stars for him. Not liking the shape of the first and complaining that the second was way below the night sky, as "It is supposed to be in the sky," Luke asked his mother to draw a third star. He continued his drawing by depicting "Mummy and I. We are walking. By night. Because it was dark." So, while at the content level, the focus was on creating a dark starry sky, at the meaning level, Luke's drawing focused on his close relationship with his mother.

## Rain and rainbows

Rain features in four of Luke's drawings, sometimes with clouds, a rainbow, and the sun. Prompted by his mother, Luke used these drawings to combine what he knew from being out after a rain shower with the appearance of a rainbow. Luke explained, "I drew a rainbow because there was the rain and the sun. These are the clouds and then the rainbow" (*LH5*, Figure 5.19).

Luke particularly liked rainbows, a feature of many children's drawings (Coates & Coates, 2006). He could recall the times when he saw a rainbow, and at school, he frequently sang *The Rainbow Colours Song* (Jenkins, 2010) with his peers, where he liked to order the colours accordingly. Luke said that drawing rainbows put him in a cheerful mood, "Give me all the colours so that I will draw a rainbow. Singing a rainbow song. It is a rainbow. It is a rainbow. It is a beautiful, beautiful, rainbow."

Luke's drawings were a reflection of himself, his characteristics, and his contrasting interests. Fantasy and reality linked myth with real events in his drawings, which combined action and soft imagery.

## Notes

1 Any drawings mentioned, but not included in this book, are available on the companion website. They can be located by using the image code (ex. *LS1* can be found under Luke's School Folder, drawing number 1). https://sites.google.com/view/childrenmakingmeaning
2 The companion website contains all the children's drawings. They are saved under each respective chapter and in the order they are mentioned in the chapter, for e.g. Figure 5.1. Each figure has a code that indicates the name of the child and the chronological order in which it was drawn by the child. *LH1* (Luke, home drawing 1). https://sites.google.com/view/childrenmakingmeaning
3 A film clip of Luke drawing Me carrying a bag of candy (*LH49*, Chapter 5, Video 1) is available at https://sites.google.com/view/childrenmakingmeaning
4 Ben Ten is a cartoon character who can transform into ten powerful aliens.
5 A film clip of Luke drawing *Ben Ten (2) fight* (*LS18*, Chapter 5, Video 2) is available at https://sites.google.com/view/childrenmakingmeaning

# 6  Thea's story

*Figure 6.1* A Man Dressed as a Koala Bear (*TS1*) – by Thea.

## Getting to know Thea

Thea (4:3) was the youngest child in the study. She lived with her parents and sister, Erica (6), in a comfortable, spacious, first-floor apartment located in a small, quiet, rural hamlet, outside the main town, and overlooking an unspoiled valley. Thea's apartment overlooked a small church, visible from her kitchen window. Maternal aunts and uncles lived in adjoining apartments, and Thea made the 10-minute journey to school in the main town by school transport.

The well-equipped kitchen, the family gathering space, had a large central table and a television on one side. Her father's well-maintained fish tank by the kitchen door held shrimps and small fish. Thea and Erica shared a bedroom, and their neatly organised playroom contained dolls, soft toys, and games.

Thea's mother was following a part-time bachelor's degree in early childhood and care at the University of Malta and attended lectures most weekday evenings. Thea and Erica went to their grandparents' house after school until their father collected them after work, then headed home to cook for them and settle them for the night. He enjoyed regular quality time with them. Family tasks were shared by both parents, and grandparents (who adored their granddaughters) regularly had supper with the family and played a significant role in the girls' lives. Cross-generational support was strong: parents and grandparents supported each other to provide a harmonious, affectionate, and calm family environment for the children who had close bonds with their paternal grandparents. They also participated in the study, sometimes helping Thea with filming, prompting her, and identifying links between Thea's drawings and family experiences.

Thea's mother adopted a seemingly business-like approach to helping Erica with homework, regularly giving her extra written work and frequently directing conversations towards letter sounding and spelling, with Thea often listening. When Thea drew, her mother's attitude was similar, prompting her to remain on task and complete her drawing. Studying meant that the mother had limited time for her own artistic and creative activities, which she encouraged in her children. She accepted "purposeful mess" (Pahl, 1999, p. 104), providing accessible, open-ended art material, neatly organised, for independent use. Both siblings could use such resources flexibly and creatively, with the "mess" confined to the kitchen table.

A bank manager, Thea's father was an articulate, knowledgeable man who exercised regularly. Thea was close to her father, often drawing him. They shared an interest in fish, doing technical things, and watching "The World's Strongest Man" (International Management Group, 2011) on television. Thea's relationship with her sister Erica seemed good, despite sometimes complaining that Erica was domineering when she played "teacher" and demanded things of Thea.

Thea's mother described her as caring, affectionate, and sensitive; she loved nature, animals, and the outdoors. Thea had a good sense of humour but was short-tempered and did not like being laughed at. She was very creative, enjoying dancing, acting, and painting; seemingly very outgoing and funny; she liked to act, joke, and make others laugh. Thea was particularly interested in how things worked; she drew playground slides that went up and down, aeroplanes with switches that helped her formulate her concepts of how planes fly, food that went inside her tummy, and butterflies that came out of their cocoons. Thea's kindergarten teacher portrayed her as "a very smart child, versatile and precise in her work ... a good leader and good communicator with an unassuming attitude." She said Thea was a diligent worker, had respect towards adults, followed their instructions, and was eager to please. Thea loved learning, was very confident, and seemed somewhat superior to her peers, eagerly sharing what she knew without dominating them. Her sense of superiority perhaps came from her excellent knowledge of letters and numbers, which the school valued. Thea was very organised, setting out all her materials before beginning to draw. She meticulously replaced caps on pens, organised drawing materials in their corresponding containers, and encouraged others to do likewise.

At school, Thea enjoyed construction toys and playing fun games with her peers; at home, she seemed to prefer more solitary play, such as drawing and playing with a toy cash register. According to her mother, Thea liked online games on children's websites and watching children's television. Thea was frightened of witches, which emerged in several of her drawings.

Halfway through the study, Thea's demeanour changed; usually cheerful and talkative, she became withdrawn and very irritable; and sometimes, nothing seemed to make her happy. She usually enjoyed drawing but, for a while, refused to do so. It transpired that Thea was being bullied on the school bus, and the arrival of a student kindergarten educator also brought temporary instability. When Thea drew during this period, she seemed to use drawing for catharsis. From using *complex modes* and drawing *complex themes*, her drawings became simpler and more repetitive, yet she still spent a considerable amount of time creating them. Thea's mother successfully intervened to stop the bullying, and Thea slowly became her happy self again, her positive demeanour again being reflected in her drawings.

## Analysing Thea's drawings: simple-complex modes and themes

Thea's home and school drawings and drawing time in each setting are summarised in Table 4.1 (Chapter 4), which shows that Thea drew extensively in both settings: over 31 hours throughout the study, taking anything from 33 seconds to over 58 minutes to finish a drawing. She preferred to draw at home, where she seemed more at ease and did not have to share resources. Drawing and role-playing were her favourite activities at school, providing her with freedom of self-expression.

Thea's 84 drawings are plotted on her *Data Cross-grid* (Figure 6.2). The school drawings coded *TS (Thea School)* (purple-top); the home drawings coded *TH (Thea Home)* (orange-bottom). Most of Thea's 84 drawings (17 home and 21 school) were in *complex modes* and *complex themes* (Figure 6.3 bottom, right).

Thea's story    73

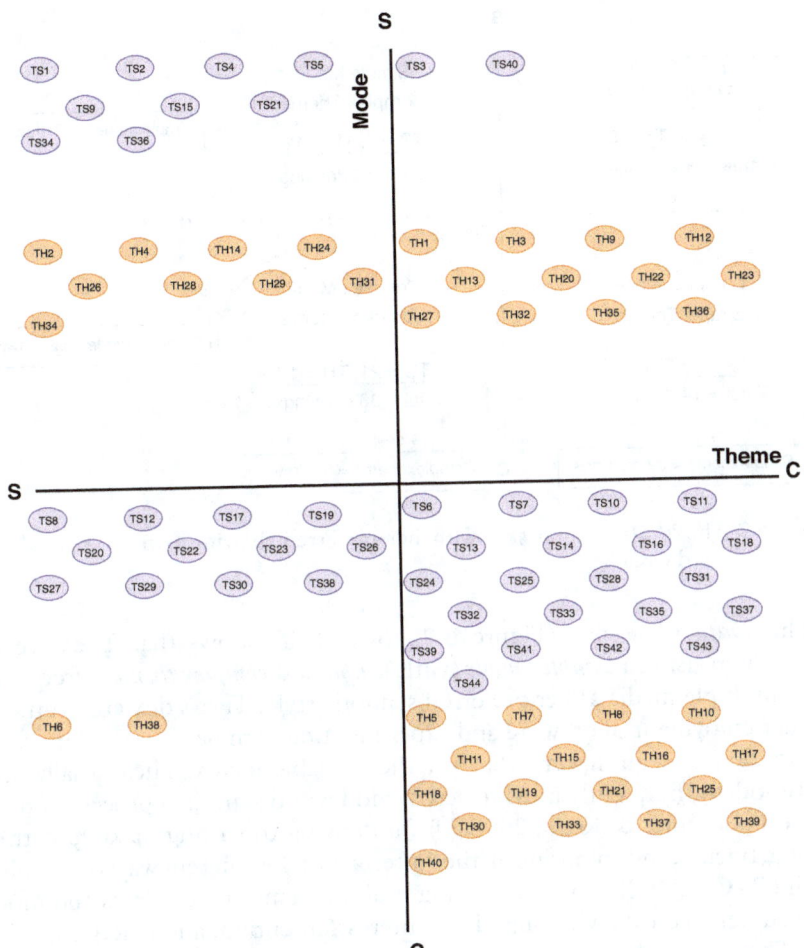

*Figure 6.2* Thea's *Data Cross-grid* represents her home (orange) and school (purple) drawings.

## Thea's use of simple-complex modes

Of Thea's 84 drawings, 32 were created using a *simple mode* (Figures 6.2 and 6.3), suggesting this was her favoured semiotic style. The first five drawings made in each setting at the start of the study were done using mainly pencil colours; perhaps because Thea was so accustomed to being limited to using her own set of pencil colours at school, that initially, she kept to this medium. Once Thea understood that she could use the material available, she quickly adjusted to using multiple modes. Most of Thea's *simple-mode* drawings used crayons, markers, pens, pencils, cardboard, tape, and ready-made foam cut-outs.

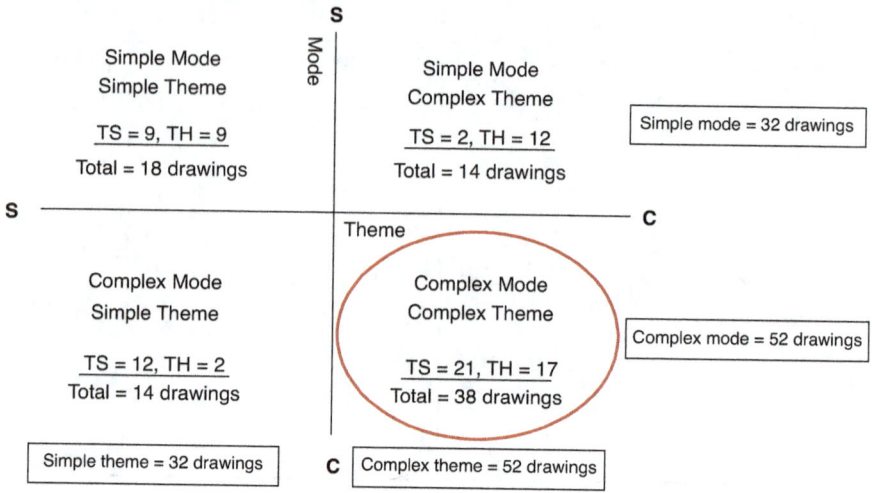

*Figure 6.3* Thea's *Data Cross-grid* with her preferred drawing pattern marked with a red circle.

The *Data Cross-grid* (Figure 6.2, lower half) shows that Thea created 52 drawings using a *complex mode* (with *simple* and *complex themes*), frequently using multiple media as her preferred semiotic style. Thea's dexterous attitude and her enjoyment of drawing and experimenting with new material make her an experienced sign-maker, whatever the available media. Thea usually drew multimodally, frequently moving across modes and signs in a process of transduction (Bezemer & Kress, 2008); from drawing to writing, talking, cutting, pasting, tracing, and colouring, in the "interplay of the different ways of meaning-making" (Cox, 2005a, p. 122). Using multiple semiotic resources and modes enabled her to create what suited her interest, intention, and emerging meaning. Thea's confidence, dexterity, and interest in experimenting may have been stimulated by the multiple novel and varied resources available, which often triggered enthusiasm to draw, sometimes making several drawings in succession.

Jo showed Thea how to trace pictures using the newly introduced tracing paper. Thea then showed her peers how to integrate tracing into their drawings. Thea often asked, "What am I going to use?" when the semiotic material provided kinaesthetic pleasure and repeatedly inspired her drawing content and use of modes, changing plans as materials influenced the flow of her thoughts.

### Thea's choice of simple-complex themes

Fifty-two of Thea's drawings had *complex themes* (Figures 6.2 and 6.3 right), indicating her preference to draw more than two objects in a scene or narration.

*Thea's story* 75

*Figure 6.4* Examples of Thea's drawings in *simple-to-complex modes* and *themes* corresponding to each section of the grid.

76  *Children making meaning*

Such scenes frequently included home and outdoor scenarios with animals, people, or objects, inspired by her lived experiences. Her narratives amalgamated real life with imaginary stories of fairies, princesses, monsters, giants, and witches. These appeared to help her convey her thoughts, interests, and emotions as she communicated love towards her family and peers, happiness, wishes, fear, and concern. Thea made 32 drawings (Figures 6.2 and 6.3, left) with *simple themes* with one or two objects, without narration or explanation. Most of these drawings documented everyday life, featuring flowers, fruit, aeroplanes, cars, people (mainly family members), and animals (butterflies, sharks, and snails).

## Thea's use of complex mode and complex theme

Thea's preferred drawing pattern was *complex mode* and *complex theme* at home (17) and school (21). She invested time and attention in the *content* and *form* of her drawings, most including decoration and embellishment with different media, to create drawings using *complex modes* with elaborate scenes that frequently resulted in *complex themes*. Both the decoration and content of the drawings were important for Thea. Figure 6.4 illustrates four drawings that typify each section of Thea's *Data Cross-grid*.

## Simple mode, simple theme

Figure 6.4 (top left) shows four out of 18 drawings made using a simple mode and simple theme. *A Woman Wearing Many Clothes (TS4)*, *The Wicked Witch (TS21)*, and *A Man Dressed as a Koala Bear (TS1)* were made at school using crayons, while *The Holy Mary (TH2)* was made at home, using markers. When Thea used just one mode (drawing) and one resource (crayons or markers), she always used more than one colour. This was an important feature, especially where in TS4, each colour connoted a different layer of clothes.

### *A Man Dressed as a Koala Bear*

Thea's made her first drawing of the study, *A Man Dressed as a Koala Bear*, at school (*TS1*, Figure 6.1 above) using a *simple mode* and a *simple theme*; it seemed to develop in different layers. After drawing the sun at the top corner, Thea drew her first layer of the drawing. Using a peach colour, Thea drew a stick outline of a man with a body, arms, legs, and hands (not visible in the finished drawing), saying, "I am drawing a man." A second layer followed, in yellow, light brown, and pink, which, according to Thea, represented the man's shirt covering his body outline, seemingly aimed at "dressing" the man with a layer of clothing made of a thick, black, circular boundary line.

Talking about the completed drawing, her mother said that Thea had recently been to an animal circus show with her grandparents, where they posed with a man holding a cross-bred panda bear, so perhaps Thea's drawing reproduced that experience. She seemed to combine this real-life experience with her schematic interest in "enveloping and containing" (Athey, 2007, p. 124). Thea's drawing seemed to have defined a reality (a man dressed as a koala bear and wearing layers of clothes) from seeing a panda bear and discussing animals in school.

## Simple mode, complex theme

Four drawings (Figure 6.4, top right) show a *simple mode* and a *complex theme*. Even in her choice of a *simple mode*, Thea used different modes in different drawings. In *My Family at Home* (*TH22*), she used the single mode of drawing; in *Dad Coming Home* (*TH20*), she combined drawing with attaching a heart-shaped sticker. In *Travelling in a Car and Aeroplane* (*TS40*), Thea used the mode of writing to add her name and her main character's invented name as part of her drawing. In *Animals Playing Hide and Seek* (*TH27*), Thea used the mode of glueing ready-made cut-outs with drawings of the animals' faces, adding a pom-pom for the sun. Even when using *simple mode*, Thea experimented with a variety of materials.

These drawings are classified as *complex themes*, each comprising two objects that together depict a scene or narrative. The theme of "family" emerged in the four drawings (Figure 6.4). *Dad Coming Home* (*TH20*) represented Thea's father arriving home from work, and *My Family at Home* (TH22) reflected the family returning home on a windy day. While at the content level, *Animals Playing Hide and Seek (TH27)* and *Travelling in a Car and Aeroplane (TS40)* did not appear to be related to the theme of family, at the meaning level, they were. *TH27* was a combination of a scene and narration where Thea created a story about animals playing in a forest, simultaneously reflecting personal feelings and her family's support. Similarly, *TS40* began as a story about fictional characters that she co-authored with Neil, a friend at school, but during the telling, Thea focused on family life.

### *Travelling in a Car and Aeroplane*

At school, sitting next to Neil, Thea drew *Travelling in a Car and Aeroplane* (*TS40*, Figure 6.5, Image 1). Using a *simple mode*, the drawing was mainly developed by "copying" Neil; it was unusual for Thea to follow and not take the lead. This drawing in *complex theme* shows a superhero and Thea in a car. Adapting some of Neil's ideas (Figure 6.5, Image 2) in the subject matter and the modes and media used, Thea gave meaning to her drawing by drawing a car, which she then transformed into a van being driven to the airport. The van became an aeroplane, first piloted by Thea and then by her father, taking them to Sweden to visit Aunt Victoria.

78  Children making meaning

*Figure 6.5* Travelling in a Car and Aeroplane (TS40) in *simple mode* and *complex theme* [1], with Neil's similar drawing [2].

Thea's story 79

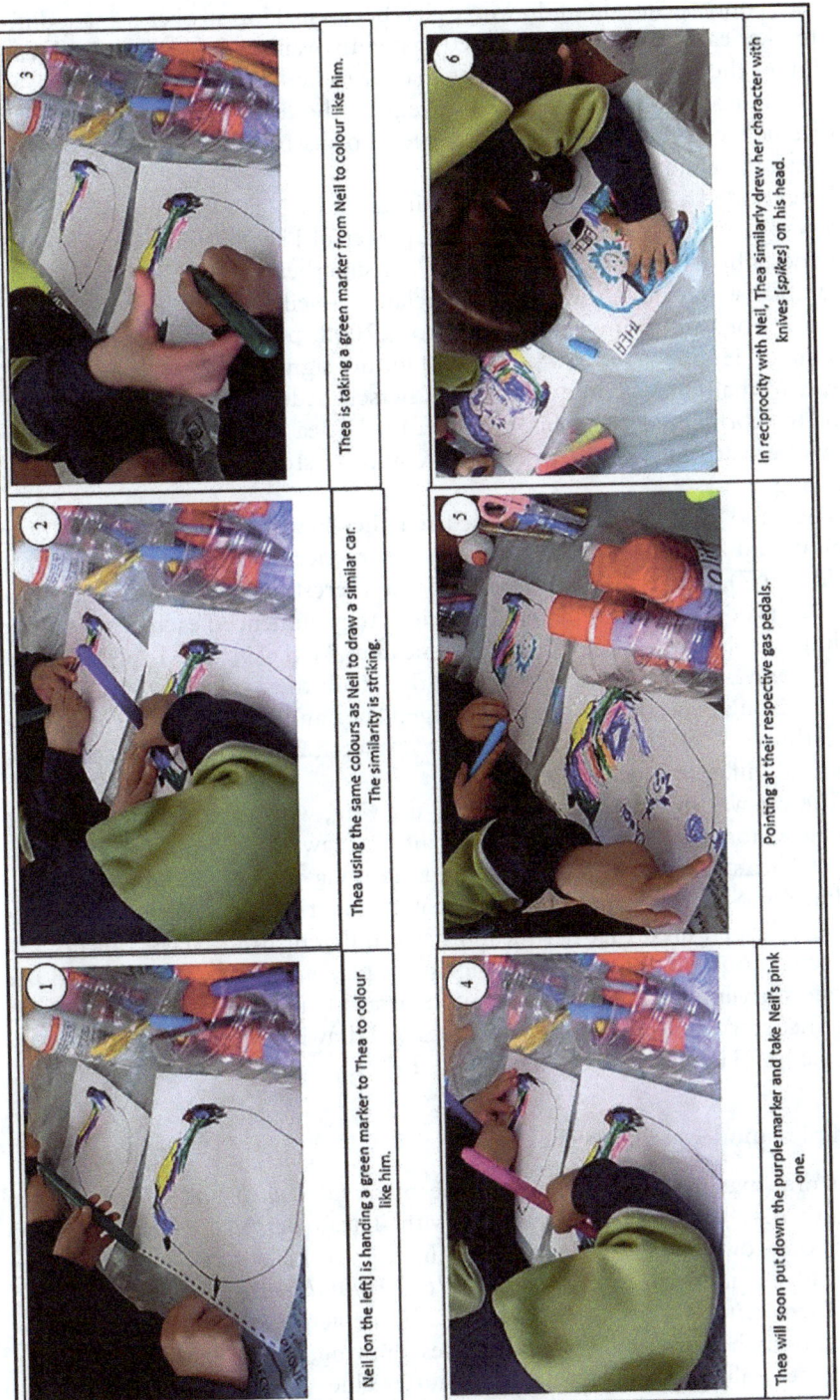

*Figure 6.6* Snapshots of playful interactions between Thea and Neil in *TS40*.

Using only the mode of drawing, Neil began making strokes using a different marker each time; Thea followed, patiently waiting for him to finish each section of the colouring and pass the marker to her (Figure 6.6, Images 1–5). The sequence of the whole drawing reflects the level of copying, the similarities between the drawings, and the level of harmonisation and reciprocity between the children.

Thea added a superhero, seemingly inspired by Neil's drawing of *Sonic the Hedgehog* (Sega Corporation, 2013), a powerful Play Station hero who runs fast and fights "bad guys." Thea named her superhero "Fuel"; however, being unfamiliar with Sonic, she could not relate to Neil's text, so she engaged in a process of "authoring self" (Edmiston, 2008, p. 198), considering other meanings (Hopperstad, 2008b, p. 145) for her signs. She transformed "Fuel" into a woman and, subsequently, into herself. Adding a stick figure, which initially represented her, this then became Thea "as-a-boy," and immediately afterward her daddy, to create a complete story with finely articulated meaning.

Thea and Neil continuously discussed the drawing, creating similarity in content and meaning – "a collaborative emergence of conversation" (Sawyer, 2002, p. 67), where they expressed mutual interests and intentions. Through their co-produced and animated discussion, they influenced each other's ideas, adding details to the "joint shaping of meaning" (Mavers, 2011, p. 49), making it *complex* in *theme*. In this process, they built their collaborative drawings while sharing experiences and knowledge. Thea and Neil co-constructed and co-authored a "collective social product" (Sawyer, 2011, p. 29) with complex, new, and different meanings.

The car was the main subject of the drawing, which transformed into the "'vehicle' for invention … and possibility" (Hawkins, 2002, p. 215). This shows Thea's distinctive ways of thinking, meaning-making, and reinterpreting in drawing. She identified herself with a male superhero, and through her narration, Thea ensured that her meaning was different from Neil's; objects and characters took on different dimensions and personalities as Thea created her unique storyline. Reading the signs of her drawing in a new way, Thea created a distinct story, reflecting her experiences and drawing on her unique funds of knowledge (Hedges, 2011; Chesworth, 2021).

## Complex mode, complex theme

Four drawings in Thea's preferred style of *complex mode* and *complex theme* (Figure 6.4, bottom right) connect with Thea's personal experiences and funds of knowledge, merged with imagination, to make sense of and process her understandings. *The Reindeer (TH10)*, *Animals not Allowed (TH37)*, and *The Interactive Whiteboard Activity (TS31)* depicted real and imagined episodes. In each, Thea used multiple modes: drawing, attaching stickers, glueing paper and lollipop sticks, and dabbing glitter glue.

*Thea's story* 81

### *Erica and Mum Before I was Born*

In a multimodal ensemble typifying Thea's style of interweaving of modes, *Erica and Mum Before I was Born* (*TH8*, Figure 6.7)[1] was in *complex mode*, where Thea used different resources to create new meaning and knowledge (Tűrkcan, 2013).

Prompted by her mother, Thea assembled all available resources, including a packet of ribbons, a novel resource for her. She associated one ribbon with hair, exclaiming, "This is like hair … I am going to use them for hair." This contextualised her drawing and stimulated her to draw people. First, using markers and glitter glue, she drew her usual sky and earth lines. Next, Thea drew her mother and sister, in red dresses (their favourite colour). She attached "hair" to each of them, "Now I am going to do your (mother) hair black… I am going to make her (mother's) hair curly." Thea had an eye for detail, thinking carefully about the best ribbon to represent their respective hairstyles. She attached a thick ribbon to reflect Erica's fair, wavy hair and glued a brown, frizzy ribbon on her mother's head, mirroring her thick, curly hair. Thea next used a different type of ribbon because the form, shape, materiality, and colour reminded her of Christmas decorations, "These (the ribbon glued at the top of the drawing) are Christmas decorations." The materiality and specification of the medium allowed Thea to experiment and investigate how the different types of ribbons could "have different effects … on the relationship between form and meaning" (Mavers, 2011, p. 11). Guided by

*Figure 6.7* **Erica and Mum before I was Born** (*TH8*) – by Thea.

colour, form, and texture, she used each ribbon to shape her drawing in complex orchestration with each other, creating a cohesive and balanced meaning.

On occasion, within the same drawing, Thea, *a priori*, had a clear idea of what she wanted to draw and the meaning she wanted to convey; she conscientiously selected the most appropriate materials to suit her needs. After drawing her mother and her sister, Thea drew around a homemade pencil holder on glossy yellow paper to make a circle and cut it out. Her dexterity, flexibility, and ingenuity were impressive. She drew an outlined image of herself on the plain side of the circle and glued it to the drawing. Drawing herself separately rather than on paper, she produced her intended meaning to separate herself from her mother and sister at a time before she was born. The choice and combination of different modes can enrich the meaning-making potential of children's intentional and systematic drawings (Hull & Nelson, 2005). Finishing her drawing, Thea wanted to draw some toy boats, "Because over here there is some sea." Using glossy paper, she cut out two triangular shapes and glued them to the left to represent the familiar sight of boats in the sea around Malta.

With a variety of novel and familiar resources, Thea improvised a response as mediated by her ideas, skills, and senses. Acting "in-the-moment" (Edmiston, 2010, p. 202), and relying on culturally familiar resources, Thea made meaning with available materials, creating a scene from before she was born. She intermingled practices, experiences, and things she liked in the present (boats and Christmas decorations). Through her reactions and uses of resources, Thea was engendering her agency and identity with personal meanings.

## Complex mode, simple theme

Four of Thea's drawings in *complex mode* and *simple theme* (Figure 6.4, bottom left) have been selected from 14 such drawings, the majority (12) done at school. In these drawings, Thea made successive transitions between modes: from drawing to cutting, glueing, taping, and dabbing. The themes were simple, each illustrating a single subject: herself, a snail, grass, presents and fruit, a pair of glasses, a flower, and the strongest man. Most of these ideas were triggered by peers or recent events. The remaining drawings in this category featured fast-moving vehicles and travel, mainly aeroplanes. *Romina's Aeroplane* (*TS30*, Figure 6.4) is about her cousin returning by plane from England, while *A Ship* (TS38, Figure 6.4) features Thea as the captain. Planes and boats are familiar to children who live in Malta; the busy island airport, large cruise ships, and small fishing and sailing boats are visible daily. In contrast, *The Strongest Man* (TS27, Figure 6.4) represents a heavy weightlifter in a TV programme that Thea and her father enjoyed.

### An Aeroplane that Flies

One of a series of drawings featuring aeroplanes was *An Aeroplane that Flies* (TS23, Figure 6.8),[2] reflecting Thea's recent, new experience of her dad

*Thea's story* 83

*Figure 6.8* **An Aeroplane that Flies (TS23)** – by Thea.

travelling on a business trip. She chose novel resources that day and, using a *complex mode*, attached a dried leaf with tape. She then crumpled two small pieces of craft paper, one orange and one blue, taping them to the left side of the leaf. Putting glue on and around the leaf, she scattered some loose glitter. She switched between crayons and markers to draw a circular shape around the leaf, then taped a piece of thin, blue corrugated paper next to the leaf.

Thea drew this the day her father left on his business trip after she, her mother, and sister had seen him off at the airport. The subject of the drawing was *simple*, and Thea explained the various parts of the aeroplane represented in each part of the drawing. Using "drawing as manipulation" (Adams, 2003, p. 222), Thea could develop her thinking about aeroplanes – exploring and refining different possibilities as they made sense to her. Starting with the leaf, Thea first said it represented the passengers' seats, which were still empty because "people were still at the airport." The leaf later became the fuel tank, "It goes down and then, it takes petrol… There will be that big truck filled with petrol and once I saw it giving fuel to the aeroplane." Thea explained that the thin blue corrugated paper and the green circular line with the red blotches made the aeroplane wings.

Influenced by her airport visit, Thea was trying to organise, sequence, make sense of, and communicate what she knew. One intriguing aspect of Thea's meaning-making revolved around the two small pieces of paper that she positioned next to the leaf, which she described as buttons or switches:

84  *Children making meaning*

> The blue button is for the plane to start and the orange one is for it to get down… I saw him [the pilot] pressing the [blue] button and I saw it [the aeroplane] fly… (while pressing the blue switch) I am going up… The pilot presses this [orange button] and it goes down… He will press the orange switch tomorrow… And yesterday he pressed this one [the blue button] to fly.

Thea tried to convey the inside of an aeroplane and conceptualise how control switches, make it take off and land, and how once grounded, it is refuelled. Through detailed explanations, she identified the various, essential components of the aeroplane: "wings," "fuel tank," and "switches," conveying her persistent curiosity around how things work. Thea was enthralled by aeroplanes and their engineering. Stemming from events around her, Thea, for a time, drew several aeroplanes.

## Inventory of content: emerging themes in Thea's drawings

The two most frequently drawn themes across Thea's 84 drawings were *Animals* (53) and *People* (45).

### *Animals*

The theme of *Animals* included wild animals (16), flying creatures (11), water creatures (9), farm animals (8), pets (4), mini-beasts (3), and fantasy creatures (2).

Children spontaneously and frequently draw animals (Villarroel et al., 2018). Thea's animal drawings were varied and included mini-beasts (principally snails); farm animals (horses, cows, a hen, and a rabbit); and pets (dogs and cats). Most commonly, Thea's drawings featured wild animals, mainly featuring lions and elephants but also including squirrels, snakes, a zebra, a reindeer, a crocodile, and a tiger. Water creature drawings included fish, shrimps, crabs, and frogs. She also drew flying creatures – birds, butterflies, and several fantasy creatures (monsters and animated cartoon animals from children's television programs). At school, they were discussing animals; children sang songs, coloured, painted, and did craft activities relating to animals. However, most of Thea's animal drawings (Figure 6.9) seemed inspired by family visits to the countryside and a farm. The prevalence of birds and fish perhaps emanated from her family's interests, especially those of her grandfather and father.

### *Wild animals*

Thea's 16 drawings featuring wild animals were filled with action, fantasy, and Thea's feelings of fear and death. *A Snake Story* (*TS41*, Figure 6.9) describes a fat man who fell on a snake, killing him. Other animal drawings carried storylines of monsters and animals falling and killing others. Thea described *Freeing Animals Stuck in a Tree* (*TS35*, Figure 6.9) as a group of invisible

Figure 6.9 Examples of Thea's drawings on the theme of *Animals*.

*Figure 6.10* Animals Hide and Seek (TH27) – by Thea.

animals eating from a tree and a monster who wanted to eat them. The animals jump into the tree trunk to avoid capture, while Thea becomes the strong hero, rescuing the animals by killing the monster. *The Reindeer* (*TH10*, Figure 6.9) features an evil dog-like animal that wanted to kill a reindeer but "they put him in a cage" to protect the reindeer.

Thea described *Animals Hide and Seek* (*TH27*, Figure 6.10) as: "These are animals in the forest. A zebra, a lizard, a leopard, a cow. That is their food [the pom-pom in the middle]." Thea then focused her description on the friendship between the lizard and leopard, "The animals are playing on their own. They are playing hide and seek." Thea was clear to point out that there were no adults around. She continued:

> These two [the lizard and the leopard] are playing together. The lizard and the leopard are happy. They make friends and they play together. The zebra wants to play with them. They are friends. But the zebra is going home now because no one is playing with him. He is sad.

Thea did not elaborate further; however, her mother saw parallels with Thea's experience of being bullied on the school van. Through her drawing, Thea expressed her emotions, particularly as she was finding it unusually challenging to talk about them. The metaphorical representation in her drawing communicated her feelings and need for support without explicitly referring to being bullied. It is relatively common for young children to communicate feelings and experiences through drawings indirectly, especially if they struggle to express themselves verbally, giving adults insights into their experiences and feelings (Solomon & Grimley, 2011; Rudolph, 2014).

*Flying creatures*

Thea's 11 drawings of flying creatures mainly featured birds and butterflies. Her maternal grandfather loved the outdoors, while her paternal grandfather was a member of a local bird protection organisation. perhaps inspiring Thea's interest in drawing birds. In *My Loveable Grandpa* (*TH9*, Figure 6.9), Thea drew her paternal grandfather surrounded by birds because "he loves birds," while in *Myself* (*TH13*, Figure 6.11) and *Me in a Muddy Puddle* (*TH14*, Figure 6.9), Thea drew herself with "a lot of birds."

*Water creatures*

Nine of Thea's drawings included water creatures. Her interest in drawing fish probably emanated from her father's, who grew up in a small town with an aquatic shop next to his house. His parents still lived there, and whenever Thea visited them, she saw the shop, which they often visited, sometimes to look at the aquaria and fish, and occasionally to buy fish and shrimps

*Figure 6.11 Myself (TH13)* – by Thea.

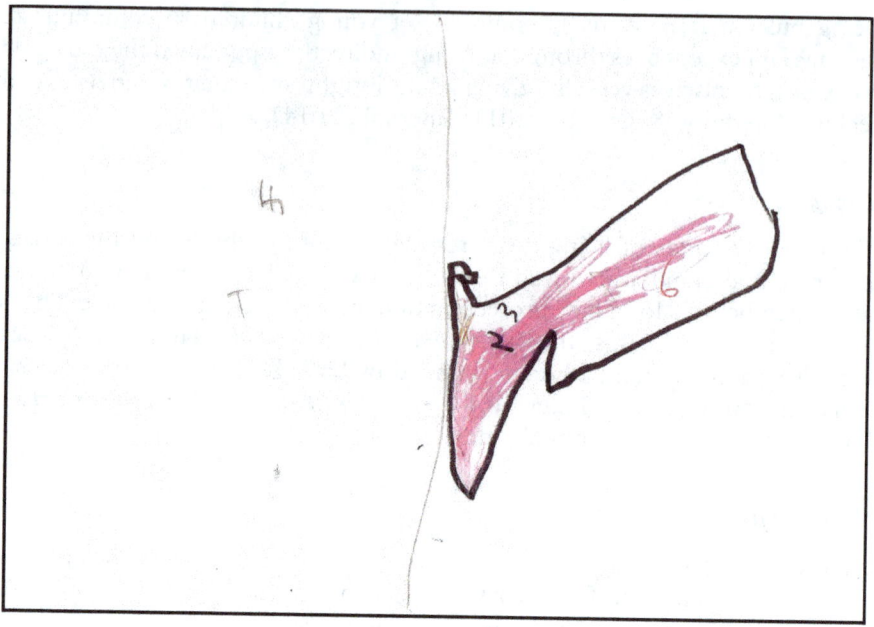

*Figure 6.12 Fish in an Aquarium (TH24)* – by Thea.

for their aquarium. *The Aquarium Shop* (*TH23*, Figure 6.9) illustrates two aquaria – side by side – with fish, seaweed, and light. Thea explained, "We are at the pet shop. I drew two aquaria... (red thick lines) These are the fish. The shrimps are here. The shrimps have died ... But the fish were still alive." Two other aquaria featured in *Dad Coming Home* (*TH20*, Figure 6.4), which included the shrimp aquarium on one side, and *Fish in an Aquarium* (*TH24*, Figure 6.12) with a recently bought fish, Thea explained, "This is only an aquarium. The pink is the fish." These three drawings are examples of how children sometimes draw on, catalogue, and celebrate significant events at home that capture strong interest and memories (Anning & Ring, 2004).

Other drawings featured several water-living creatures, mainly crabs and frogs, which were indicative of the cross-over between Thea's home and school influences. During the study, the class was learning a song about frogs, and the educator told the children facts about frogs, showed pictures, and asked them to colour templates of frogs. However, when talking about *Frog in the Sea* (*TH19*, Figure 6.9), Thea referred to her experiences with frogs, "Once I saw frogs ... In the muddy puddles. They were all muddy ... Once we saw a dead one ... poor him."

Thea's three drawings of crabs included *A Card for Eman* (*TH5*), a birthday card for a friend, to which she had attached a rubber picture of a frog by the water; *A Crab* (*TS5*), Figure 6.13, Image 1); and *Me as a Crab*

Thea's story 89

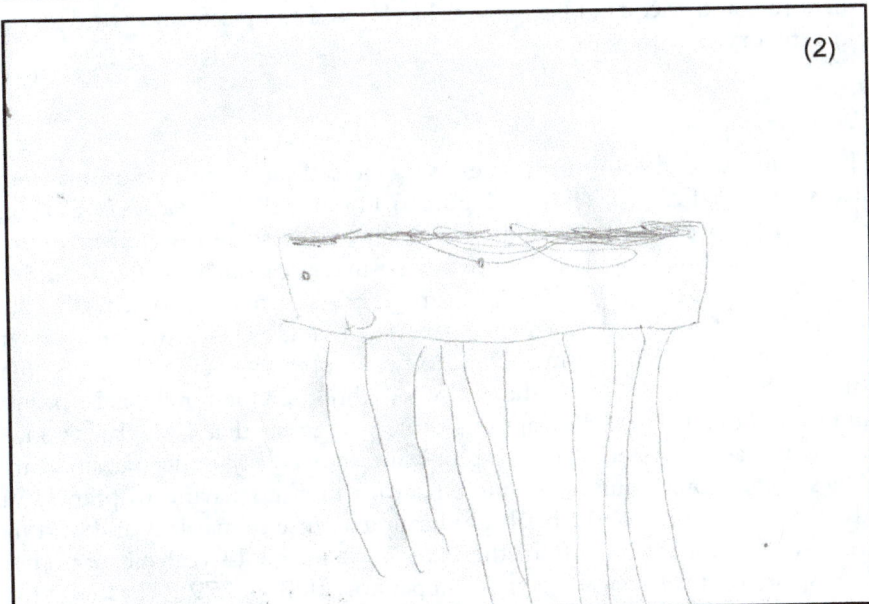

*Figure 6.13* The Crab *(TS5)* [1] and *Me as a Crab (TS9)* [2] – by Thea.

(*TS9*, Figure 6.13, Image 2), each made after Thea read from a book that included a picture and sentence about a crab stating, "Today, I am going to draw Thea the crab" (*TS9*). She drew hurriedly, without her usual attention to colour and detail, perhaps because this drawing had a different meaning for her. Her mother explained Thea's experiences with crabs on days at the beach, "In summer she plays with crabs with her father. She looks for them in the rocks and counts them." Thea's encounters with real crabs and images in the book perhaps helped to form her "private meaning" (Kress, 2010, p. 109) of crabs with "a big, smooth back, eyes and mouth, orangey colour, as well as many long legs," as in *A card for Eman* (*TS5*). Children's multimodal ways of expressing meaning involve them in making connections, blending, and connecting home and school experiences. These examples encapsulate the influence of context and significant others on children and what they choose to represent (Rose et al., 2006; Woolford et al., 2015; Burkitt et al., 2019).

### People

Thea's second prevailing theme was *People* (45), which we categorised under six sub-categories: self (13), family (10), fantasy (10), unnamed (8), named others (3), and friends (1). Figure 6.14 shows a sample from each drawing sub-category.

### Myself

Thea made several self-portraits, drawing herself alone and occasionally in places she liked. *Myself* (*TH13*, Figure 6.11) and *Me in the Rain* (*TH15*, Figure 6.14) were two drawings where Thea represented herself in future roles or in ideal or imagined identities (De Ruyter & Conroy, 2002; Kendrick & McKay, 2004). *Myself* (*TH13*) features Thea as a ten-year-old, and in *Me in the Rain*, Thea is a pregnant woman. Thea said, "This is the baby's boat ... the baby is in her tummy. The mother is preparing everything for the baby ... She has lots of toys. She has two umbrellas. One for the baby in her tummy and one for her." Perhaps this content suggests that Thea (the youngest child) was interested in growing up? She showed her understanding that babies come from "mummies tummies" with mothers having to prepare in advance for the birth of their baby, indicating a sense of maturity and nurturing care. During the narration, the baby grew into a 14-year-old boy. In a process of "re-imagination" (Ahn & Filipenko, 2007, p. 279), Thea used the narrative to make sense of human development and, through imagined images that flowed over space and time, constructed a hypothesis about herself in her possible future.

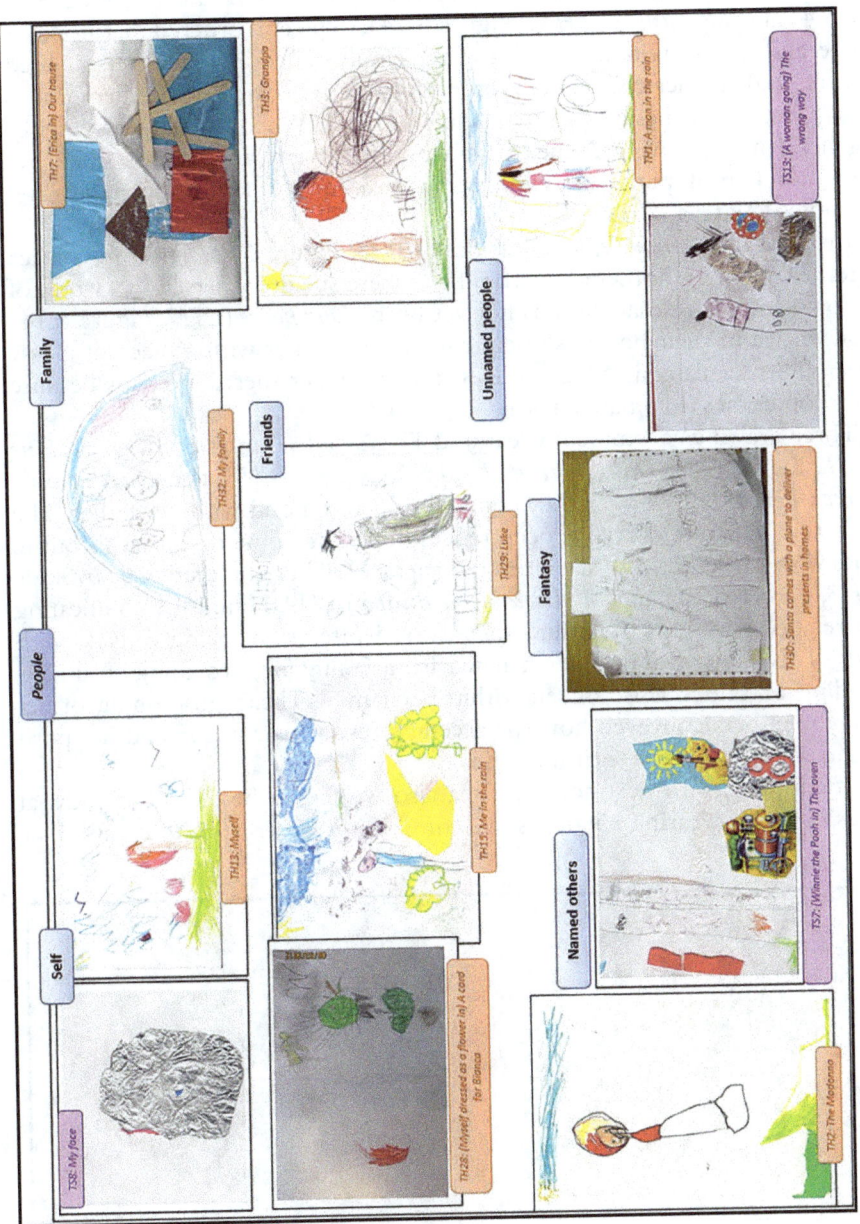

*Figure 6.14* Examples of Thea's drawings on the theme of *People*.

### Family

Ten drawings featured family members, suggesting the importance of family life to her. Two drawings of Thea's family, *My Family at Home* (*TH22*, Figure 6.4) and *My Family* (*TH32*, Figure 6.14), depict an ordered, harmonious home and Thea's relationships with her family. Thea included personalised features and characteristics: her mother's distinctive curly hair and her father's short, receding hair signified with spots (*TH32*). When drawing or describing her family drawings, Thea began by identifying her parents, then her sister, and herself, perhaps suggesting her awareness of family hierarchies and dynamics (Zlateva, 2019).

In *Erica and Mum Before I was Born* (*TH8*, Figure 6.7), Thea drew Erica together with her mother away from her, where she drew herself in a world of her own to convey that she was not yet born. *Our house* (*TH7*, Figure 6.14) shows Erica in their house, subsequently covering her with a piece of glossy paper. Thea explained, "Because I do not want her there," perhaps because Erica sometimes dominated Thea.

Three drawings prominently featured Thea's dad *(Daddy in) An Aeroplane* (*TS18*, Figure 6.8), *Dad Waking Up* (*TH36*, Figure 6.15), and *Dad Coming Home* (*TH20*, Figure 6.4), indicating Thea's close bond with her father. The latter two illustrate everyday occurrences including some of Thea's favourite times with her father. She also drew two pictures of her grandfathers, *Grandpa* (*TH3*, Figure 6.14) and *My Loveable Grandpa* (*TH9*, Figure 6.9), indicating her relationship with them and their shared interest in being outside with birds. This suite of drawings emanated from family life, providing an understanding of Thea's sense of self within her family. Thea's positioning of her family members conveyed how she acceded, resisted, or negotiated her position as she constructed their identities.

Identifying with her mother, Thea also wished to be like her daddy, at times enjoying wearing his tie, as in *Dad Coming Home* (*TH20*, Figure 6.4).

*Figure 6.15* Dad Waking Up *(TH36)* – by Thea.

She also enjoyed doing things with her father: "Erica will be with my mum, hanging clothes on the roof, and I will be with my dad. We switch on the TV and we watch The Strongest Man." The male figures in Thea's family strongly influenced her identity, including conveying a perception of herself as "strong" as in *The Strongest Man* (*TS27*, Figure 6.4), "I have muscles. I am the strong man." She emphasised strength in other drawings such as *The Snake Story* (*TS41*, Figure 6.9), where she drew herself running fast, or *Freeing Animals Stuck in a Tree* (*TS35*, Figure 6.9), where she killed the monster. Discussing Thea's keenness to portray herself as strong, her mother suggested, "Thea sometimes picks up a broomstick and pretends that she is doing weights. Sometimes she picks up a bottle of water and pretends that it is heavy, and she is pushing it upwards. And grandpa called her 'the strongest girl.'" This perception of Thea could have been interpreted as forming part of her "ideal identity" (De Rutyer & Conroy, 2002, p. 510).

Thea used her drawings to draw objects and people she loved and to communicate her feelings, knowledge, and ideas to others. Her drawings helped her to externalise and make meaning of her self-perceptions, her position within her family, community, and culture, as well as her relationships with other people.

### Notes

1 A film clip of Thea drawing *Erica and Mum before I was born* (*TH8*, Chapter 6, Video 1) is available at https://sites.google.com/view/childrenmakingmeaning
2 A film clip of Thea drawing *An Aeroplane that Flies* (*TS23*, Chapter 6, Video 2) is available at https://sites.google.com/view/childrenmakingmeaning

# 7 Bertly's story

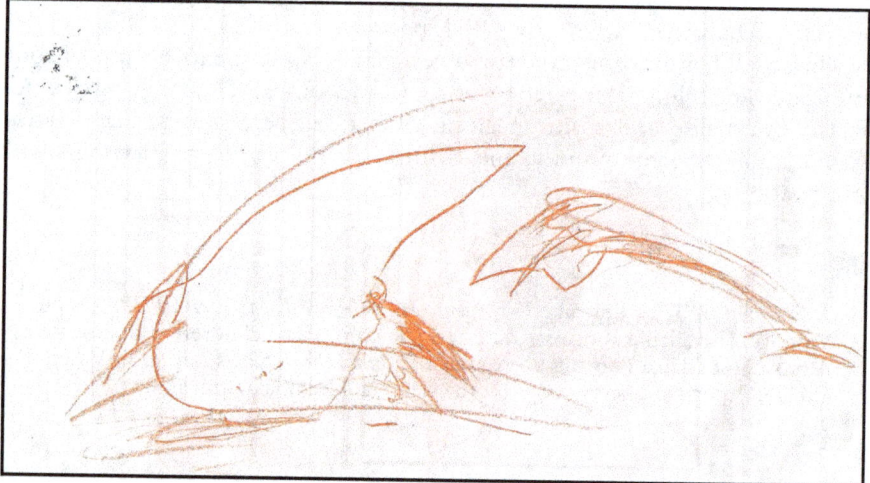

*Figure 7.1* Fireworks (BS16) – by Bertly.

## Getting to know Bertly

Bertly (4:5) and his sister Jael (6) attended the same school, which was a walking distance from their home. They lived in a first-floor apartment with an entrance area used by the family as a kitchen-dining-living space, where the children also watched television, stored their toys and books, and played. A television and a laptop in the same space were switched on when the siblings came home from school.

Bertly's mother described him as very sensitive, shy, and withdrawn; very organised and possessive taking time to do things and to get to know people. Similarly, Bertly's kindergarten teacher described him as a "Reserved child who becomes very self-conscious when given special attention … It takes him a while to trust and become confident." Bertly did not seem to have a best friend at school or to talk or interact much with his peers, especially those who were more

DOI: 10.4324/9781003427582-7

boisterous. He was often silent and seemingly out of place in the chaotic and noisy class environment. His demeanour at school contrasted considerably with that in his peaceful home environment, where Bertly was often outspoken and bubbly.

At home and school, Bertly enjoyed construction toys, play dough, dramatic play, riding his bicycle, going to the playground, playing computer games, and watching cartoons on television. *Pinocchio* (Disney, 1940), *Pink Panther* (MGM, 1963), and *Fireman Sam* (Mattel Television, 1987) were favourites. Bertly spent considerable time watching television or videos or playing on the computer, capable of operating the computer, accessing the internet, finding his way around new gadgets, and downloading video clips from his favourite cartoons.

At the beginning of the study, Bertly's mother and kindergarten teacher said that he did not enjoy drawing, often saying, "I don't know how to draw. I only know how to scribble." His mother felt his lack of confidence in drawing stemmed from having his apparent inability to draw confirmed on several occasions at school. During the project, Bertly's self-esteem and confidence levels grew; he seemed to believe that his drawings were good and worthy of adult attention. His voice was heard more in class; when the other children teased his scribbling, he stood up and refuted this.

Bertly was very close to his mother and sister, enjoying watching television, visiting relatives, shopping, and going to the playground and public gardens together. His mother cared for the house and children full-time, organising space and time in the home, controlling television viewing and Bertly's and Jael's use of a laptop. She was involved in the Parents-Teachers Association and helped with extra-curricular activities at school. Bertly's father, a construction worker, worked long hours and consequently spent less time with Bertly, who loved weekend time at his father's field, visiting Max, the pet rabbit. Bertly seemed to regard his sister highly; she was warm, caring, protective, and nurturing towards him. They were accomplices in play and each other's endeavours, sharing ideas, thoughts, and skills. Bertly had a close relationship with his extended family, where uncles played an important role, as did his maternal grandmother, whom he visited frequently.

When Bertly drew at the kitchen table, his mother and sister were always close by, coaching and encouragingly interacting with him. There was remarkable reciprocity in their interactions, which Bertly did not experience at school. He frequently asked for his mother's advice when drawing, and sometimes asked her to draw things for him. His mother and sister encouraged realistic drawings, and Bertly tended to depend on their influence around what and how he should draw.

## Simple-complex modes and themes

Bertly's home and school drawings and drawing time in each setting are summarised in Table 4.1 (Chapter 4). He drew for longer at school, though he made almost twice as many drawings at home. He spent from 35 seconds to over 33 minutes to finish a drawing.

Bertly's 59 drawings are plotted on his *Data Cross-grid* (Figure 7.2); school drawings, coded *BS (Bertly School)*, and in green-top; home drawings, coded *BH*

## Children making meaning

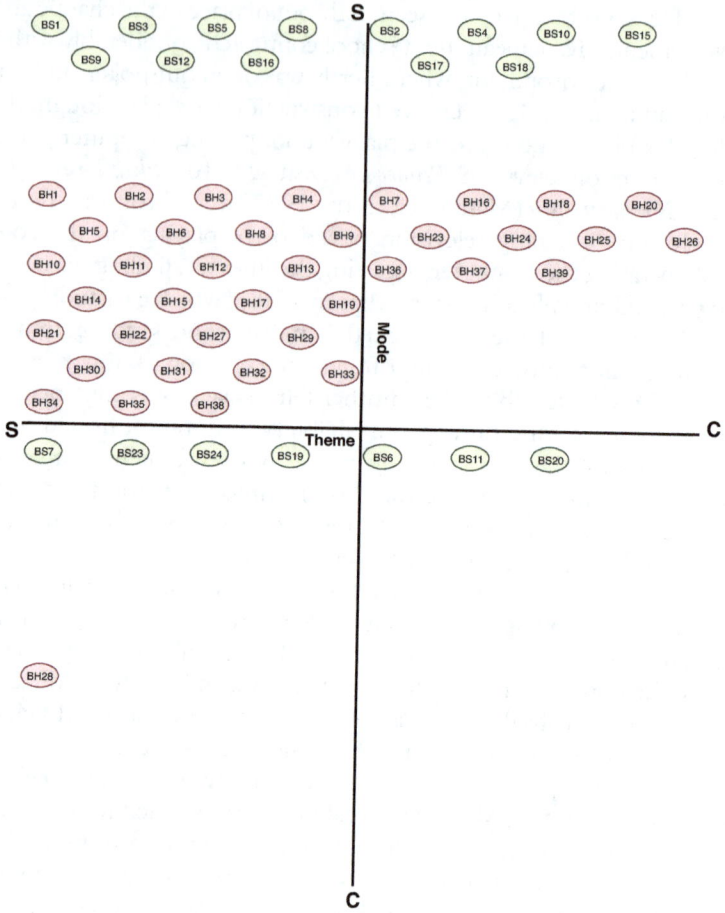

*Figure 7.2* Bertly's *Data Cross-grid* represents his home (orange) and school (green) drawings.

*(Bertly Home)*, and in red-bottom section. Figure 7.3 shows that Bertly made 34 drawings (top left) in a *simple mode* and a *simple theme* (27 home & seven school).

### Bertly's use of simple-complex modes

The majority of Bertly's drawings (51 of 59) were created using a *simple mode* (Figure 7.2 top), showing this as his dominant drawing style. Using a *simple mode*, Bertly preferred pencil colours, making 40 drawings exclusively in this medium, even with other materials available. He often drew with one or a few colours, again reflecting the *simple mode* preference. Bertly's choice to limit his use of media and modes could be a matter of convenience, routine, or confidence. Bertly's drawing style emphasised the use of a *simple mode* and

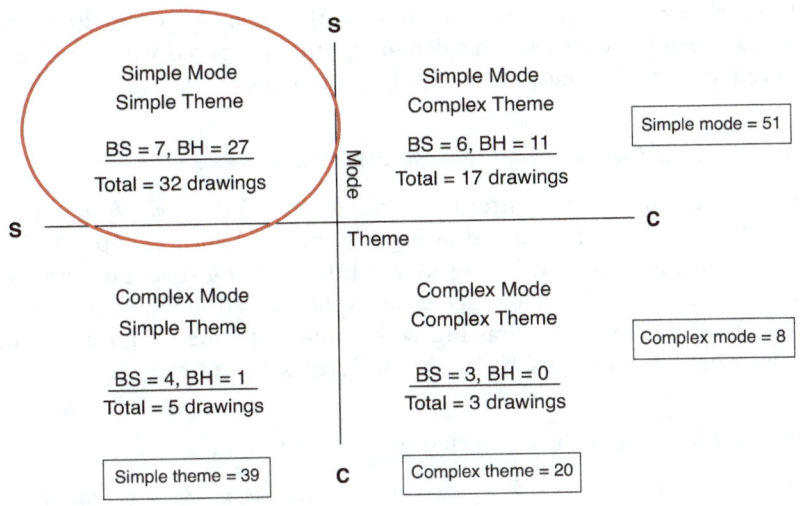

*Figure 7.3* A summary of Bertly's *Data Cross-grid* with his preferred drawing pattern marked with a red circle.

paralleled his lack of experience with other media. Bertly's mother described him as "not as yet able to use particular modes such as using scissors, sticking with glue, and dabbing glitter glue." Without such skills, children are less likely to use a *complex mode*.

Over time, and after considerable exposure and observation of his peers, who persistently made use of *complex modes*, Bertly grew in confidence, becoming more adventurous in using different media. Drawing multimodally, he seemingly tried to make connections between the relatively novel resources available, experimenting with using them and eventually moving across different modes, including cutting, glueing, sticking, and dabbing, to create new forms of drawing and meaning.

Bertly made eight (of 59) drawings using a *complex mode*. Figure 7.2 (bottom) shows seven of the eight complex mode drawings were made at school, perhaps because Bertly was influenced by his peers who were also experimenting with different media. In *complex mode* drawings, Bertly used a variety of media, including tape, glitter glue, pens, crayons, corrugated paper, wrapping paper, lollipop sticks, ribbons, and pipe cleaners. He tended first to observe his peers before beginning his drawing, using similar materials, media, and modes. Bertly incorporated their ideas and techniques to create his drawings, spending considerable time exploring materials, and forms available to shape his meaning. Sometimes, the similarity between Bertly's and his peers' school drawings was noticeable.

### Bertly's choice of simple-complex themes

Bertly made 39 drawings in *simple themes* (Figures 7.2 and 7.3 left), clearly indicating his preferred drawing style, which mainly featured one or two

## 98  Children making meaning

subjects related to animals, people, and weather. He also drew 20 drawings in *complex theme*; scenes from his daily life, often peppered with imagination, conveyed ideas and wishes, which Bertly struggled to verbalise.

### Bertly's preferred drawing pattern: simple mode, simple theme

Bertly's preferred drawing pattern was *simple mode* and *simple theme*, at home (27) and school (7); 34 (of 59) drawings (Figures 7.2 and 7.3 top left). There could be many reasons why Bertly adopted this drawing style, but perhaps his limited drawing confidence restricted his experimentation with new modes or his keenness to elaborate a drawing with complex themes. Figure 7.4 shows four drawings that typify each element of Bertly's *Data Cross-grid*.

### Simple mode, simple theme drawings

Bertly made four (of 34) drawings using a *simple mode* and *simple theme* (Figure 7.2, top left). Characteristics across these drawings included the sketchy style and the minimal use of modes, media, and colour. All four drawings use limited medium, pencil colours alone, and few colours. The theme in each drawing was also simple, depicting one object: *Leaves* (*BS8*, Figure 7.4); *Grass in Our Field* (*BH30*, Figure 7.4); *More balloons for Grandma's Birthday* (*BH35*, Figure 7.4), and *Fireworks* (*BS 16*, Figure 7.1).

### Fireworks

In *Fireworks* (*BS16*, Figure 7.1), drawn at school, Bertly used an orange pencil colour to make several marks across the page, which we define as *simple mode*. The *theme* 'fireworks' is *simple* too. Bertly was silent while drawing, eagerly talking about it afterwards:

> That is the sky. Psh! Those are fireworks. Here and here and here and here (pointing towards different areas on the paper). Psh! Psshhhhh! The fireworks are in the sky … Once I was in a restaurant and saw fireworks in the skies … Fireworks shoot up in the sky. They are shot with a gun. My father detonates the fireworks. He also shoots with a gun.

Bertly showed great interest in and knowledge of fireworks, communicating enthusiastically to construct and interpret his drawing through expressive vocalisations, sounds, words, gestures, and facial expressions. Bertly's eager explanation of his drawing contrasted considerably with his usual silence and shyness around adults.

*Fireworks* was laden with complex relevance for Bertly, who went beyond a simple depiction to represent his time at an open-air restaurant with his family when he saw fireworks in the sky. Watching fireworks is a very common local summer experience in Malta. Bertly had an insider view, making

*Figure 7.4* Examples of Bertly's drawings in *simple-to-complex modes* and *themes* correspond to each section of the grid.

connections between his father's interests in detonating fireworks and shooting target plates with a gun. Linking the fireworks and gunshots, Bertly continued his narrative, connecting his drawing to the notion of fire in a chimney in the story *The Three Little Pigs*:

BERTLY: But we do not have a chimney.
JO: Why would you want a chimney?
BERTLY: To go in it.
JO: Oh my! Would you like to go in a chimney? It will be hot!
BERTLY: It will have fire in it.
JO: Yes, it will have fire in it. And then what?
BERTLY: But the wolf went in the chimney.
JO: And what happened to the wolf when he went down the chimney?
BERTLY: He went up.
JO: Right. Why did he go up? What happened to the wolf?
BERTLY: He burned his bottom. Even if he falls into the pot, he will still get burned ... His tail gets burned.

Children can connect ideas and spontaneously construct links between different ideas, creating new genres and styles that help them make sense of the diverse socio-cultural experiences around them. *Fireworks* – with Bertly's accompanying narrative – provide insights into social and cultural contexts and funds of knowledge that go beyond the drawing alone.

Bertly's funds of knowledge were in play here, as he connected fireworks, gunshots, and the chimney in the story. While adults know that fireworks, gunshots, and a chimney are fire-related, only the chimney has a flame. Fireworks make a visual display of colours in the sky, and gunshots produce a loud sound. While the word "fireworks" in English links includes the word "fire," in Maltese, the equivalent word "murtali" (fireworks) does not sound like the Maltese word "nar" (fire); however, sometimes Maltese locals use the words interchangeably referring to "murtali" as "nar."

The connection Bertly made to the chimney in the story also reflected different cultural knowledge acquired through a traditional children's story. Popular media influences children's lives and thinking processes. Bertly merged popular media and social conventions with his communal and personal experiences to generate an understanding of fireworks, gunshots, fires, chimneys, and *The Three Little Pigs*. Ultimately, he put a personal hallmark on meaning.

### Simple mode, complex theme

Four drawings using a *simple mode* and a *complex theme* (Figure 7.4, top right) were again dominated by Bertly's preferred mode: mark-making and drawing. *Killing a Dragon (BS4)* and *Jack and the Beanstalk (BH7)* combined these two modes, while *The Choo-choo Train (BH23)* and *An Apple and a Mandarin Orange in a Box (BS10)* seem to be more discernible images with the single mode of drawing. What makes these four drawings complex in theme is that they each comprise more than two objects involving the composition of a scene or a narration.

### The Choo-choo Train

*The Choo-choo Train* (*BH23*, Figure 7.5)[1] was made at home. Using the *simple mode* of drawing and colouring-in in red, black, and yellow pencil colours – his preferred medium – Bertly drew a sightseeing train with considerable detail, including six carriages, two big wheels, the driver, himself, his family, and other passengers. He also included a fantasy character on the train, subtly blending reality and imagination. Before beginning the drawing, Bertly proudly showed a local sightseeing tourist train brochure, enthusiastically explaining that the previous Saturday he rode on the train with his mother, sister, and maternal grandmother. This was a long-awaited, exciting, and memorable experience for Bertly, whose peers at school had also been on the train on other occasions. The drawing combined glimpses from recalled experiences merged with Bertly imagination to create a related narrative. Bertly invested time, thought, and detail in his drawing, which took him fourteen and a half minutes to complete. He drew from memory and also referred to the train brochure to confirm specific details while holding a continuous, unfolding discussion with his mother about their shared experience. Bertly's train depicted things that captured his culture, social practices, places, and time as he re-constructed his experience.

*Figure 7.5* The Choo-choo Train (BH23) – by Bertly.

Bertly approached this drawing with a planned intent to document and share his experience, making this clear from the start. This is not uncommon in children's drawings (Matthews, 1999; Coates, 2002; Hopperstad, 2008b), but it contrasts with many of Bertly's drawings, which seem more spontaneous. Bertly and his mother had talked about and planned for the drawing of the train experience even before the train ride. Bertly began by voicing his plan to draw the train carriages and counting them while he drew, "One carriage. Two carriages. Three carriages. Four carriages. Six carriages ... That is the carriage."

*The Choo-choo Train* was developed with a continual interplay between intention and mark; throughout, Bertly communicated what he planned to add next. After drawing the six carriages, Bertly's conversation with his mother conveyed his intention, as he followed his mother's suggestions to help him create a realistic representation of the journey:

BERTLY: How am I going to draw Bertly now? ... And mummy?
MOTHER: ... And who else was with us?
BERTLY: Grandma.
MOTHER: Grandma, and who else? There was mummy, grandma, Bertly and who else was with us? Did you forget Jael? Did you forget that she was with us?
BERTLY: Then what?
MOTHER: Would you like to draw Bertly and Nanna in the carriage?

After drawing himself, Bertly said, "My face is peach ... I am going to draw Bertly here." Then he explained that he was drawing his grandmother Guza with peach lines to represent "her ears ... up above." After some time, he announced, "I am going to draw the wheel" while drawing a big yellow circle with black inside. A different set of lines in black represented "my legs, Jael's legs, and mummy's legs." He continued by drawing a tadpole figure with two dots for eyes, a dot for the nose, and a line for a mouth "That is the driver." Several studies have found similar communication of intention by children, who spontaneously and voluntarily state their drawing intent, naming and adding details as ideas develop during conversations (Coates, 2002; Hopperstad, 2008b). Matthews (1999) argues that children's intentional action is to communicate their meaning to others; they often engage in intentional, active thinking (Cox, 2005a) as they bring shape, order, and meaning to their ideas.

Sometimes, the intent of a drawing can be deduced from observation, only becoming apparent as the drawing emerges (Cox, 2005a). This was the case when Bertly drew "two ladies" in the second carriage. He said that he planned to draw them, then added that he was drawing one of them wearing boots. Bertly made his intention clear in the formation and sequence of the drawing, the purpose being more apparent when Bertly counted the women. The structure of his drawing sometimes showed his intention; when Bertly drew two tadpole figures in the fifth carriage, he did not explain them at the time, but later it became clear that they represented the two people at the back of the train. The following extract gives a flavour of Bertly's intentions in the drawing context:

MOTHER: There was a lady sitting at the front who gave you some chocolate.
BERTLY: But I am not going to draw her at the front. I am going to draw her in this carriage at the back.
MOTHER: Where was Bertly sitting?
BERTLY: He was sitting next to Grandma Guza …
MOTHER: Who was sitting behind you in the carriage? … There was mummy and Jael.
BERTLY: Who was in this carriage?
MOTHER: Which carriage? The first carriage? There was that lady, right? How many women were sitting in the front carriage?
BERTLY: Three?
MOTHER: Three. There were three.
BERTLY: But the other one is at the back.
MOTHER: We cannot see the third one.
BERTLY: Who was sitting in this carriage?
MOTHER: There were other two people at the back. There was another woman and a man.
BERTLY: Pssst. Pssst. Pcoo. Pcoo. Pssst. Pcoo. Pcoo. Pcooo. Kick. Kick (while drawing) … Nee-no. Nee-no. Nee-no.

Soon after, Bertly lifted the drawing and, holding it vertically facing him, moved it forward on the table, animating his narrative with sound effects and explaining, "Then we did, Nee-no, nee-no, nee-no. And then someone else got on the train." This example of "playing *at* drawing" (Wood & Hall, 2011, p. 274), where Bertly used the drawing as a prop combined with vocalisations and sound effects to enhance his narrative, reflects his kinaesthetic and oral enjoyment in transforming his static, flat drawing into a prop for play through movement and chanting.

During this conversation, Bertly's mother was a "communicative prompt and prop" (Flewitt, 2005, p. 212), explaining and guiding Bertly, making links to the event, and providing suggestions in a process of co-construction that helped him develop his drawing. Such talk and endorsement through shared, detailed dialogue (Rose et al., 2006) helped Bertly sustain his drawing intent and improve his drawing. Children sometimes seek and receive verbal instruction and positive reinforcement from more knowledgeable others to help them achieve the visually realistic drawing they desire, and which they perceive adults value highly.

Once Bertly had drawn all the people on the train, his mother regarded the drawing as complete because, according to her, it represented a factual picture of the event. Bertly, however, wanted to develop the story further. First, he said he was going to add *Pink Panther*, quickly adapting this to add his friend Alexander. Even though he knew that Alexander was not on the train,

Bertly wanted to include him, thus reflecting Bertly's ability and agentive role to move between past and present, experience and imagination, as he creates an unpredictable, fluid, and unique drawing (Jewitt, 2009a).

Bertly's narrative was a combination of genres – an autobiographical memoir combining fiction, fact, graphics, narratives, and action. Bertly had last seen Alexander months before the train ride. The same day that Bertly drew the tourist train at home, he drew an octopus at school (*BS7*, Figure 7.7). The octopus drawing reminded Bertly of a summer day when he swam in the sea with Alexander, and they saw a man coming ashore holding an octopus. Bertly wanted to include Alexander in his train drawing even though "He was not in the choo-choo train." As with his *Fireworks* drawing, Bertly was making new associations and connections as meanings emerged in the process of drawing: from the octopus drawing to remembering Alexander, and then to including him in the train drawing. Bertly drew on his past, social, and cultural experiences to create new meanings at a particular point in time. Such "points of fixing" (Stein, 2008, p. 39) are a potpourri of past, present, and future, forming a semiotic chain of meaning-making that provides "concrete traces' of socio-cultural worlds of making" (p. 99). Bertly was making meaning of his life occurrences, moving across virtual and real spaces, contexts, media, activities, and time, while coherently integrating meaning.

## Complex mode, complex theme

Bertly did three school drawings using a *complex mode* and a *complex theme* (Figure 7.2, bottom right). The use of a *complex mode* was quite rare for Bertly. In these drawings, Bertly experimented with new techniques, media, and modes using cutting, glueing paper and sequins, and dabbing glitter glue. The *theme* in the three drawings (Figure 7.4) was *complex* too, where *Cooking Chicken in the Oven (BS20)* and *Animals on a Plane (BS6)* each illustrate a scene, and *A Party at Sea (BS11)* illustrates a story.

### *A Party at Sea*

*A Party at Sea* (*BS11*, Figure 7.6) took Bertly 16 minutes to do while sitting next to a classmate, Sandra. He intertwined *complex modes*, including drawing, scattering and dabbing glitters, and glueing sequins, to create and communicate meaning in multi-layered, multimodal ways. Bertly's constant observation of and discussion with Sandra may explain her influence on techniques and ideas in this drawing and its emerging theme.

The theme of *A Party at Sea* was also complex; Bertly made a scene where people were having a party at sea. The drawing denotes a night picture, but later, talking with his mother and sister at home, Bertly changed the time of the party:

*Figure 7.6* *A Party at Sea (BS11)* – by Bertly.

BERTLY: They had a party at sea.
MOTHER: Was it at night?
JAEL: I think so. Here are the stars, and here is the moon (referring to some of the sequins patterns).
BERTLY: No, it was not at night. It was not night.
MOTHER: So what time was it? Was it in the morning?
BERTLY: Yes, it was in the morning.
MOTHER: Was there a sun or not? I am not seeing a sun. I am seeing a moon.
BERTLY: It was a sunny day but there were also clouds.

Children's descriptions of their drawings can reflect their distinctive, culturally shaped, complex interests, traits, and characteristics. Bertly's *A Party at Sea* communicated his love of the sea, born from his geo-cultural heritage. While Bertly labelled the glitter as stars flying from the sea to the sky, Sandra decided that her drawing represented people flying across the sea. Thus, while Bertly was inspired by Sandra and copied her theme, content, and some techniques (Boyatzis & Albertini, 2000), he was not a "compliant respondent" (Mavers, 2011, p. 3). He constantly made decisions about the meanings he wanted to make and what he would use to make them, adding his thoughts and ideas to the drawing as he negotiated, interpreted, and challenged what Sandra was doing while he developed his drawing. Bertly made personal and subtle changes to his drawing that were almost imperceptible but significant. His ability to imitate, led him to create a drawing with a *complex mode* and a *complex theme*, following Sandra's use of and movement across different modes.

## Complex mode, simple theme

Four drawings (of five) are *complex* in *mode* but *simple* in *theme* (Figure 7.4, bottom left), an atypical, experimental style for Bertly. Three drawings were done at school, where Bertly could observe and be influenced by his peers' styles and use of different modes and media. In *A Gate (BS19), A Portrait of Myself with a Moustache (BS13), An Octopus in the Deep Sea (BH28)*, and *An Octopus (BS7)*, Bertly made use of multiple modes, including drawing, glueing, taping, and dabbing.

The *themes* in these drawings are *simple*, each featuring a specific object with no accompanying narration. Bertly seemed inspired by the resources available, and the suitability of the chosen materials represented his intended meaning.

### *An Octopus*

*An Octopus* (*BS7*, Figure 7.7)[2] was drawn at school in *complex mode*. Bertly glued and taped lollipop sticks and made some marks; the shape of the lollipop sticks perhaps prompted Bertly to create the many "legs" of the octopus. Bertly brought his interest in water creatures and his factual and fictional knowledge about octopuses to his drawing, conveying his thinking that an octopus has many legs and two hands. He also drew its head and tummy, represented by the red marks, and said, "I saw it in the deep sea. That is an octopus. Those are its legs."

Bertly took 25 minutes to complete the drawing while sitting next to Thea, occasionally looking at what she was doing. He began by drawing the red part at the centre of the page. Simultaneously, Thea (*TS20*) began attaching lollipop sticks to the top of her paper. Taking cues from Thea, Bertly conscientiously glued five lollipop sticks vertically towards the top, securing them with transparent tape. Bertly's finished picture looked similar to Thea's, but his meaning – an octopus – was entirely different from Thea's "fan."

Children sometimes consider various interpretations to create a new meaning (Wright, 2003); therefore, while Bertly drew on what was happening around him and Thea's use of modes, descriptions, and development of their drawings, he maintained his intent in his emerging drawing. Subsequently, he expanded its existing meaning through his accompanying drawing-narrative. The dynamic development of Bertly's drawing can be seen as a transformative process of the resource that shaped his making according to the meaning he applied.

*Figure 7.7* **An Octopus (BS7)** – by Bertly.

## Inventory of content: emerging themes in Bertly's drawings

Many of Bertly's 59 drawings featured *People* (17) and *Animals* (16).

### People

With 17 drawings of people, this theme was the most prevalent in Bertly's drawings, with subcategories of fantasy characters (such as *Pink Panther* and *Pinocchio*) (5), self-portraits (4), family members (4), unnamed people (3), and a friend (1).

In the following sections, we discuss one of each of Bertly's drawings that are featured under *Fantasy, Self, Family, Unnamed,* and *Friends.* Figure 7.8 shows examples of drawings from Bertly's content theme of *People.*

### Fantasy

Bertly drew five pictures that included fantasy characters (Figure 7.8), four inspired by children's cartoons or television series. Bertly drew scenes from

108  Children making meaning

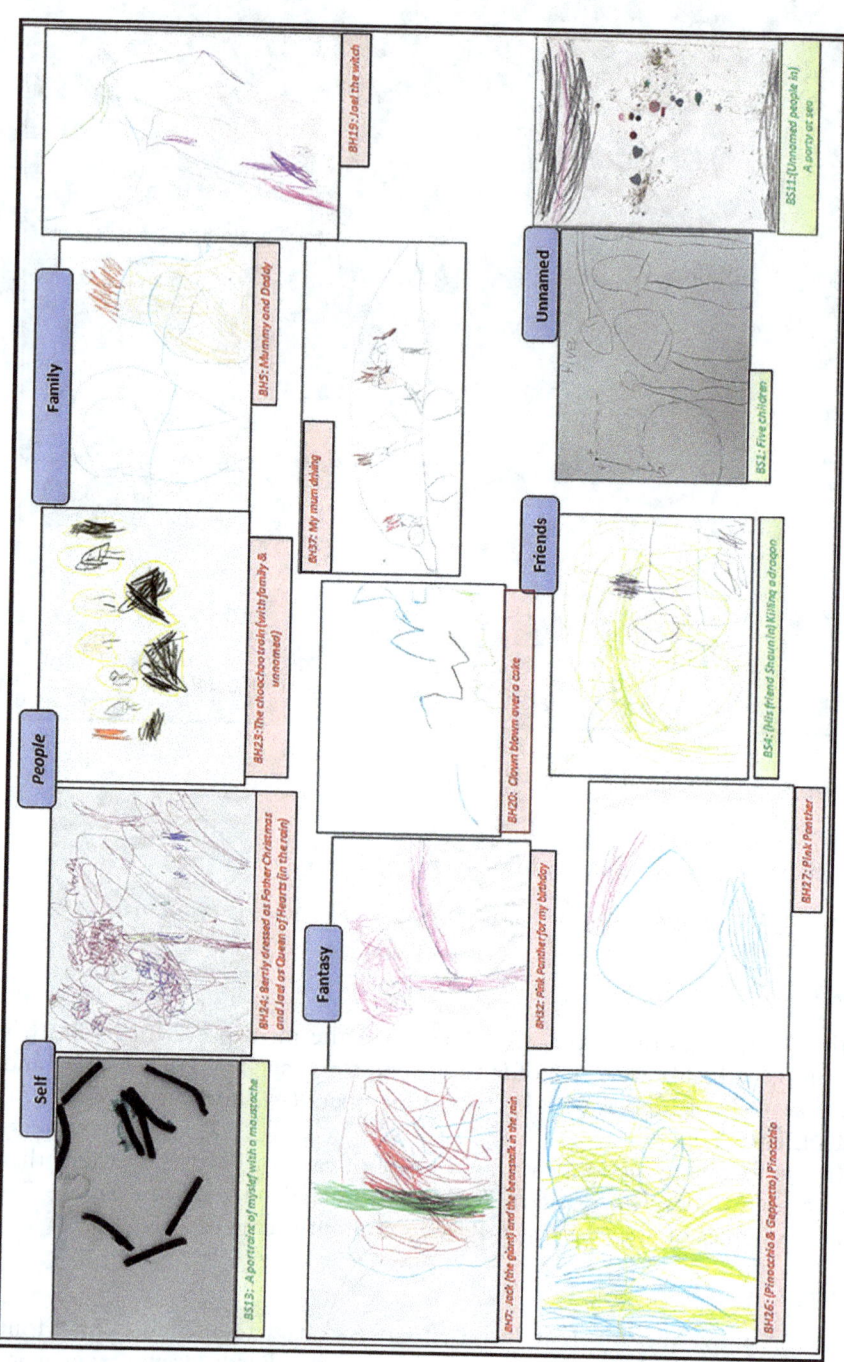

Figure 7.8 Examples of Bertly's drawings illustrate the theme of *People*.

the *Cartoonito Tales* (Cartoon Network, 2013): *Jack and the Beanstalk (BH7)* and *Pinocchio (BH26)*. Two drawings featured *Pink Panther (BH27, BH32)*, Bertly's favourite cartoon character. The fifth picture was an imaginary character of a clown blown over a cake (*BH20*). All were done at home, where Bertly was most exposed to popular media culture.

Whenever he drew *Pink Panther*, including *Pink Panther for my Birthday* (*BH32*, Figure 7.9), Bertly narrated the same story from one *Pink Panther* episode:

> He (Pink Panther) sleeps on the iron. Then the phone rings and he is talking on the phone. Then the iron board falls on his tummy. Then he places a clock on his tummy. Then we would need to go to the hospital. Pink Panther is going to the hospital.

Bertly showed his ability to narrate stories while trying to make sense of real experiences. Theorising about the burning effect and consequence of leaving an iron on clothes, he concluded that if someone is burned with an iron, (including *Pink Panther*), they would need to be hospitalised.

### Self

Bertly drew four pictures of himself, including *A Portrait of Myself with a Moustache* (*BS13*, Figure 7.10), which seemed stimulated by some black

*Figure 7.9* Pink Panther for my Birthday (BH32) – by Bertly.

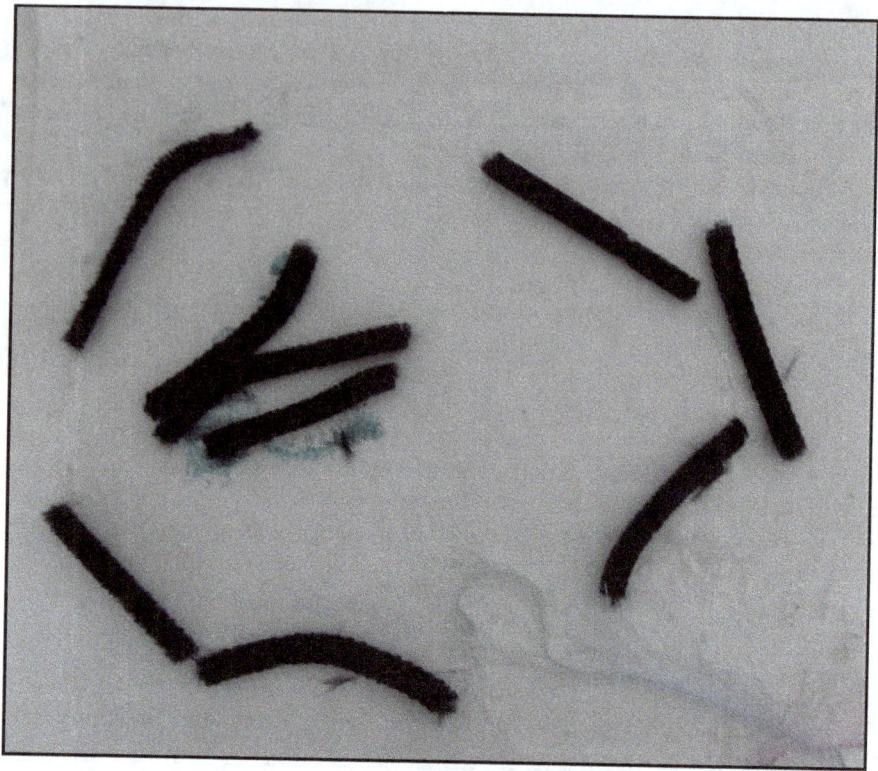

*Figure 7.10* A Portrait of Myself with a Moustache (BS13) – by Bertly.

pipe cleaners that the children at school were curious about, and someone suggested they might be moustaches. Squeezing glitter glue on his sheet and attaching small pieces of pipe cleaner to form a circle, Bertly said (to himself) "moustache." Bertly said the outlined circular shape was the face, onto which he attached three pieces of pipe cleaner to the middle, representing the moustaches, and added colourful ribbon for the hair. Bertly enclosed the whole thing in a border of transparent tape to complete a portrait of a boy, explaining, "Yes, it is a boy: me. Bertly with a moustache."

Bertly seemed to imply that he made a drawing of himself in an ideal, imagined future identity (De Ruyter & Conroy, 2002; Kendrick & McKay, 2004). This drawing was experimental in several ways: he tried a different style of drawing and used a different material, moving from pencil colours. He also experimented with a new way of thinking and visualising himself as an adult man with a moustache. None of his relatives had moustaches, but Bertly explained that *Fireman Norris*, from the *Fireman Sam* series (Mattel Television, 1987), had a moustache – another example of children's popular culture influencing content in Bertly's drawing.

## Family

Bertly made four drawings featuring family members, including two representing a family outing in transport. All four drawings were done at home; all stemming from cultural events. Bertly drew all his family in *My Mum Driving* (*BH37*, Figure 7.8), showing an everyday event: his mother, with her distinct red spikey hair, driving the family. *Mummy and Daddy* (*BH5*, Figure 7.8), drawn around St Valentine's Day, was the only drawing of his mother and father that explored the love and well-being he experienced at home. Bertly's father (left) and his mother, with her red spikey hair (right), were joined by a line. When the drawing was complete, the two people had become Jael (Bertly's sister) and Grandpa Peter.

*Bertly dressed as Father Christmas and Jael as Queen of Hearts* (*BH24*, Figure 7.11) shows Jael (centre) wearing her Carnival costume from the previous year. Bertly did not have a Father Christmas costume but drew himself as his favourite small Father Christmas toy, putting the small plastic toy on the paper and drawing around it (blue, left).

Exhibiting the characteristics of a "patterner" (Gardner, 1980, p. 47), Bertly included details in his drawings: boots for Father Christmas and a crown for the queen. Other marks signified food in their kitchen, and the zigzag lines were rain. This drawing seems to intertwine the past with imagination and dramatic play.

*Figure 7.11* Bertly dressed as Father Christmas and Jael as Queen of Hearts (BH24) – by Bertly.

112  *Children making meaning*

*Figure 7.12* Examples of Bertly's drawings of *Animals*.

## Animals

With 16 drawings featuring *Animals*, this was the second most prevalent theme in Bertly's drawings, which included water creatures (4), fantasy animals (3), farm animals (2), pets (2), flying creatures (2), mini-beasts (2), and wild animals (1).

Bertly's interest in animals perhaps stemmed from a class theme, when children frequently sang songs, coloured templates, and did structured crafts focusing on animals. Home experiences – the animals at his father's field, their home next to the sea, fishing trips, and swimming – connected with this theme. Figure 7.12 shows examples of Bertly's drawings, including different animals.

### Water creatures

Six drawings focused on sea and water features, including *A Shark* and *A Shark in the Sea* (*BH14; BH21*, Figure 7.12), *The Whale at the Beach* (*BH18*, Figure 7.14), *An Octopus and An Octopus in the Deep Sea* (*BS7, BH28*, Figure 7.13), and *A Fish, a Cricket and a Cat* (*BH26*, Figure 7.12). Bertly's interest in sea creatures was perhaps influenced by his father's.

*A Shark (BH21)* and *A Shark in the Sea* (*BH1*, Figure 7.13) show Bertly's knowledge about sharks:

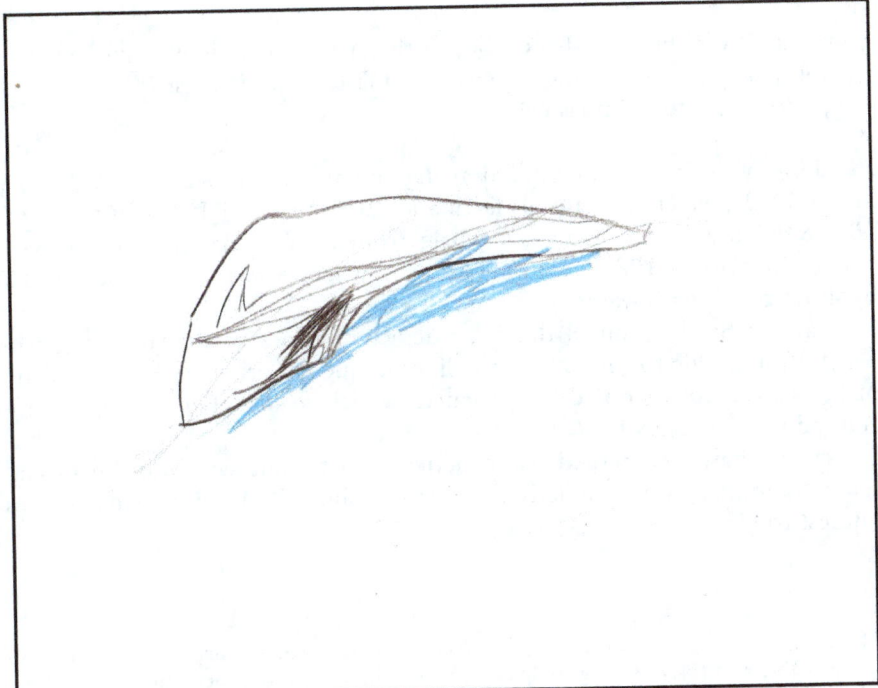

*Figure 7.13* *A Shark in the Sea (BH14)* – by Bertly.

114  *Children making meaning*

*Figure 7.14* A Whale at the Beach (BH18) – by Bertly.

> A shark is very big … a shark is bigger than us … will it do like this [open mouth action] and eat me? Do we swim faster if it bites us? If he wakes up, do I have to swim faster?

In addition to the two octopus drawings mentioned above (*BH28* & *BS7*, Figure 7.12), which indicate his fascination with them, *A Whale at the Beach* (*BH18*, Figure 7.14) features a whale from an episode of *Fireman Sam* (Mattel Television, 1987) cartoon character, where *Fireman Sam* had saved it by showering it with water.

Many of Bertly's animal drawings depicted stories or drawing-narratives which brought life to them. His storylines frequently originated from a blend of books, cartoons, and real experiences, which formed Bertly's rich socio-cultural funds of knowledge.

Bertly's drawings merged real experiences with fantasy; the ordinary and the extraordinary were similarly important to him. Bertly drew what was of interest to him.

### Notes

1. A film clip of Bertly drawing *The Choo-choo train* (*BS23*, Chapter 7, Video 1) is available at https://sites.google.com/view/childrenmakingmeaning
2. A film clip of Bertly drawing *An Octopus* (*BS7*, Chapter 7, Video 2) is available at https://sites.google.com/view/childrenmakingmeaning

# 8 Form and content in children's drawings

*Figure 8.1* The Reindeer (TH10) – by Thea.

### Form in children's drawing: the use of simple-complex modes

Having discussed Luke's, Thea's, and Bertly's drawing stories, we now focus on *form* and *content* in their drawings, highlighting their preferred modes to identify their respective semiotic styles. We distinguish each child's drawer identity as we bring together their *configuration styles* and choices of *simple-complex themes* with their *drawer patterns* and *types of drawing*. We then consider the prevailing themes that emerged across all three children's drawings.

Luke (Figure 5.3, Chapter 5) favoured drawing in *simple mode* with a *complex* theme. Most of Thea's drawings (Figure 6.3, Chapter 6) were in *complex*

DOI: 10.4324/9781003427582-8

## 116  Children making meaning

*mode* and *complex theme*, and Bertly's drawings indicated his preference for *simple mode* and *simple theme* (Figure 7.3, Chapter 7). Preferred use of *simple-complex modes* (*semiotic style*) and *themes* (*configuration style*) are summarised in Table 8.1 (bold defines each drawer profile).

*Table 8.1* Summary of the children's semiotic and configuration styles, indicating drawer profiles

| Name of child | Number of drawings | | | | Drawer profile |
|---|---|---|---|---|---|
| | Semiotic style | | Configuration style | | |
| | Mode | | Theme | | |
| | Simple | Complex | Simple | Complex | |
| Luke | **63** | 17 | 26 | **54** | **Simple mode, Complex theme** |
| Thea | 32 | **52** | 32 | **52** | **Complex mode, Complex theme** |
| Bertly | **51** | 8 | **39** | 20 | **Simple mode, Simple theme** |

Figure 8.2 shows the distinctive drawing preferences and unique *semiotic* and *configuration styles* of the three children as plotted on the *Data Cross-grid*.

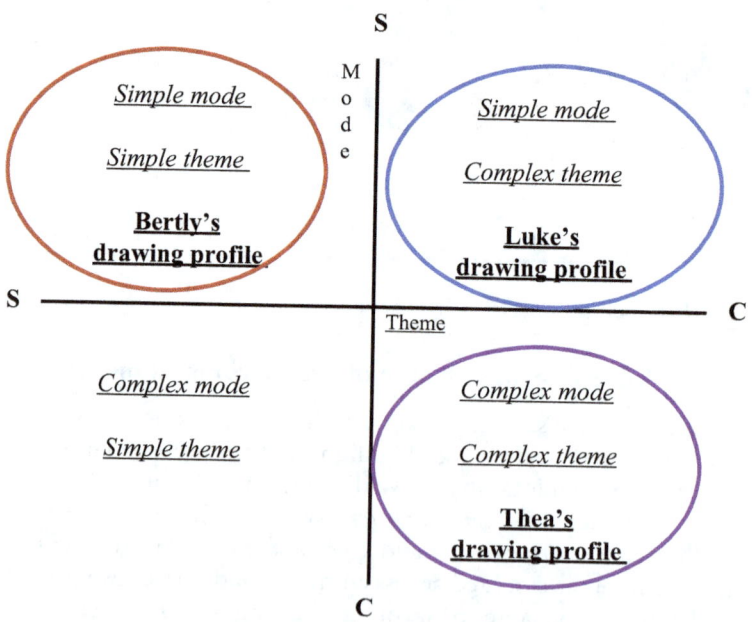

*Figure 8.2* A summarised representation of the three children's drawing preferences.

## Children's semiotic styles: use of modes

To establish which modes Luke, Thea, and Bertly used, we analysed their data according to their respective *Data Cross-grids* (Figure 5.2, Figure 6.2, Figure 7.2). Combining their respective drawer identities, we see that each child's drawings seem to have a distinct mode preference. Luke and Bertly favoured a *simple mode*, while Thea preferred a *complex mode*.

Building on our broad definition of "drawing," we have seen that Luke and Bertly used few embellishments. Bertly's preferred drawing medium was pencil-colours, often using one or a few colours. Luke preferred to draw with crayons, gem markers, or a combination of both, regularly restricting his sketchy, *simple mode* drawings to the use of one medium and one colour and occasionally experimenting with multiple media within the same *simple mode* drawing. Over time, both tried unfamiliar semiotic resources, often after watching their peers using *complex modes*. Bertly and Luke spent considerable time exploring the materials when using multiple modes.

Thea's *semiotic style* was dominated by a *complex mode*. Her dexterity, motivation, and experimentation made her capable in any medium. Though drawing was often featured in her graphic representations, Thea usually worked multimodally – often moving between modes: drawing, writing, talking, cutting, glueing, tracing, and colouring. She made effective use of the properties of available media, fluidly shifting across multiple modes and semiotic resources to enhance her meaning-making while maintaining her core meaning (Hull & Nelson, 2005; Mavers & Newfield, 2012). Children's *semiotic styles* and preferences emanate from personal and social experiences: Thea's love for drawing, her familiarity with diverse media, her inquisitiveness to try new ones, her kinaesthetic enjoyment of semiotic resources, and the inspiration that materials sometimes evoked, fuelled her *complex mode*. Even when working in a single-mode drawing, she frequently incorporated several media, using crayons, pencil colours, markers, gel pens, or pens in different colours.

Our focus on three children means we are not generalising but setting out their unique, drawing portraits.

## The influence of modes in children's drawings

From a funds of knowledge perspective (Moll et al., 1992), the environment can inform and shape a drawing, and the semiotic resources available can influence the content. Before the project, Luke, Thea, and Bertly experienced a limited variety of semiotic resources and experiences at kindergarten, though Thea had a rich range of resources at home. This may have limited the boys' aptitudes, explaining their hesitancy to experiment with new media and limiting their broader drawing skills. Perhaps this explains why Luke and Bertly used a *simple mode* and stimulated Thea's ready use of *a complex mode*.

The wide variety of novel materials sparked Bertly's and Luke's new interest and experimentation, yet their preferred *semiotic style* was to draw in a *simple mode*. Thea drew mainly in *complex mode* when materials were introduced at school, occasionally drawing in *simple mode*. Luke, Thea, and Bertly selected modes – depending on the meanings they wanted to convey. Their *semiotic styles* reflected their personal drawing preferences and distinct identities. Irrespective of any apparent prevailing *semiotic style*, the children shifted between *simple-complex* modal forms. Luke and Bertly seemed mostly to prefer drawing in a *simple mode*, occasionally using *complex modes*, while for Thea, the opposite was the case.

A *simple mode* did not restrict the children's ability to create *complex themes* and meanings. Luke's dominant drawing style was a *simple mode* in his sketchy, monochrome drawings, seemingly offering more flexibility to focus on the complexity of his theme and his creation of intricate drawing-stories. Rather than diversifying his attention by orchestrating the interplay between modes, Luke seemed focused on creating his meaning; the *simple mode* of drawing enabled him to efficiently create his particularly *complex theme* drawings. A lack of interaction with different resources could result in limited acuity in the simultaneous use of modes, where a *simple mode* drawing can offer unique meaning-making opportunities. A *simple mode* allowed Luke to develop *complex themes* as he drew.

### *The potential of modes in meaning-making*

Luke, Thea, and Bertly explored a variety of modes across media and meaning, manipulating modes in *simple* and *complex* forms. In some drawings, they seemed to select modes for their potential to represent meaning; in others, the choice of mode and medium preceded and shaped the meaning. This was done in mainly two paradigms: (i) meaning is stimulated by the choice of mode and (ii) meaning-making as the result of modal functioning.

#### *Meaning is stimulated by the choice of mode*

During their meaning-making processes, children play and experiment with the form and materiality of available media, choosing the mode that best suits their intentions (Kress, 2004; Hopperstad, 2008a). The children sometimes seemed to have clear intentions around what they wanted to draw, purposefully choosing their mode according to its semiotic potentialities for their meaning and how they wanted to communicate it. The next three examples show how modes may be selected for their affordance and meaning-making potential, depending on children's interests.

Thea drew a reindeer (*TH10*, Figure 8.1), opting for the materiality and dimensionality of the yellow pipe-cleaner, which she cut and taped to signify antlers.

In *Me Carrying a Bag Full of Candy* (*LH49*, Figure 5.1, Chapter 5), Luke had planned to draw a bag and wanted to include a rod to hold it. This perhaps prompted him to use a lollipop stick to represent the rod. Its shape and wooden texture were an apt modality, for his intended meaning. Similarly, wanting to communicate flying, in *Animals on a Plane* (*BS6*, Figure 7.12, Chapter 7), Bertly used glitters to convey flying and perhaps magic, having watched his peers using glitters to represent pixie dust that fairies might use to make things fly.

*Meaning-making as a result of modal functioning*

The appeal and materiality of media often inspire children. Blended with their curiosity about how to manipulate a new resource, this provided a starting point for meaning-making. Tape, glitters, lollipop sticks, ribbons, and pipe-cleaners, for example, offered kinaesthetic pleasure and sensual experimentation (Price et al., 2012). Multisensory materials can act as catalyst media that children integrate into their meaning-making processes, as Bertly did when he decided the black pipe cleaners could be a moustache (*BS13*, Figure 7.10, Chapter 7). Thea, likewise, used ribbons for hair (*TH8*, Figure 6.7, Chapter 6), and colourful, ready-made cut-outs of animals and greenery inspired Luke's garden scene (*LH30*, Figure 5.4, Chapter 5). The semiotic resources, together with the chosen mode, became starting points for drawings, which stimulated the meaning. The modes children select may deeply influence the content, style, and meaning of a drawing (Kress, 2004; Price et al., 2012).

## Drawer identities

Every child is unique, and it is important that we see children and their drawing identities as unique too. This is a matter of right as well as being a way of seeing them more clearly. Combining each child's use of *simple-complex theme*, their choice of *simple-complex mode*, and their *types of drawing* with their *drawer patterns*, we arrive at a *drawer identity* for each. This means bringing together analysis of the children's *semiotic styles* and *configurations* as plotted in *Data Cross-grid* (Figure 8.2) with direct observations and analysis of the products and processes of drawings.

*Luke: person-centred, narrator, dramatist*

Luke made (54 of 81) drawings in *complex themes*, indicating his preference for drawing multiple objects to create scenes and narratives. We think of these drawings as tableaus of fact and fiction, combining imaginative themes, highly influenced by popular culture, conveyed through active mythical characters.

Luke's *types of drawings* varied; most featured people, making him a *person-centred* drawer (Gardner, 1982) for whom relationships are important. Home drawings tended to be *autobiographical*, frequently depicting family events. Many were *graphic-narrative* types, frequently using a *simple mode* to make complex action stories. Primarily influenced by superhero characters, these *person-centred* drawings were fuelled with "personal fantasy-based" storylines (Wright, 2007, p. 1), impregnated with imagination, character, and plot stimulated by popular media. Luke's narratives were full of adventure and tension, embellished with mythical and fictional chronicles. Luke mainly used his drawings as a way of thinking and moving (Adams, 2004), while processing the moral and ethical values of power, justice, and mortality.

Luke often drew in a solitary way, engaging in ongoing dialogue with himself. He gave his images a strong sense of narrative: dynamic descriptions explaining actions, enfolding stories, or dramatising scenes whilst highlighting moral and life dilemmas. As an *"inveterate verbaliser"* (Gardner, 1982, p. 117), he frequently moved in and out of the drawing, between real and pretend features, while fluidly and intensely developing extensive narratives. The animated narration that accompanied *The Lobster Story* (*LS11*, Figure 8.3) exemplifies:

> Psht! Psht! Psht! ... The bad guys are shooting at the lobster. No, the good guys are ... Then they eat the lobster ... I am shooting the lobster .... Puff! They will put it in the pot and cook it. I am going to put on some purple glitter glue on it so that he will surely die ... It is killing him. He is dying.

*Figure 8.3* *The Lobster Story (LS11)* – by Luke.

"Playing *at* drawing" (Wood & Hall, 2011, p. 274), Luke accompanied his drawing with gestures, vocalisations, and banging with the drawing material (e.g. gem markers) on the table to simulate shooting, thus animating his narrative. Luke accompanied many of his drawings with dramatic elaborations, which suggests his *drawer pattern* is also "*dramatist*" (Gardner, 1982, p. 118). Luke often seemed reluctant to draw, especially at school, but once he started drawing, he became totally immersed, transforming himself into a conductor, scriptwriter, narrator, and performer of his drawings, which he packed with energy and inventive plots.

### *Thea: subject matter generalist, person-centred, object-centred, patterner*

Thea mainly drew in *complex themes*, frequently drawing home and outdoor scenes of animals, people, or objects. She drew narratives that amalgamated real life with imaginary stories of fairies, princesses, monsters, giants, and witches. Thea's *complex theme* drawings distinguish her as a "*subject matter generalist*" (Thompson, 1999, p. 155) where objects or persons often dominated her drawings, making her a "*person*" and "*object-centred*" drawer (Gardner, 1982, p. 118). Family members, household objects, vehicles, and outdoor scenes of varying complexity proliferated in Thea's drawings as she incorporated new and elaborate elements. In *Our House* (*TH7*, Figure 8.4, Image 1) and *Dad Coming Home* (*TH20*, Figure 8.4, Image 2), Thea drew her house, first from the outside, emphasising the skylight (brown triangle), and in the second, on the inside, including her dad returning from work, the front door and the apartment door, with the connecting staircase (pink).

*My Family TH22* and *TH32* (Figure 8.5, Images 1 & 2) are examples of Thea's people-centred drawings, featuring her family, emphasising personal characteristics, including distinctive hair features, and representing family dynamics and hierarchies.

Thea seemed almost always motivated to draw. She was full of contrasts and appeared to have a fluid *drawer pattern*. Sometimes she drew silently, absorbed in creating drawings full of patterns, decorations, and detail, characteristic of "*visualisers*" and "*patterners*" (Gardner, 1982, p. 117–118). Thea was also a *dramatist* (Gardner, 1982, p. 118), enthusiastically filling her drawings with imaginative narrations. She sometimes began a drawing with a clear and meticulous plan of what to draw; on other occasions, she drew spontaneously, seemingly without a plan. Thea's approach was never rigid, her thoughts changed fluidly. A "self-starter" (Gardner, 1982, p. 117), Thea rarely needed encouragement to draw, often spending considerable time engrossed in her drawing. She demonstrated ephemeral interest in what she drew, frequently shifting attention from one section to another to express different meanings. Some drawings lost their permanence after a few days, and she did not always remember what she drew; once drawings were finished and discussed, they often lost significance. What seemed to matter to Thea was creating something aesthetically pleasing in the moment.

122  *Children making meaning*

*Figure 8.4  Our House (TH7)* [1] and *Dad Coming Home (TH20)* [2] – by Thea.

*Form and content in children's drawings* 123

*Figure 8.5* **My Family *(TH22)* [1] and *(TH32)* [2]** – by Thea.

Thea often seemed to use her drawings to change or invent possibilities (Adams, 2003); playing with ideas to make connections and invent new possibilities, as might a structural engineer. Thea's *An Aeroplane* (*TS23*, Figure 6.8, Chapter 6) is an example; other invention drawings are discussed in Chapter 9.

### Bertly: autobiographical, visualiser

Bertly preferred to draw *simple themes*, often adopting a *simple mode*, mainly featuring single symbols and objects such as animals, people, or weather. These *autobiographical* drawings provided a snapshot of his experiences, a bricolage of his immediate experiences and memories, sometimes intertwined with the imaginary. *Fireworks* (*BS16*, Figure 7.1, Chapter 7) was an autobiographical drawing dominated by mark-making. *An Octopus* (*BS7*, Figure 7.7, Chapter 7), in a *simple theme* was done in a *complex mode* and carried complex meanings and connections reflecting another *autobiography* memoire; it reflects Bertly's attunement with past and present experiences and his funds of knowledge that crossed home-school boundaries. Many drawings show how Bertly actively defined his reality, bringing shape and order to his experiences.

Drawing in a *simple theme*, Bertly frequently appeared silently detached from his surroundings, immersed in his drawing. We consider Bertly to be mainly a *patterner* or a *visualiser* (Gardner, 1980). Occasionally, he drew *complex themes*, drawing stories of life events, actions, and fantasy tales. In the style of a *dramatist* and *verbaliser*, he energetically and enthusiastically described his drawings in "joint involvement episodes" (Schaffer, 1992, p. 101), mainly with his mother, where they reconstructed narrations based on shared experiences.

Bertly could be described as an unpredictable, episodic drawer, seeming indifferent towards drawing if nothing interested him. When he found things interesting, he was eager to draw, often producing several related drawings in quick succession.

## Three different drawers

The children were each different types of drawers. Luke's drawing preferences reflected a *simple mode* and *complex theme*, with his main focus being on the content and complexity of his theme rather than form. Thea mostly drew in a *complex mode* and *complex theme*, experimenting with the form of her drawing while valuing the content and meanings she conveyed. Bertly mainly drew in *simple mode* and *simple theme* to make the content of his drawing understandable for others; he seemed less interested in complex *form* or *content*. Drawing in *simple or complex modes* and *themes* worked in different ways for the children.

The children's *types of drawings* were interpreted according to three types of content: *autobiographical, subject matter generalists,* or *graphic-narrative*. Bertly's drawings and many of Luke's home drawings were *autobiographical*. Luke's school drawings were mostly *graphic-narrative* in type – centring on people and their actions. Thea's drawings were mainly object- or *person-centred*, classifying her as a *subject-matter generalist*. Observations suggested that Bertly and Thea mostly adopted the roles of *patterner* or *visualiser*, preferring to draw silently; talking only when necessary. We describe Luke as a *dramatist* or *inveterate verbaliser* (Gardner, 1982), making elaborate narratives and sound effects integral to his drawing process. Table 8.2 summarises

*Table 8.2* Drawer identities of Luke, Bertly, and Thea

| Child | Drawer identity | | | |
|---|---|---|---|---|
| | Semiotic style | Configuration style | Types of drawing (Thompson, 1999; Wright, 2007) | Drawer patterns (Gardner, 1980, 1982) |
| Luke | Simple mode | Complex theme | Autobiographical Graphic narrative Person-centred | Dramatist/ verbaliser |
| Thea | Complex mode | Complex theme | Subject-matter generalist | Patterner/ visualiser |
| Bertly | Simple mode | Simple theme | Autobiographical | Patterner/ visualiser |

the four components of each child's *drawer's identity*, including their *semiotic style*, *drawing configuration*, *types of drawing*, and *drawer patterns*.

Figure 8.6 below shows how the four components – *semiotic style*, *drawing configuration*, *types of drawing*, and *drawer patterns* – connect at *form*, *content*, and *meaning* levels. It shows how the *Data Cross-grids* and observations were used to develop each child's *drawer identity* at the time. As children's drawing preferences change, so might their drawer identity.

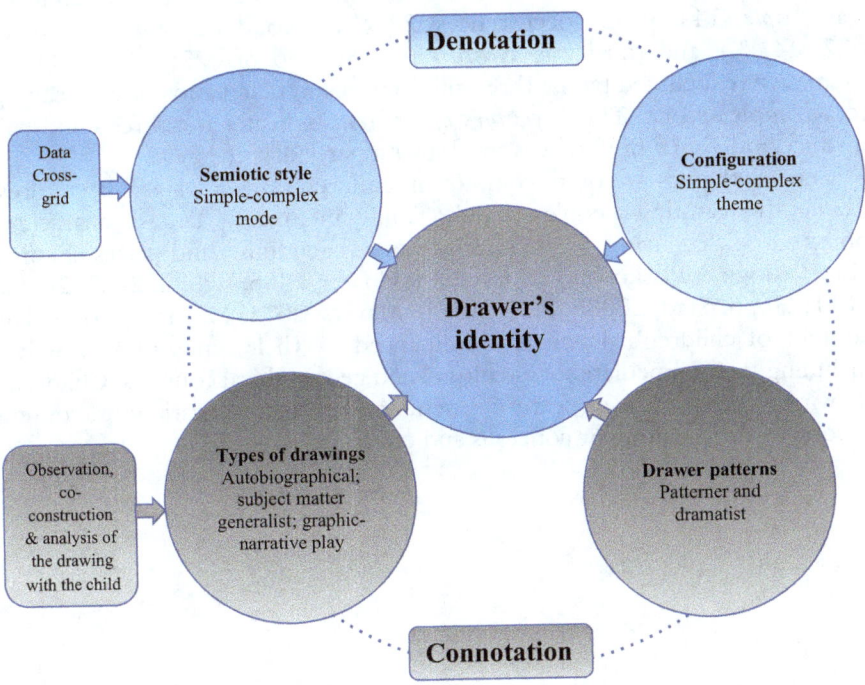

*Figure 8.6* The interplay between *semiotic style*, *configuration style*, *types of drawing*, and *drawer patterns* to form the drawer's identity.

Our classification of the children's *types* and *patterns* of drawings solely relates to their preferred styles. All three children experienced shifts from *patterners* to *dramatists*, sometimes in different drawings and sometimes within the same drawing, depending on the purpose, mood, time, and context. Children move between patterns, even if they seem to favour one; therefore, children should not be labelled as having one particular, fixed pattern. Our approach to categorisation can help to understand the development of *drawer identity*, yet it must not inhibit attending to the intricate complexities and uniqueness of each child's fluid drawer identity.

## Content themes arising from the data

The *Inventory of Content* (Chapter 4) itemises the 13 themes in the children's drawings. This shows the connection between *content* and *meaning* and provides interpretations of the children's case studies. Such classification is difficult because drawings often feature multiple objects, scenes, or stories. Categorisation has limitations and risks losing the complexities and rich visual acuity of children's drawings (Coates & Coates, 2006; Hall, 2010b); thus, sometimes a drawing is classified under several theme headings and sub-categories to maintain the variety of content in our analysis.

The *Inventory of Content* (Table 8.3) shows the number of occurrences of each theme for each child. The most popular theme for all three children was *People* (144 of 627 occurrences; 22.9%), second was *Animals* (90 of 627; 14.4%), and third was *Weather and Sky* (86 of 627; 13.7%). Other themes were included by the three children to add detail and enrich meaning to a complex scene. The *Inventory of Content* indicates the three children's distinct, individual preferences for drawing particular themes.

Generic themes are quite common in children's drawings across cultures, frequently featuring people (mainly family members), fantasy characters, objects, vehicles, living things (animals and vegetation), and places children visit (Kellogg & Plaskow, 1972; Coates & Coates, 2006; Wright, 2007, 2010a, 2011; Hopperstad, 2008b; Hall, 2010b; Mavers, 2011; Machón, 2013). The content of children's drawings is influenced by their funds of knowledge, including their immediate socio-cultural and geographical contexts. Children's drawings, the world over, feature generic themes, cultural variations, content unique to them, and their concerns and contexts.

*Form and content in children's drawings* 127

*Table 8.3* The *Inventory of Content* shows the number of occurrences by each theme for each child

| Themes<br>Sub-categories | Number of occurrences of the themes | | | | |
|---|---|---|---|---|---|
| | Luke | Thea | Bertly | Total | % |
| **People**<br>(family, self, fantasy, unknown, friends, and named others) | 82 | 45 | 17 | 144 | 22.9% |
| **Animals and other creatures**<br>(mini-beasts, farm, pets, wild, water and flying creatures, and fantasy) | 21 | 53 | 16 | 90 | 14.4% |
| **Weather and sky features**<br>(sky, stars, sun, rainbow, and rain) | 52 | 18 | 16 | 86 | 13.7% |
| **Miscellaneous objects**<br>(digital equipment, warfare equipment and trophies, and everyday objects) | 25 | 35 | 3 | 63 | 10.1% |
| **Natural features**<br>(flowers, pond, river, lake, water, sea, beach, trees, leaves, grass, mushrooms, stones, rocks, and mountain) | 14 | 36 | 10 | 60 | 9.6% |
| **Vehicles**<br>(aeroplane, boat/ship, car, van, crane, motorbike, rocket, and train) | 15 | 17 | 4 | 36 | 5.7% |
| **Writing**<br>(letters, names, and numbers) | 4 | 24 | 7 | 35 | 5.6% |
| **Shapes and symbols**<br>(circle, square, kiss, and heart) | 7 | 16 | 7 | 30 | 4.8% |
| **Food**<br>(fruits, ice cream, Easter egg, sausage roll, bread, candy, ravioli, cake, and food) | 12 | 11 | 6 | 29 | 4.6% |
| **Toys and play equipment**<br>(balls, Wii, Trampoline, and pink goo) | 8 | 7 | 5 | 20 | 3.2% |
| **Manufactured objects**<br>(pool, road, roundabout, tunnel, and well) | 8 | 6 | 3 | 17 | 2.7% |
| **Buildings**<br>(apertures, houses, castle, church, and farm) | 1 | 9 | 1 | 11 | 1.8% |
| **Elements**<br>(fire and water) | 2 | 0 | 4 | 6 | 0.9% |
| **Total number of occurrences** | 251 | 277 | 99 | 627 | 100% |

# 9 Drawing identities

*Figure 9.1 Only Me (LH11)* – by Luke.

## Introduction

The next three chapters focus on the meanings children conveyed through their drawings. Our interpretation of the children's drawings uncovered layers of symbolic meaning, sometimes complex, unpredictable, and obscure. The children sometimes spontaneously made sudden changes in their drawings, elaborating and adapting their narratives with reasoned intention in a dynamic

DOI: 10.4324/9781003427582-9

and fluid way that reflected their present thinking. Three core meanings in Luke's, Thea's, and Bertly's drawings showed that they used drawings to:

- Construct their identity
- Communicate their emotional self
- Process knowledge

These core functions form a conceptual framework derived from the analysis of their drawings, where their socio-cultural context is integral. The construction and interpretation of meaning is complex, where meanings intertwine throughout the drawing process, simultaneously supporting the development of multiple functions within a drawing. For example, the drawings that we identified as ways to *process knowledge* also contributed to the children's *construct of their identity* and their ways of *communicating their emotional selves*.

## Drawing as a construction of identity

Identity is developed through continuous cultural construction, where drawings act as symbolic and semiotic spaces (Brockmeier, 2001). Children's layering of meaning across their multimodal drawings is a way of mediating their voices and their individual identities (Hall, 2010b). Their drawings can be considered "tools of identity" (Holland et al., 1998, p. 43), through which children reveal their ways of being, doing, and becoming (Edmiston, 2008; Hawkins, 2002). Our interpretations and categorisations of the three children's drawings as constructions of their identity lead us to suggest that children use drawing to explore four perspectives of identity, drawing themselves in:

- The present: "*Who I am*"
- The past: "*Me before I was born*"
- The future: "*Who I might become*"
- Fantasy roles: "*How I can change*"

Children often mingled these identities in one drawing.

### *The Present: who I am*

Luke and Thea drew themselves alone and with their families, while Bertly only drew himself with his family. Luke made four drawings of himself in the present, two of which are *Only Me* (*LH11*, Figure 9.1) and *Me Stretching* (*LH25*, Figure 5.17, Chapter 5). Of the latter, he said, "That is me. My hands. And my legs, tall. Tall a lot. I am stretching." Luke was representing himself on a particular day in the present when he drew himself sleeping, and after he was woken by Jacob, he stretched his hands and legs, making them seem tall. In *Two of Me* (*LH28*, Figure 5.16, Chapter 5), Luke drew two versions of himself, pointing to the second stick figure and saying, "This is me again."

130  *Children making meaning*

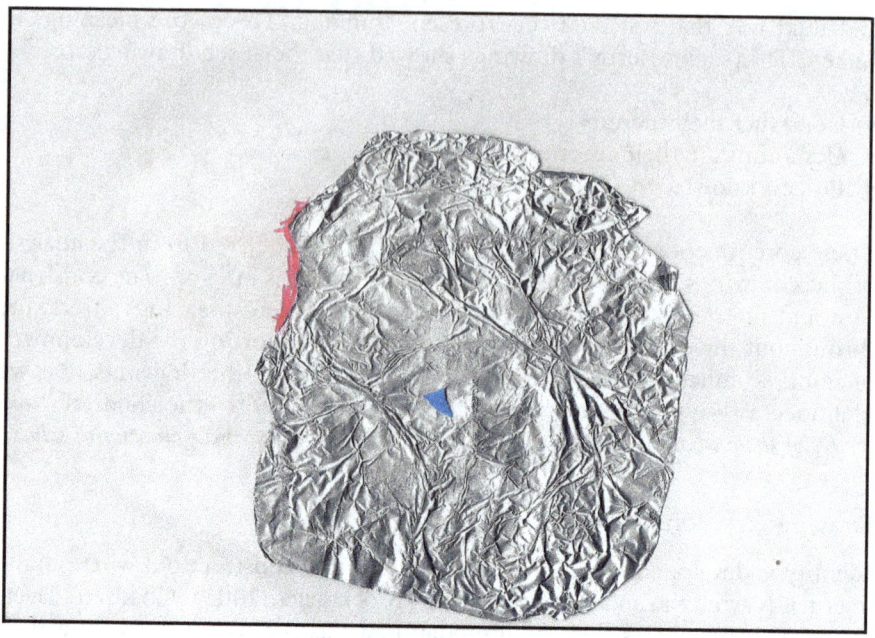

*Figure 9.2* *My Face (TS8)* – by Thea.

*Figure 9.3* *Things Falling in my Dream (TS16)* – by Thea.

Thea made only two drawings of herself alone *in the present*, with little elaboration. She drew *My Face* (*TS8*, Figure 9.2) with blue eyes, a nose, and pink cheeks (pink line on the left).

She also drew herself dreaming while asleep in *Things Falling in my Dream* (*TS16*, Figure 9.3), saying:

> I drew myself ... I was dreaming. This is me ... I was thinking I was a fairy. I was dreaming that I was in bed ... Then I stopped dreaming ... and then all the sweets and the other things fell down ... I was dreaming that I was a fairy.

Thea was moving between the image of her real self and a fantasy role, with some fantasy that she was a fairy and had sweets.

### The Past: me before I was born

Luke and Thea drew themselves before they were born. *My family* (*LH1*, Figure 5.10, Image 1, Chapter 5) represents an unborn Luke, who said to his mother:

> This is you making belly with daddy ... getting married to daddy ... This is me in your tummy. Let me draw myself in your tummy because you are going to marry Daddy and Matthias will be in your tummy as well.

The figure on the right shows Luke's mother with unborn Luke inside her and his father (second from the left). Luke added himself unborn and then born, saying, "Now this is me when I was born ... No, that is me as a grown-up baby." Luke seemed to be sequentially processing the development of his family; his parents married and his mother became pregnant – first with his brother and then with himself. Neither the drawing nor the narrative referred to his younger brother. Luke seemed focused on processing how his family evolved up to his birth, situating himself in the past to make sense of where and who he was before birth.

Thea's drawing, *Erica and Mum Before I was Born* (*TH8*, Figure 6.7, Chapter 6), indicates her processing ideas of how life was "before she was born." Thea drew her mother and sister, who seemed to be having a good time together; her father is not included. Thea drew herself in a circle (corner, right), physically separated from her mother and sister in a world of her own (with a separate sun and grass line). Thea seemed to understand that, as an unborn baby, she was with them but alone, "This is Erica, this is mummy and I was in mummy's tummy. This is me when I was a baby." This is an example of drawing "as perception" (Adams, 2004, p. 6), epitomising the ordering of Thea's thoughts and feelings while negotiating her role within her family and her identity, helping her understand "the external world of people, objects and events as well as the inner world feelings ... and imaginings" (Adams, 2004, p. 6).

Children's representation of themselves as one of many components of their picture indicates a movement from an inner view of themselves to acknowledging others as part of their world. Identity issues were important for Thea. To ensure she could be identified, she drew her fringe (a characteristic of which she was proud) and emphasised her ownership by adding her name. She explained the changed spelling, A-E-T-H, was because the letters "did not fit because of the grass."

Thea and Luke drew their unborn selves differently. Drawing themselves as unborn or small babies indicates that Luke and Thea were aware of their size, possibly representing age, where the self was partly defined in relation to others. Luke and Thea seemed, in these examples, to be integrating past and present events, memories, and their images of themselves to create unique amalgamations. In connecting their internal and external worlds, Luke and Thea each positioned themselves as unique human beings in their family contexts. A drawing can provide fragments of children's concepts of identity, and in the drawing process, children can actively transform and develop their distinct identities. Meaning-making emerging from their drawings enabled Luke and Thea to organise and interlace their realities with concepts of their identities.

Considering the notion of the "authoring self" (Edmiston, 2010, p. 198), we can see Luke and Thea constructing and reconstructing their own distinct identities, forming, for each, their "process of forming a self-identity" (Ahn & Filipenko, 2007, p. 287), as they found a way to understand their place as it once was in the world.

### *The Future: who I might become*

The children often drew themselves alone in their future roles. Bertly's *Myself with a Moustache* (*BS13*, Figure 7.10, Chapter 7), and Luke's *Myself* (*LS12*, Figure 9.4), as an adult with a moustache, were inspired by the men in their lives. Bertly described his drawing (*BS13*) as "It is a boy. Yes, it is a boy with a moustache. Me." Luke's description of "Myself with a moustache" (*LS12*) sees him transforming the man into himself, portraying himself as a man with a knife and a gun in his pocket "A man without hands … they are in his pockets … He has a gun in his side pockets. This is me shooting." Luke seems to have given himself his "ideal identity" (De Ruyter & Conroy, 2002, p. 510), as a man with the power to fight the "bad guys." This shows Luke's "perception of self-image" (Hall, 2008, p. 3); he has created himself as "strong, powerful, aggressive and almost anti-social" (Marsh, 2000, p. 211). Thus, Luke's imagined self has merged identities: an imagined identity in the future and a fantasy identity, fighting his older brother.

Thea drew herself in a variety of "ideal" and imagined future identities, including herself as a ten-year-old (*TH13*, Figure 6.11 Chapter 6), a pregnant woman (*TH15*, Figure 6.14, Chapter 6), and in career-oriented roles, where in *Travelling in a Car and Aeroplane* (*TS40*, Figure 6.5, Image 1, Chapter 6),

*Drawing identities* 133

*Figure 9.4* Myself *(LS12)* – by Luke.

she drew herself as the driver of an elaborate car that changed into an aeroplane, and she became a pilot, saying, "This is the aeroplane. I am driving the plane." Thea seemed proud of herself in this role, reflecting her sense of ownership by writing her name.

Thea drew herself as captain of *A Ship* (*TS38*, Figure 9.5), explaining:

> It is a ship… I am the captain. This is me and this is my name [referring to her written name]. I am driving the ship. And here there is written 'Thea' so that they would know who I am.

Thea depicted herself in future roles, seeming ambitious to take control of large modes of transport, perhaps inspired by her cultural capital, which included familiarity with ships and planes.

*Figure 9.5* *A Ship (TS38)* – by Thea.

### Fantasy Roles: how I can change

The children drew themselves as fantasy characters, exploring how to become their ideal characters and doing things in drawings that were beyond their realities. In *I am Ben Ten* (*LH23*, Figure 9.6, Image 1), Luke drew himself as the superhero *Ben Ten* saving his family and the world. Luke was fascinated by *Ben Ten* and his superpower ability to transform himself to fight evil. Luke drew himself in *Cutting Out the Bad Guy 2* (*LH22*, Figure 9.6, Image 2) as big and powerful, and the bad guy (far right) as small and weak. Luke physically cut out the bad guy with scissors, killing him. Engaged in heroic drawing-narratives fighting evil, Luke portrayed himself as a powerful hero using weapons to fight evil and kill the enemy.

Bertly drew himself as a fantasy hero, *Killing a Dragon* (*BS4*, Figure 9.6, Image 3), claiming he was not afraid of the dragon, even if it bit his finger. He drew his imagined self as a strong, powerful hero who threw the dragon into the water, shooting him, stabbing him with a knife, and throwing stones at him, killing him. Bertly's drawing of himself as *Father Christmas and Jael the Queen of Hearts* (*BH24*, Figure 9.6, Image 4) was discussed in Chapter 7.

The fantasy roles Thea assigned to herself were somewhat soft in nature. Thea drew *Me as a Crab* (*TS9*, Figure 9.6, Image 5), explaining, "That is me ... That is my forehead. These are my eyes. That is my mouth ... Those are my legs ... I have many legs." Thea liked the crab she saw in a book and perhaps wished to try on the character. *The Fairy Princess* (*TS10*, Figure 9.6, Image 6) sees Thea as a fairy princess labelled with a word sticker. She drew a "naughty" monster at the bottom, going into the castle (the foil shape) to steal the princess's things, but the fairy did not allow such a bad thing to happen and transformed the bad monster into a good boy.

*Figure 9.6* Luke, Bertly, and Thea in fantasy roles. *I am Ben Ten (LH23)* [1], *Cutting Out the Bad Guy 2 (LH22)* [2], *Killing a Dragon (BS4)* [3], *Father Christmas and Jael the Queen of Hearts (BH24)* [4], *Me as a Crab (TS9)* [5] and *The Fairy Princess (TS10)* [6].

The children seemed to use their drawings as an "authoring space" (Edmiston, 2008, p. 98), where they identified, related, and fluidly formed their identities.

## Drawing as a communication of the emotional self

The *United Nations Convention on the Rights of the Child* (United Nations, 1989) stresses the importance of children being heard; their drawings offer a way for us to listen to their views and emotions. In this section, we show how the children's used drawings to understand and communicate feelings (Fourie, 2020; Palvan et al., 2021; Talu, 2019; Schirrmacher, 2002).

136  *Children making meaning*

*Anger*

Luke communicated anger towards family members in five drawings. Describing *My Family and I Shooting the Bad Guys* (*LH17*, Figure 9.7), he said, without elaborating further, that he was angry at his father because "he fights … with me."

This resonates with *My Mother Tied Up* (*LS8*, Figure 5.12, Chapter 5), where Luke vented his anger towards his mother for not giving him sweets. He came to school saying, "Do not talk to me. I am very angry." After hours of not talking to anyone and frowning, making his anger apparent, he made this drawing, saying, "I tied her up … because she does not always give me sweets." After making the drawing, Luke's mood seemed to improve, as he later talked and laughed with his friends. The power of drawing as an emotion regulator and an outlet for feelings has led to claims that drawing can have short-term affective benefits for children and help to elevate negative feelings (Drake & Winner, 2013; Fourie, 2020; Drake, 2023).

In three of his drawings, done consecutively on the same day, Luke voiced his anger towards his brother Jacob (*LH25*, *LH26*, and *LH27*). In *Me Stretching* (*LH25*, Figure 5.17, Chapter 5), Luke explained that he drew himself (stretching and) angry as he was woken up by his younger brother Jacob, describing the drawing and saying, "Now I woke up and I am angry … because Jacob woke me up … I shouted, 'Jacob' [shouting angrily] … and I scared him." In *Throwing Pink Goo at Jacob* (*LH26*, Figure 5.14, Chapter 5),

*Figure 9.7* *My Family and I Shooting the Bad Guys* (*LH17*) – by Luke.

Luke was still angry at Jacob for waking him. To spite him, he "put" pink goo on Jacob (marked with fervently pink lines) to "stick forever," something that angered Jacob, as both boys hated pink, using it only to deride each other. *Two of Me* (*LH28*, Figure 5.16, Chapter 5) was made when Luke was still angry with Jacob, telling him, "I am angry to the top. I want to kill you." These examples show how Luke used drawing to express anger and the reason for it. Drawing can be useful to adults seeking to understand anger in young children as expressed through their drawings (Fourie, 2020).

*Fear*

Children use drawings to explore feelings and experiences of fear (Driessnack, 2006; Talu, 2019; Konleczna & Talu, 2023), as did Thea and Bertly. Thea expressed her fear of monsters (*TS31*, *TS32*, and *TH35*) and witches (*TS21*), while Bertly conveyed his fear of sharks (*BH21*). Thea's *A Monster Story* (*TH35*, Figure 9.8, Image 1) tells of a fearful, big monster (enclosed yellow and red lines) who was hiding behind a rock (enclosed line) while observing (eye-shape on the right) a smaller monster (green and red lines, left) who was walking slowly. The big monster wanted to catch and eat the little monster, which scared Thea. Similarly, *The Monster* (*TS32*, Figure 9.8, Image 2), which Thea said was a monster who "is killing the bird and the owl. It broke the ladder and he is killing the mushrooms … the monster came from the prison." Perhaps Thea was using the bird and owl as metaphors for herself and other children, fearing that someone bad would catch them.

*The Interactive Whiteboard Activity* (*TS31*, Figure 9.8, Image 3), depicting Thea's fear of monsters, originated from an incident at school. Thea began by drawing the front of her classroom, with detail of the whiteboard where she was writing the letter "m." She attached a pile of papers on top of each other (right), claiming, "This one is crushing the papers … because he is a naughty guy. He gets on everybody's nerves, even the teacher's … these are giants … many giants … monsters on top of each other… they come from the prison." It seemed that the papers represented giants that turned into monsters, whereas Thea was referring to two handymen who were doing some maintenance work in the class. One of them frightened the children by threatening to take the naughty children away. Representing the men as monsters, Thea conveyed her fear about this instance.

Thea communicated her fear of witches when she drew *The Wicked Witch* (*TS21*, Figure 9.8, Image 4), after listening to the story of Hansel and Gretel at school. Thea drew the witch (bottom corner), making her seem small and thus powerless, perhaps to make her less scary. The picture could be interpreted as the witch from the story scaring Thea because "she catches people and puts them in the fire." Talking about her fear of witches to Jo, Thea explained:

*Figure 9.8* Drawings communicating Thea's fears. *A Monster Story (TH35)* [1], *The Monster (TS32)* [2], *The Interactive Whiteboard Activity (TS31)* [3], *The Wicked Witch (TS21)* [4].

At night I go next to mummy because I am scared of the witch … One night, we were at home and I dreamt of the witch and went next to mummy and daddy … And I said to mummy, "Mummy, can we throw all the witches' DVDs away?" … And she threw them away.

This drawing seemed to convey Thea's general fear of witches, which was so strong that she was having nightmares. The drawing enabled Thea to express her fear and find a resolution. While her mother's disposing of the DVDs may have helped dissipate Thea's fear, her experiences at school, including stories and role-play involving pretending and talking about witches and monsters, sustained her fear.

Bertly communicated his fear of sharks in *A Shark in the Sea* (BH21, Figure 9.9). Drawing a shark at the bottom of the paper, where it "lives in the deep seas," Bertly asked his mother what if "it bites our slippers … Will it do like this [open mouth action] and eat me?" Here Bertly communicated his thinking that sharks are big, scary fish who eat people. While his mother tried to dispel his fear by reassuring him that sharks stay in the deep seas and do not come close to where people swim, Bertly asked, "Do we swim faster if he

*Figure 9.9* A Shark in the Sea (BH21) – by Bertly.

140  *Children making meaning*

bites us? If he wakes up, do I have to swim faster?" These questions indicate that Bertly knew of the possibility of shark attacks and was thinking of the best ways to escape.

Thea's and Bertly's fears were perhaps influenced by "culturally shared fears" (Higgins, 2004, p. 38) acquired from books, stories, accounts at home and school, and watching cartoons and documentaries (Konleczna & Talu, 2023).

*Happiness*

Bertly and Luke used drawings to communicate happiness. The weather was an important aspect of Bertly's family life; they followed the daily weather forecast to decide how to prepare for the day, especially important for his father, who worked outside. The weather affected Bertly greatly, impacting his mood. Discussing *A Nice Scribbled Rainbow* (*BH12*, Figure 9.10), Bertly's mother told him, "You were happy on that day ... There was daddy cooking." Bertly's mother knew the rainbow communicated his happiness about his father's cooking at home, which was relatively a rarity. Bertly did not specifically draw what made him happy (his father at home cooking) but rather what symbolised his happiness (Bakr, 2019).

Several of Luke's drawings communicated happiness, frequently represented by a light blue sky and a big, bright yellow sun, natural phenomena that children often draw to convey happiness (Bakr, 2019; Moula et al., 2021). *My Mother and I Playing with Ball* (*LH38*, Figure 5.11, Image 2, Chapter 5), and *Nicholai and I*, which was later changed to *Mum and I* (*LH39*, Figure 9.11,

*Figure 9.10* *A Nice Scribbled Rainbow (BH12)* – by Bertly.

*Figure 9.11* Drawings reflecting Luke's happiness *Mum and I (LH39)* [1], *An Ice-cream in the Sun (LH40)* [2].

Image 1) were made immediately after each other. Luke drew a bright, yellow sun over blue skies and his mother (and/or friend) playing or running with him, something special to him. *An Ice-cream in the Sun* (*LH40*, Figure 9.11, Image 2), which was drawn next, represents things that made Luke feel good.

*Figure 9.12* Wishes for pets. Luke's *Cousin James Jumping in the Pool with a Dog* (*LH51*) [1], Bertly's *A Dog in a Box* (*BH11*) [2] and Thea's *Animals Not Allowed* (*TH37*) [3].

*Drawing identities* 143

*Wishes*

All three children used drawings to communicate their wishes to others. They all wished for a pet, something currently being discussed by the class. Luke drew his *Cousin James Jumping in the Pool with a Dog* (*LH51*, Figure 9.12, Image 1); neither had a dog, but both wanted one. Luke's father explained that Luke and his brothers had talked that week about their wish for a pet. Bertly too expressed his wish for a pet dog when he drew *A Dog in a Box* (*BH11*, Figure 9.12, Image 2). *Animals Not Allowed* (*TH37*, Figure 9.12, Image 3), drawn by Thea, tells her story about "a king" (a foam sticker of a zebra) who did not allow animals in the castle because they were dirty. Using a catapult and pixie dust, the animals entered the castle through the windows. This metaphorical drawing seems part of Thea's perpetual communication of her disappointment at not having a pet cat because "the fur will come down and it will dirty everywhere," while reiterating her wish to her mother, trying to convince her to allow them a pet – a wish that (unlike the boys') came true!

The three children communicated other wishes in their drawings. *Jacob in a Volcano* (*LH31*, Figure 9.13) depicts Luke's birthday wish: "This is me with roller skates. I wish I had real roller skates or a skateboard to skate with … I never skate." Then to his mother, "Mum, can you buy me a skateboard for my birthday?"

*Myself* (*LS12*, Figure 9.4) shows Luke's wish for headphones, "I will draw him his ears and a pair of headphones … because I wish to have headphones." The same drawing included another wish: "I wish I could see a real

*Figure 9.13* *Jacob in a Volcano (LH31)* – by Luke.

*Figure 9.14* Bertly's *(BS20)* [1] and Thea's wishes *(TS30)* [2] *(TS18)* [3], *(TH3)* [4], *(TH18)* [5], *(TS39)* [6], and *(TS44)* [7].

speedboat." *Me Carrying a Bag Full of Candy* (*LH49*, Figure 5.1, Chapter 5) shows Luke with a bag full of sweets, communicating, "Let me put candy in … all for myself," and *Mum, Dad, and I Eating Ice-cream* (*LH15*, Figure 5.10, Image 2, Chapter 5) shows Luke and his parents eating ice-cream:

> You [mum] say, "We [parents] do not want ice-cream. I do not want ice-cream. I do not want ice-cream." But I say, "I want one. I want ice-cream. One ice-cream, two ice-cream, three ice-cream. Can I have three ice-creams?" And you say, "Yes."

Bertly drew his wish to "swim with the dinghy … like Uncle Stephen" (*A Shark: BH14*, Figure 7.13, Chapter 7) and to have a piano as his sister Jael (*Cooking Chicken in the Oven: BS20*, Figure 9.14, Image 1) who would like to learn how to play it: "That is a piano … A piano for myself and another for Jael. A pink one for Jael and a red one for me."

Some of Thea's wishes included making a playground for her sick cousin Romina (*Romina's Aeroplane: TS30*, Figure 9.14, Image 2) to help her feel better, riding a plane (*An Aeroplane: TS18*, Figure 9.14, Image 3), and riding a motorcycle with a helmet all the way to Sweden to visit her auntie (*Travelling in a Car and Aeroplane: TS40*, Figure 6.5, Image 1, Chapter 6), playing ball with her grandpa (*Grandpa: TH3*, Figure 9.14, Image 4), and hide and seek with her friends (*Animals Hide and Seek: TH27*, Figure 6.10, Chapter 6). She also conveyed her wish to see a real mouse (*The Warehouse Mouse: TH18*, Figure 9.14, Image 5) and to have the courage to eat snails, like the many people she saw at a feast "One day I will try snails. I will eat real snails" (*A Snail Playing a Guitar: TS39*, Figure 9.14, Image 6), represented by a blue sticker of a snail in her tummy (*Inside my Tummy: TS44*, Figure 9.14, Image 7).

Above all, Thea wished to wear her daddy's tie (*My Dad Coming Home: TH20*, Figure 8.5, Image 2, Chapter 8). Drawing a large tie, Thea said, "This is the tie he wears for work. He is going to work with it … I wish to have one… Look how nice it is." Her father was her role model, and she wanted to be like him; dressing smartly with a tie was one way for Thea to do this.

*Wishes in greeting cards*

Bertly and Thea made greeting cards to communicate particular wishes. Drawing a birthday card for his grandmother, *Happy Birthday Grandma* (*BH34*, Figure 9.15, Image 1), Bertly said, "I did it for Grandma Guza … That is Happy Birthday. Because tomorrow we are going for her birthday. I want to give it to her tomorrow. It is for her birthday. There is written, 'Happy Birthday.'" The same day, Bertly drew *Balloons for Grandma's Birthday* (*BH33*, Figure 9.15, Image 2) and *More Balloons for Grandma's Birthday* (*BH35*, Figure 9.15, Image 3), saying, "I drew the balloons for grandma's birthday … more balloons for grandma. I am going to draw her many pictures for her birthday." Making drawings as gifts seems to show Bertly's increased

*Figure 9.15* Happy Birthday Grandma (BH34) [1], Balloons for Grandma's Birthday (BH33) [2] and More Balloons for Grandma's Birthday (BH35) [3] – by Bertly.

*Drawing identities* 147

*Figure 9.16* *A Birthday Card for Eman (TH5)*, outside [1] and inside [2]; *A Birthday Card for Belle (TH28)*, outside [3] and inside [4]* – by Thea.

self-esteem and confidence in drawing. At the beginning of the study, Bertly said, "I do not know how to draw, I only know how to scribble."

Thea made several greeting cards communicating her wishes for people. *A Birthday Card for Eman* (*TH5*, Figure 9.16, Image 1), with the front comprising "A flower in the sea, a sun in the sky and grass in the sea. And a frog … I drew him a lot of hearts because I love him. I love him a lot." Inside the card (Figure 9.16, Image 2), Thea wrote her name and drew hearts for Eman. She also drew *A Birthday Card for Belle* her cousin (*TH28*, Figure 9.16, Images 3 & 4). On the outside (Image 3), Thea drew herself dressed as a flower, a costume she had worn for Carnival; on the inside (Image 4), she wrote her name. Thea explained that the card was for Belle, "Because I love her … she had her birthday. One day I will give it to her. We went to give it [at home] to her but she was not there." Thea's card drawings were of a similar format to commercial cards with a front cover and the message written inside, showing her understanding of greeting card formats.

The children seemed to feel safe using drawings to express and communicate different emotions; these examples convey the potential of drawing to promote emotional intelligence (Fourie, 2020).

## Drawing to process knowledge

The children used drawings to construct, mediate, and communicate their knowledge (Kress, 2003b; Kress & Van Leeuwen, 1996). Drawings can be used for "manipulation" (Adams, 2003, p. 222) or "invention" (Adams, 2004, p. 6), where children draw to help them think as they inquire, try out, discard, refine, and develop their evolving hypotheses.

Examples from the three children's drawings show how they used their personal "funds of knowledge" (Moll et al., 1992) in complex, meaningful ways. Luke, Thea, and Bertly communicated their knowledge of animals, weather, fireworks, various objects and how they work, and how cars and planes operate. The following examples illustrate how drawing content often reflects children's cultural contexts.

### Knowledge about animals

Luke's drawing of *A Worm* (*LS16*, Figure 5.7, Chapter 5) with many legs, long fur, a head, and a brain conveyed his thinking and knowledge about the physiology of a worm. He used this drawing to mediate his knowledge and imagination to create a convincing image of a worm. Similarly, *A Butterfly-monster Story* (*TS28*, Figure 9.17) communicated Thea's knowledge of the life cycle of a butterfly, "This is the cocoon. Then the cocoon comes out and then it turns into a butterfly … It is going to open its wings."

Thea and Bertly were both interested in fish, each making a series of pictures communicating their knowledge of fish and other water creatures. *My Dad Coming Home* (*TH20*, Figure 8.5, Image 2, Chapter 8) and *The Aquarium Shop* (*TH23*, Figure 9.18) both show Thea's knowledge, gleaned from regular visits to a pet shop with her father, to look at the aquaria and buy fish.

*Drawing identities* 149

*Figure 9.17* *A Butterfly-monster Story (TS28)* – by Thea.

*Figure 9.18* *The Aquarium Shop (TH23)* – by Thea.

150  *Children making meaning*

She drew two well-lit aquaria, explaining, "We are at the pet shop ... this is the aquarium shop ... sometimes I go with daddy and see many aquaria ... the shop is next to grandma's house." Here, Thea conveys her knowledge about the pet shop, where aquaria are sold. Thea continued by describing what she was drawing:

> I am going to draw two aquaria. This box is the aquarium. These are the fish ... I am going to draw shrimp. I am going to draw them large because they have grown up. The yellow is the light ... this is the grass ... The shrimps have died. Here they died but the fish are still alive ... These are the small fish. And this is the big shrimp.

Thea's drawings show her knowledge of living conditions for fish and shrimps, "We have food for shrimps and food for fish. We went to the pet shop and we bought fish, food for the fish, and food for the shrimps."

Bertly was interested in sea creatures, drawing sharks (*BH14*, Figure 7.13, Chapter 7 and *BH21*, Figure 9.9) and octopuses (*An Octopus: BS7*, Figure 7.7, Chapter 7 and *An Octopus for You: BH28*, Figure 9.19), conveying concepts of size, strength, and perspective. Bertly's shark drawings communicated his knowledge, "blue and black ... sharks are also grey ... a shark has a tail, lives in the sea," as he "watched on TV." He said, "A shark is bigger than us ... it has big eyes," and that it could eat people. Referring to his drawing (*BH28*) and a television documentary about sea life he had watched with his father, Bertly

*Figure 9.19* *An Octopus for You (BH28)* – by Bertly.

stated that his octopus is "hiding at the bottom of the seabed ... it hides ... it will be in the very deep sea." Bertly referred to a real-life experience when making an octopus with "many legs".

## Knowledge about the weather

*The Storm – Thunder, Rain and Wind* (*BH16*, Figure 9.20) is an example of a knowledge-based drawing where Bertly drew three weather elements, describing that "It was very windy on that day. The wind was blowing and it was raining. It is the sun, the wind, and the rain. A chaos of wind and rain ... There was a storm outside." This drawing may appear to be insignificant, random mark-making, but it reflected Bertly's knowledge about the experience of local autumn storms. It represents the dull, thunderous, wet weather typical of the Mediterranean region and Bertly's use of specific vocabulary – similar to his parents' conversations and watching the daily weather forecast with his father, which formed his "networks of exchange" (González et al., 2005, p. 12). The conversation between Bertly and his mother provides a rich description of such storms, the meaning Bertly attributed to his drawing, and his theory about why the sun might look green on particular days:

BERTLY:   That is the sky. There is a lot of thunder. It is raining ...
          ... look at how the sun looks with the wind.
          It is not yellow anymore. Look at it.
MOTHER:   It turned green with the wind.

*Figure 9.20* The Storm (BH16) – by Bertly.

BERTLY: Yes. It came like this
MOTHER: Did it get dirty?
BERTLY: Yes.
MOTHER: So it is not nice anymore.
BERTLY: Because the sun got wet. It is being washed.

To fully appreciate this conversation and Bertly's knowledge, one has to have experienced the idiosyncrasies of Maltese weather on some autumn days when southern storms from the Sahara Desert blow brownish particles that culminate in stormy, thunderous clouds and murky rain covering everything with dust. The sun is partially obscured by a thin layer of grey clouds, making it appear a shady green. Bertly's conversation with his mother gives an insight into his thinking and understanding of the weather. Using his drawing and narrative as a way of reorganising and reconstructing meaning, he developed his theory to explain the changed sun and surrounding atmosphere; his hypothesis that the sun got dirty with the wind and was being washed with the rain, leaving a lot of "dirt" behind is a plausible, complex conjecture for a four-year old.

This, and other examples in this book, show how drawing can be a mediating tool in the learning process (Anderson et al., 2014; Kampeza & Delserieys, 2020), as children actively reflect on their knowledge and portray their understandings.

### *Knowledge about how cars and planes work*

Thea made many drawings where she played with ideas and made connections to construct knowledge and to invent and theorise how vehicles work. In *Travelling in a Car and Aeroplane: TS40* (Figure 6.5, Image 1, Chapter 6), Thea drew a car, which she then transformed into an aeroplane. Drawing on her knowledge of steering a car, by using *"il-pedala tal-gas"* (the gas pedal – bottom right, oval-shaped lever in blue and outlined in black) (Figure 6.46, Image 5, Chapter 6) to drive it, Thea explained how pressing the gas pedal makes a car work: "This is the gas pedal. Every car has a gas pedal … Pressing the gas pedal makes the car drive faster." Referring to her understanding of using and needing a helmet (on top of the red figure's head), Thea engaged in a process of complex sign-making and narrative to develop and convey her understanding of a car. In *Romina's Aeroplane* (*TS30*, Figure 9.14, Image 2), Thea shows her understanding of how the inside of an aeroplane is constructed, with wooden sticks for wings, pink lines to denote the entrance, and blue corrugated paper to signify the seats. *An Aeroplane* (*TS18*, Figure 9.14, Image 3), *An Aeroplane that Flies* (*TS23*, Figure 6.8), and *Daddy's Aeroplane* (*TS26*, Figure 9.21) assisted Thea's thinking about how aeroplanes fly, exploring, refining, and practising different possibilities and alternatives that made sense to her. In Thea's first drawing of an aeroplane (*TS18*), she added dark red glitters at the back of the plane to denote pixie

*Drawing identities* 153

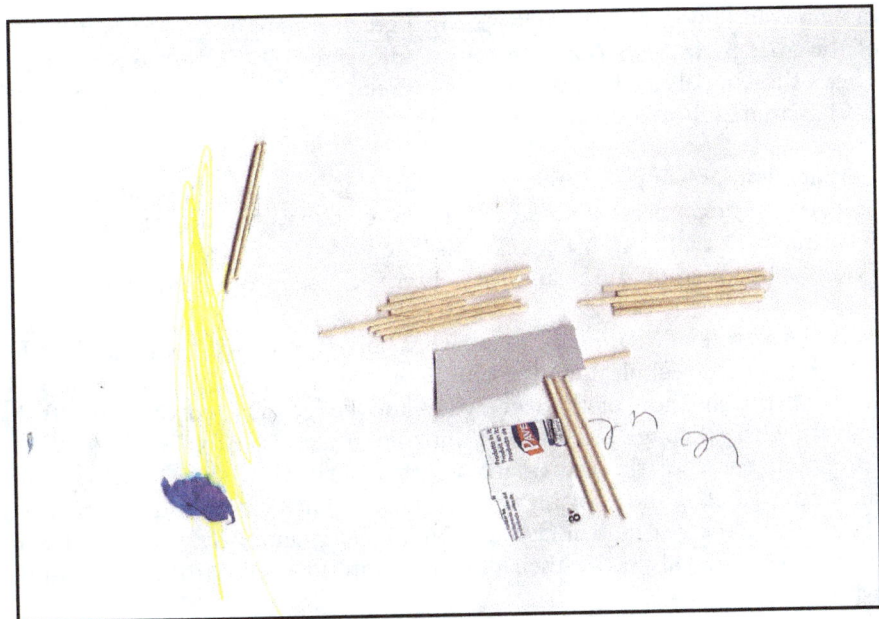

*Figure 9.21* **Daddy's Aeroplane (TS26)** – by Thea.

dust, concluding that aeroplanes fly with the help of fairies, who "scatter the pixie dust [on the aeroplane], and on themselves to make it fly." Drawing on her cultural practice and using ideas and knowledge obtained from her network of exchange, Thea used magic (Egan, 1998) as an explanation of how an aeroplane flies. Thea's hypothesis changed in two later drawings (*TS23* and *TS26*), where the idea of making an aeroplane fly with pixie dust was replaced by the notion of pressing switches. When Thea drew the aeroplane (*TS23*) on the day her father flew by plane, she attached two paper balls in the middle of the paper, explaining that pressing the orange one made the aeroplane fly while pressing the blue one made it land. Interestingly, in *Daddy's aeroplane* (*TS26*), which she drew the day her father returned, Thea attached only one blue paper ball to represent the only switch needed to make the aeroplane land. There appears to be a clear progression in her reasoning of how aeroplanes fly, from being helped by fairies and pixie dust to the idea that a pilot makes a plane take off and land by pressing switches. The plane drawings became Thea's tool for "possibility thinking" (Craft & Chappell, 2016, p. 407), where she used the drawings to meet her "urge to actualise" (Knight, 2009, p. 15) and to develop her emerging concepts. She made connections between the aeroplane, its flight, and the use of switches in everyday life to extend her thoughts and try out possible solutions.

Thea used drawing as an invention in other examples, showing her remarkable construction of knowledge. *A Ship* (*TS38*, Figure 9.5) shows how the captain could hoot the horn by pressing a green rectangular shape at the back of the image. *Animals Not Allowed* (*TH37*, Figure 9.12, Image 3) conveys Thea's thinking about how a "see-saw" (green wooden stick, right) could be used as a catapult to launch animals:

> When you press here ... this see-saw like this [the left side of the green wooden stick representing a catapult], the animals could fly and go up in the castle ... the animals press this [the same wooden stick] with their legs. They keep on going and they enter the castle from the windows.

As the inventors of their ideas, Luke, Thea, and Bertly used their drawings to resolve abstract, technical, and scientific problems. Drawing was a means of "cultural transmission of their everyday knowledge" (Wood & Hall, 2011, p. 270), where through intentional "thinking in action" (Cox, 2005a, p. 115), they made sense of the things around them. Through such drawings, the children organised and explained their theories, knowledge, and experiences. Drawing on the real and imagined, Luke, Thea, and Bertly used fact and fiction to continually revise their drawings until satisfied with their plausible hypotheses.

# 10 Love, power, good and evil

*Figure 10.1 A car with a heart (TH4)* – by Thea.

### Eternal themes and emotional opposites

In this chapter, we discuss how Luke, Thea, and Bertly explored concepts of love, power, good, and evil. We consider how the children addressed universal moral qualities and eternal "emotional opposites" (Wood & Hall, 2011, p. 277), which present them with ethical dilemmas (Edmiston, 2008). Interpretation of their drawings uncovers their improvised and complex portrayals of – and play with – personal thoughts and feelings about the very essence of existence.

DOI: 10.4324/9781003427582-10

## 156 Children making meaning

### Love

Luke, Thea, and Bertly communicated love differently. We explore their use of the heart as a symbol of love, their expressions of love for family members and others, and their notions of romantic love.

#### Symbolising love

The heart symbol is conventionally and universally understood to represent many facets of love. Luke, Thea, and Bertly used heart to represent love in several drawings. Sometimes they simply drew a heart, as in Thea's *A Car with a Heart* (*TH4*, Figure 10.1) and Bertly's *A Heart* (*BH15*, Figure 10.2). Without explanation, simply, the heart meant love.

Thea and Bertly both seemed to associate the heart with love, affection, and care. Several of Thea's drawings (*TS24*, *TH18*, *TH19*, *TS12*, *TH21*, and *TS22*), made in the same week, featured heart symbols to express love. *Grass, Sea, Sky and a Mountain* (*TS24*, Figure 10.3, Image 1) features natural elements and a heart symbol in yellow highlighter on the blue glitter (bottom right). Clarifying that the blue glitter signified the sea, Thea explained she drew the heart, "Because I love the sea."

Hearts were included in *The Warehouse Mouse* (*TH18*, Figure 9.14, Image 5, Chapter 9, depicting a mouse in a puddle (blue glitter, right) in the countryside surrounded by flowers. Thea explained that she added heart stickers (top left), "Because I love the mouse ... I would like to see a real one." Similarly, *Frogs in the Sea* (*TH19*, Figure 10.3, Image 2) was drawn after Thea saw frogs in

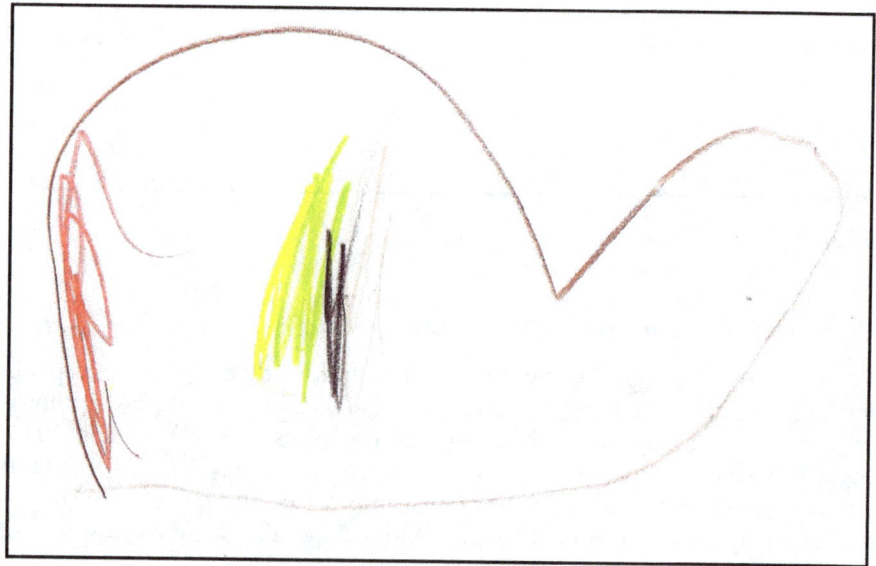

*Figure 10.2 A Heart (BH15)* – by Bertly.

*Love, power, good and evil* 157

*Figure 10.3* Grass, Sea, Sky and a Mountain *(TS24)* [1], Frogs in the Sea *(TH19)* [2], A Snail *(TH12)* [3], A Flower *(TH21)* [4], Flying Hearts *(TS22)* [5] - by Thea.

muddy puddles; several frogs (colourful lines) are in the water (blue glitter) and "A heart … because I love frogs" (red, to the right of the wooden stick).

When Thea drew *A Snail (TS12*, Figure 10.3, Image 3) eating sunflower seeds, she included two hearts above, saying, "I want to draw hearts for the snail … I drew two hearts because I love it." Thea drew *A Flower (TH21,* Figure 10.3, Image 4), which she saw on a picnic. The flower is the dominant element in the picture, the centre is depicted as a large circle with surrounding petals. Thea added glitter to the centre and pompoms to the petals, saying, "This is a flower. These are the petals. I like the flower. It is a big flower." She described the purple and green markings at the bottom of the flower as "leaves attached to a stalk," showing her knowledge of different parts of the flower. Declaring her love of flowers, Thea attached a heart sticker in the middle. The simplicity and vibrant colours of the pompoms seem to reflect her appreciation for nature's beauty and highlight her ability to capture the

158  *Children making meaning*

wonders of that flower. *Flying Hearts* (*TS22*, Figure 10.3, Image 5) symbolised love between people. Taping several hearts, Thea explained, "These are all hearts. They are flying in the sky ... The hearts are flying to Europe to pick people and then they go to their houses. A heart means we love each other."

The hearts in Thea's drawings conveyed her feelings of love and affection.

### Loving family members and others

Bertly's *Kisses* (*BH4*, Figure 10.4) reflects his understanding of how symbols can be used to convey emotions; the "Xs" represent kisses to express love to his mother on Valentine's Day. He said, "Look, mummy. I am going to draw you many kisses ... This is a card. Kisses on a card. They are for mummy."

It was mainly Luke and Thea who used their drawings to express love for people. Luke explicitly declared his love for his mother. He craved her sole attention, for which he sometimes seemed to be in friendly rivalry with his father. In three home drawings (*LH6*, *LH18*, and *LH37*), Luke drew his mother and himself. *Mummy and I* (*LH6*, Figure 10.5, Image 1) shows Luke's loving connection with his mother, giving her the drawing he kissed her, saying, "This is for you mum. I drew myself beside you because I love you. This is for you. It is yours and mine."

*My Mum and I Walking in the Dark* (*LH18*, Figure 5.11, Image 1, Chapter 5) shows a special moment that Luke shared with his mother, capturing his love

*Figure 10.4 Kisses (BH4)* – by Bertly.

for her and the emotion of their relationship. Luke conveys a sense of intimacy, with the night-time setting adding a layer of wonder to the drawing and the stars in the sky conveying awe and beauty. The stars seem to represent the enchanting nature of the moments Luke and his mother shared during their regular night-time walks. Luke said, "Myself and mummy; mummy and I … This is me and mum walking in the dark … at night." This drawing and the collaborative nature of creating it with his mother, who modelled and drew stars for him, shared ideas, and prompted suggestions, underscore their closeness and highlight the co-authorship of the ideas and meanings. Overall, this drawing is a poignant reminder of how young children can use drawings to powerfully capture and communicate complex emotions and experiences.

*You and I* (*LH37*, Figure 10.5, Image 2), as with *LH6* and *LH18*, depict Luke's loving relationship with his mother. Drawing himself (blue figure) larger than his mother (pink figure) perhaps indicates Luke's desire to emulate his father or to suggest his own prominence. Asking his mother to draw the heart and write "inħobbok" ("I love you," in Maltese) emphasises his eagerness to express such sentiment as they collaborated in a shared emotional space.

*A Cake for Mama* (*LS19*, Figure 10.5, Image 3) again shows Luke's love for his mother, with a birthday party scene including a cake and decorations. He described the drawing, saying, "I made a party and cake for mama … because she loves it … and I love mummy." The family was celebrating his grandmother's birthday, but because Luke's mother anticipated surgery the following week, perhaps he wanted to show his love by making the party for her. Drawing can be a powerful tool for expressing complex emotions and thoughts, providing children with a safe and expressive mode to process and communicate what might otherwise remain unvoiced.

Thea loved her father and grandfather. In *Dad Coming Home* (*TH20*, Figure 8.4, Image 2, Chapter 8), Thea communicated an ordinary daily event of her father returning home from work. Drawing everyday objects: the apartment doors, stairs, light, and aquarium, she described, "Daddy climbing upstairs, opening the door and coming in," conveying her anticipation and joy when her father returns. Using drawing as "a real-time depiction" (Wright, 2010a, p. 46) of waiting for her father, Thea expressed her feelings and explained the significance of the heart-shaped sticker (left), "I added the heart because I love daddy." Two of Thea's drawings reflected her love for, and connection with her two grandfathers. *Grandpa* (*TH3*, Figure 9.14, Image 4, Chapter 9), features her paternal grandfather with "his hair that goes up like that in the wind." She seemed fascinated by his hair being blown up, unlike her father's shorter hair. The drawing depicts a special moment they shared playing ball with Thea, saying, "I love my nannu (grandpa) Bert." *My Loveable Grandpa* (*TH9*, Figure 10.6, below) represents Thea's affection for her maternal grandfather, "Grandpa Cikku, Grandpa Cikku." She described his big ears and large hands – reflecting her attention to his physical features – and drew him surrounded by birds. "He loves birds" Thea explained, "I did these hearts because I love my grandpa Cikku a lot."

160  *Children making meaning*

*Figure 10.5* Mummy and I (LH6) [1], You and I (LH37) [2], A Cake for Mama (LS19) [3] – by Luke.

*Love, power, good and evil* 161

*Figure 10.6* **My Loveable Grandpa (TH9)** – by Thea.

*Figure 10.7* **Me in a Muddy Puddle and Lots of Birds (TH14)** – by Thea.

162  *Children making meaning*

In two drawings done in succession at home, Thea declared her love for herself. *Myself* (*TH13*, Figure 6.11, Chapter 6) portrays Thea in an imagined identity as a ten-year old, with hearts alongside herself [in red and blue above the grass line]. She said, "That is me. These are all hearts. I drew them for myself because I love myself," expressing her affection and appreciation for who she is, reflecting her inner confidence and the value she places on self-love.

*Me in a Muddy Puddle and Lots of Birds* (*TH14*, Figure 10.7) continues this theme of self-love, with Thea saying, "This is me. I am on the ground in the muddle puddle ... I fell down. I got dirty all over, even my teeth." Again, she added hearts (the zig-zag pink lines across the drawing), saying, "And these are all hearts because I love myself."

These two drawings show Thea's ability to reflect on herself, her experiences, and her emotions through her drawings.

We can see in the examples above how important the right to a family life is to these young children.

### *Romantic love*

Children develop an understanding of romantic love by observing the relationships of adults such as their parents (Brechet, 2015) and, as influenced by the media and wider society. Bertly's *Mum and Dad* (*BH5*, Figure 10.8) shows his unique perspective on romantic love: his Valentine's Day drawing glimpses of his understanding of his parents' relationship and the cultural

*Figure 10.8* **Mum and Dad** (BH5) – by Bertly.

*Love, power, good and evil* 163

*Figure 10.9* Rings, Hearts and Flowers for Daniel (TH16) – by Thea.

context surrounding Valentine's Day, which is highly celebrated in Malta with love symbolised in shop displays, through exchanging messages, and gifting tokens of affection.

Bertly drew his mother (right) with "Spikey hair. Your hair is spikey. Red and spikey." Then he drew his daddy, "Now Daddy … Dad's hair went away. He does not have any hair. Here I drew mummy and daddy because they love each other," joining the two figures with a blue line as if holding hands.

In two drawings, Thea communicated her love for two brothers, distinguishing her love for each. *In A Card for Eman* (*TH5*, Figure 9.16, Image 1, Chapter 9), Thea added her name with eight hearts underneath, inside the card (Figure 9.16, Image 2, Chapter 9), saying she loved him "a lot." *Rings, Hearts and Flowers for Daniel* (*TH16*, Figure 10.9) shows her feelings of affection for Daniel (Eman's brother); while Thea liked both boys, she loved Daniel more and considered him her boyfriend. Her drawing, a gift to Daniel, with leaves, flowers, butterflies, and hearts symbolised her love, and "Many rings … a lot of rings." She emphasised her love for Daniel, saying, "Everything, everything is for my boyfriend … Here I drew him hearts. They are for my boyfriend Daniel. I am going to give all these to Daniel … Because I love him. Because I love him." Explaining the central figure as "Me. And I am thinking of Daniel and the many rings and hearts to give to my boyfriend" highlights her feelings for him.

Children choose many ways to communicate love in their drawings, reflecting their personalities and emotional connections. Some children, like Luke and

164  *Children making meaning*

Thea, openly express their love for family members; others, like Bertly, seem more reticent. Bertly's drawings communicate love indirectly, with words, gestures, and actions to convey affection and understanding of personal connections. The children's drawings offer insights into their emotional worlds and relationships, showing how they differently express feelings of care for others. These examples show how children can navigate emotions and relationships, capturing their interpretations of complex concepts like love and reflecting the unique blend of personal experiences and cultural influences that shape their understanding.

## Power, good, and evil

Themes of good and evil, power and powerlessness, often intertwine in a single drawing and can indicate children's thinking about complex concepts such as authority, control, vulnerability, and fear. Sometimes these themes are also intertwined with expressions of love and protection.

Small children may use drawing to change their size and gain power (Skattebol, 2006), as Luke sometimes did, drawing himself bigger and taller than the other family members, perhaps reflecting his aspirations for power, strength, and protection (*LH25*, Figure 5.17, Chapter 5; *LS12*, Figure 9.4, Chapter 9). This strategy conveyed his desire for characteristics to enable him to overthrow the bad guys (sometimes his brothers!), thus protecting the vulnerable (De Ruyter & Conroy, 2002). Seeming keen on the role of protector, Luke drew *Matthias, Mum and I* (*LH14*, Figure 10.10), with himself (left)

*Figure 10.10 Matthias, Mum and I (LH14)* – by Luke.

bigger than his mother and Matthias and able to fight his older brother. Luke seemed to be establishing his power identity, dominance, and role of protector, saying, "I am the bigger one I am fighting with Matthias ... Matthias is small ... You (to mother) are small as well."

When drawing himself and his mother (*LH37*, Figure 10.5, Image 2; *LH39*, Figure 9.11, Image 1, Chapter 9), Luke drew himself taller and bigger than her, again emphasising the strength and protection of his mother. Interestingly, making himself bigger conveys Luke's power identity as a protector, which also conveys love.

Luke's favoured graphic-narrative style sees several of his drawings as "action-packed encounters between good guys and bad guys" (Dyson, 1995, p. 36) as he plays out the dichotomy of good and evil. In two drawings at school, Bertly, deeply in conversation with Luke, portrayed himself as strong and powerful. Perhaps Bertly's drawing-narratives were influenced by Luke. In *Killing a Dragon* (*BS4*, Figure 10.11, Image 1, below) and *When a Dragon Came to School* (*BS17*, Figure 10.11, Image 2), Bertly drew big, frightening dragons. In the latter, Bertly was fighting a monster with his friend. Projecting himself as a powerful hero, Bertly said that he threw the dragon in the water, shot, and killed him. The drawing, dominated by action lines, captures a complex story packed with fear, conflict, and heroism where reality and myth are interwoven with concepts of friendship. Uncharacteristically, Bertly may have been trying to use this drawing as "a means of entry" (Dyson, 1997, p. 47) into his friends' social world, where, by representing himself as powerful in a dangerous situation, he saved them.

Bertly embraced the narrative pattern of Luke's heroic stories, expressing similar power and control in Luke's drawing narratives. While exploring feelings of empowerment and responsibility, Bertly incorporated imagery similar to Luke's, indicating a "perception of self-image" (Hall, 2008, p. 3), and portraying an assumed persona. Luke and, to some extent, Bertly engaged in a process of "self-transformation" (Hall, 2010a, p. 106), delighting in transforming their vulnerability as four-year-old children into strong, powerful, fearless heroes. Drawing on their knowledge of mythical and fictional characters and narratives, Luke and Bertly juxtaposed real and fantasy-based elements in their drawings, reconstructing events through "playful intentions" (Cox, 2005a, p. 121). Thereby, they explored moral concerns in life's paradoxes of good, evil, and power, expressing their feelings around such strong themes (Gardner, 1982). Playing out the use of violence to kill the antihero and protect the vulnerable, positioned Luke and Bertly to make ethical choices (Edmiston, 2008) in imagined scenarios. The concept of "moral identity" (Edmiston, 2010, p. 205) becomes pertinent here as mythic narratives expose notions of assuming and exerting personal power for good.

Luke made several "good and evil" drawings (*LS1, LS14, LS17, LH17, LH21,* and *LH22*) portraying scenarios where he engaged in battles between good and evil characters, where the good guys overcame the bad guys. In *The*

166  *Children making meaning*

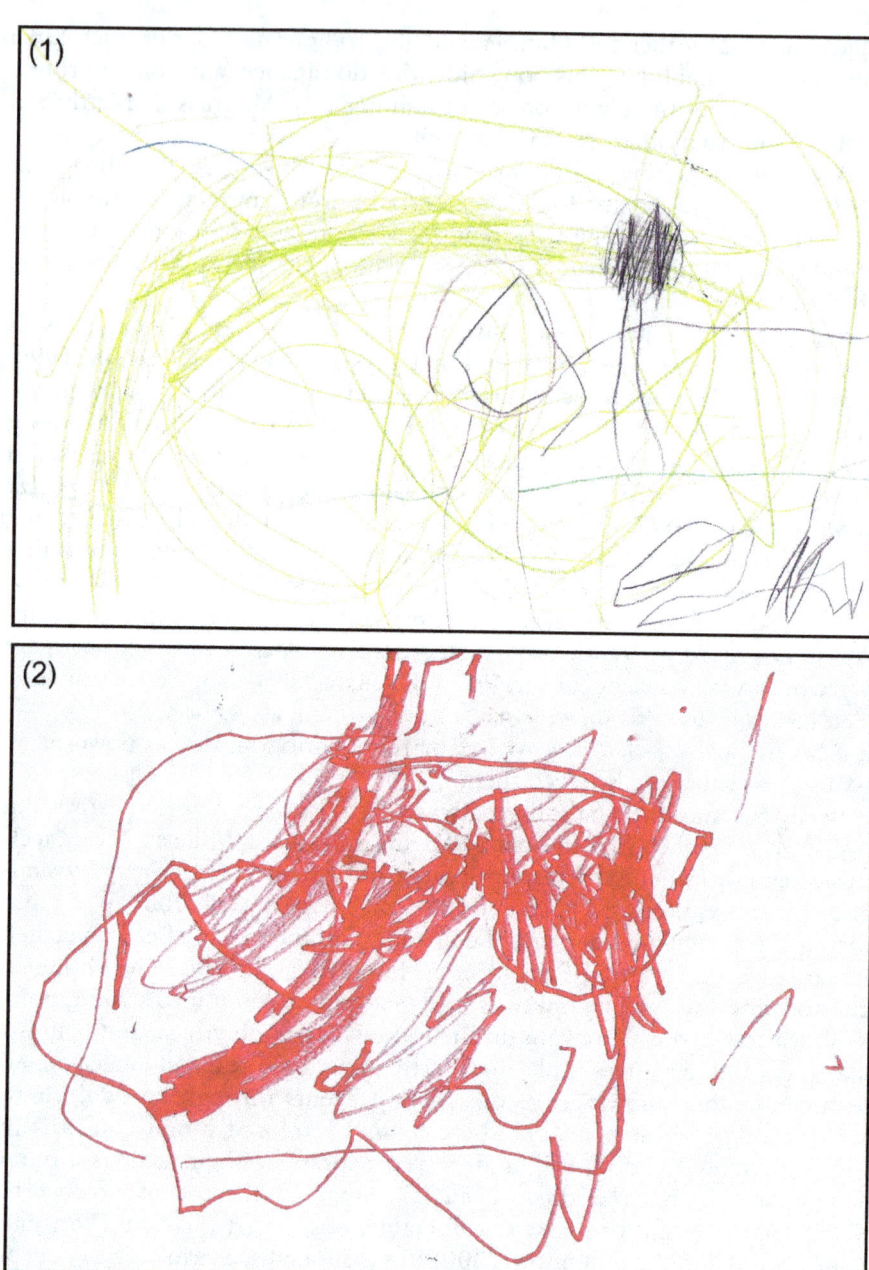

*Figure 10.11* Killing a Dragon (BS4) [1] and *When a Dragon Came to School (BS17)* [2] – by Bertly.

*Figure 10.12* The Good and the Evil (LS1) [1], A Fight between Good and Evil (LS14) [2], The Good Guy and the Bad Guy (LS1) [3] – by Luke.

*Good and the Evil* (*LS1*, Figure 10.12, Image 1), the "good guys" were the car, Eeyore and Diego,[1] while the "bad guys" included a rocket and other small entities that were not clearly visible. Luke's interaction with the drawing was vivid, as he animatedly narrated the fight, describing it as "the good guys are killing the bad guys with a knife" and using sound effects: "Puck. Picho. Puck. Picho. Pshu. Pshu. Pshu" to convey the use of weapons (while drawing lines over the paper). He continued:

> This is going to kill this one. Pshu. Pshu. Pshu. They are shooting at each other. Pum! This one. Pum! This one. Pum! And this one. Pshu. Pshu. They died. Pum! Pum! They shot them ... Now I am going to put the bad guys, in prison.

The drawing (*LS1*) reflects the struggle between good and evil, and Luke's knowledge of popular culture.

*A Fight between Good and Evil* (*LS14*, Figure 10.12, Image 2) also symbolises the struggle between good and evil. While less animated, Luke again conveyed a storyline where the "good guys" (the glitters) fired at the "bad guys." Good prevails over bad, as "the good ones killed the bad ones and took them to prison and left them there."

*The Good Guy and the Bad Guy* (*LS17*, Figure 10.12, Image 3) also encapsulates the battle between good and evil. Luke drew a "good guy" fleeing from the "bad guy" (horizontal figure at the top covered in black lines) who was shooting him. Luke began the *Good Guy and the Bad Guy* (*LS17*) by drawing "a man is running ... because he [the bad guy] is firing at his head." Using visual cues such as a series of dots in action on the paper indicating the gunshots, he created sound effects to mimic the shooting, "Yes. Pum! Pum! He will die. I want to draw him a knife," interrupting his narration to draw a knife. Similar to other drawings, Luke drew a series of black lines on the bad guy, imposing consequences on him by putting him in a cage, "because he is naughty." Intertwining his drawing with narration, Luke said, "Here he is flying ... I am going to draw *Ben Ten*. *Ben Ten* is flying." This graphic narrative concludes with Luke putting the bad guy in the cage, marked with fervently made black lines. Drawing on the popular culture character of *Ben Ten*, Luke created an imaginary story with fictional characters while occasionally moving out of the drawing to explain or enact what was happening. Luke was using drawing as a form of small-world play, where drawing is a space for a playful fantasy plot.

Other drawings (*LH17*, Figure 9.7, Chapter 9; *LH21*, Figure 5.6, Chapter 5; and *LH22*, Figure 9.6, Image 2, Chapter 9) discussed in previous chapters likewise illustrate Luke's creative exploration of the conflict between good and evil and the motif of justice and the triumph of good as prominent themes.

### *Playful storytelling in drawings of power, good, and evil*

According to Wood and Hall's (2011) notion of playing *with* drawings, children combine storytelling with graphic-narrative play to tell a fantasy-based story. By merging mythical character development, plot, and scenery (frequently borrowed from popular culture), children create playful drawing-narratives with unifying eternal themes – such as good and evil. Three of Luke's drawings (*LS1*, Figure 10.12, Image 1; *LS14*, Figure 10.12, Image 2; *LS17*, Figure 10.12, Image 3) are examples of "playing *with* drawings" (Wood & Hall, 2011, p. 276), where Luke used drawing as a narrative function to explain his drawn imaginary worlds.

Storytelling through graphic-narrative play was Luke's preferred way of drawing. Adopting a "heroic-agonistic genre" (Nicolopoulou, 1997, p. 166), which mainly included fictional characters, graphic action, and drama, Luke used his drawing as a dynamic playing field, packed with action and narrative. Playing *with* drawings resembles small-world play, where instead of using small 3D figures, Luke used his drawings as an arena for his playful plot involving fighting fantasy characters. To represent the action as it unfolded in such drawings, Luke often drew many seemingly chaotic straight and circular lines between his characters. *Ben Ten Fight* (*LS18*, Figure 4.1, Chapter 4), *The Good and the Evil* (*LS1*, Figure 10.12, Image 1), *A Fight between the Good and the Evil* (*LS14*, Figure 10.12, Image 2), and *The Good Guy and the Bad Guy* (*LS17*, Figure 10.12, Image 3) are examples where Luke described, modified, enacted, located, and relocated imaginative characters as he shifted himself in and out of the drawing, explaining what was happening.

Luke's drawing-narratives were not constricted in *form* and usually contained a range of ever-changing themes, which frequently originated from books and cartoons, as he blended ideas, scenarios, actions, and characters to create playful running narratives of good and evil where he was the powerful victor. Luke's narratives had "fluid structures" and "fleeting moments" (Wright, 2007, p. 2) that evolved through and from fantasy, without conforming to conventional, sequential, or rational storytelling.

Some of Luke's graphic-narratives feature him as the good guy in action – powerful, strong, and fully-armed; fighting, killing, capturing, and imprisoning enemies to protect the innocent. *Cutting Out the Bad Guy 1* (*LH21*, Figure 5.6, Chapter 5) and *Cutting Out the Bad Guy 2* (*LH22*, Figure 9.6, Image 2, Chapter 9) are similar drawings and storylines where Luke, as the good guy – shoots and wins over the bad guy – represented by physically cutting out the bad guy from the drawing. The two drawings were done in succession at school. Similar to *LH21* (discussed in Chapter 5), *Cutting Out the Bad Guy 2* (*LH22*, discussed in Chapter 9) features Luke as the good guy, fighting and killing the bad guy. Inspired by cartoon characters on TV (such as *Ben Ten*), Luke becomes a superhero with weapons to fight bad guys. He drew the bad guy in pink (Luke's preferred colour for insults) and smaller than Luke. Taking a pair of scissors, Luke then says, "cut the bad guy out, once again … and he will be dead" (the cutting marked with blue lines). Driven by a sense of justice and victory, Luke rewarded himself for his achievement by drawing a medal on his chest and a trophy in his hand, proudly stating, "I won! I killed him." The bad guy's fate seemed to be rigidly controlled by a predetermined script, where he would, "always die" (Paley, 1988, p. 19). Perhaps this statement was Luke's way of voicing a desire for superpowers and his interest in competition and justice – all salient values manifested in this set of drawings.

In *Cutting Out the Bad Guy 2* (*LH22*, Figure 9.6, Image 2, Chapter 9), Luke drew himself as big and tall, filling the paper, and his mother and Matthias in his pockets so that Luke could carry them with him – again the protector of the good and innocent. Armed with weapons and appropriating the role of *Iron Man*, Luke portrayed himself as powerful and strong to fight the "killers of the world." With his in-drawing power, Luke cut the bad guy's face and killed him, claiming "bad guys always die. They die with a gun. They die even with a sword."

The inclusion of weaponry in his drawings is an articulation of Luke's thoughts and emphasises the detail of a comprehensive popular culture, the warfare-narrative. He also showed his passion, insight, and exposure to objects and the vocabulary of combat. In *LH21* (Figure 5.6, Image 2, Chapter 5) and *LH22* (Figure 9.6, Image 2, Chapter 9), Luke transformed his drawings into play props by cutting them out to develop the storyline (see Dyson, 1989; Kress, 2000a; Hope, 2008). Luke's cutting out of the bad guy is a metaphor for the literal removal of the bad guy (Oksanen, 2008; Wright, 2010b) and the glorification of Luke as the triumphant superhero. Luke's use of cutting brought an additional dimension to his drawing, it being part of the complex meaning as he used drawing "to see" (Hope, 2008, p. 12). Cutting, in the two drawings (*LH21, LH22*), actually eradicated the bad guy. Using cutting to understand (Hope, 2008, p. 12), Luke established the meaning of his drawing-narrative. Dyson (1988) suggests that for children to compose change, they must have well-developed skills of analogy, just as Luke did to lithely convert the representation of a violent bad guy on paper into a dead figure that is gone. Luke's detailed descriptions during the meaning-making process helped him to follow his mental associations and appreciate his different layers of meaning: the reason behind the elimination of the bad guy, the significance it had for Luke, and his concepts about the element of the drawing-narrative suggest that such analogies are part of playful experiences that allow children the possibility of using superhero powers, making the impossible possible (Edmiston, 2008; Nielson, 2009; Wright, 2010a).

### Playing in drawings of good and evil

In *Tying the Blue Lady* (*LH24*, Figure 10.13), Luke drew his whole family; this time to fight the *Blue Lady*. The drawing emanates from a combination of imagination and real experiences from a recent family visit to a local castle. While there, they watched a short film about a *Blue Lady* who, dressed in blue and projected like a ghost, was said to haunt the castle. This frightened Jacob, Luke's brother, who cried relentlessly, "The Blue Lady fired at me." Violating

*Figure 10.13* Tying the Blue Lady (LH24) – by Luke.

any sense of logic that is only possible in play, narratives, and drawing, Luke then drew two other figures, all representing Jacob.

Children's drawings can be fluid in structure, taking drawing-narratives beyond the confinement of reality. Luke next sketched the *Blue Lady* (far right) with a pink marker (covered with black lines). Pink was an intentional and metaphoric device that Luke used to convey a desire to spite. Luke drew himself as a superhero in the drawing, explaining, "I am Ben Ten," intent on saving his brother. Luke was playing *in* drawing (Wood & Hall, 2011), assuming a fictional self in the drawing-space for imaginative play. Imitating *Ben Ten's* actions, saying "I want to catch the Blue Lady," Luke drew black lines on the *Blue Lady*, signifying her being tied with ropes. He saved his family by imprisoning her, treating his drawing as an unfolding role-play, and manipulating the characters and drawing as he imagined himself the powerful superhero, capturing the *Blue Lady*. This drawing-narrative was interwoven with elements of imagination, mythical narrative, fantasy, and a real experience – partly drawn and partly as a dramatic play alongside the drawing – where Luke became his own drawing-narrative.

As with other drawings (*LH25*, Figure 5.17, Chapter 5; *LS12*, Figure 9.4, Chapter 9; *LH14*, Figure 10.7), in *Tying the Blue Lady* (*LH24*, Figure 10.13), Luke drew himself bigger than other family members. Taking on the roles of *Iron Man* and *Ben Ten* and armed with weapons, he portrayed himself with strength and power and in full control, declaring that he was unafraid and showing confidence that he could overcome the *Blue Lady*. Luke's self-drawings portray him facing dangerous, frightening characters and challenging injustice with guns, knives, and powerfully voiced narratives, signifying strength and authority. Luke's preference for drawing action pictures with violent and dangerous creatures alongside harmless and vulnerable characters could aid his exploration of his own fears of aggression and destruction by killing evil-doers while demonstrating his own power, courage, and role of protector.

The drawing-narrative of *Tying the Blue Lady* (*LH24*, Figure 10.13) became an action story with "iconic links" (Wright, 2011, p. 166) made with pink marker, connecting the *Blue Lady* to Luke's younger brother (third on the right). These action lines signified the gunshots that the *Blue Lady* fired at Jacob. Luke's accompanying vocalisation resembled fighting, demonstrating his power:

> I am not scared of the *Blue Lady*. I am *Ben Ten* and I am going to kill the *Blue Lady*. Heyah! Heyah! Chuck. Chuck. Chuck. This is a gun. The Blue Lady had a gun. She fired at Jacob. Buff. Buff. Buff. I want to catch the Blue Lady. I am going to trap her with the rope. (the black line). Crashh! I caught the *Blue Lady*. Bvvvvvuuummmm. Bvvvvvuuummmm. I put her in prison.

This action narrative showed Luke's predisposition and competence in graphically organising and composing imaginary and dramatised narratives in a

172  *Children making meaning*

*Figure 10.14* I am Ben Ten (LH23) – by Luke.

seemingly ad hoc way. He transformed and recontextualised his drawing by experimenting with and remixing different symbolic material from real-life, popular culture, and his play.

*I am Ben Ten* (*LH23*, Figure 10.14) and *Ben Ten Fight* (*LS18*, Figure 4.1, Chapter 4) are two examples of playing *in* drawing, where Luke drew himself as the superhero succeeding in his mission to kill the "bad guys" and saving his family and the world. He drew *I am Ben Ten* just before *Tying the Blue Lady* (*LH24*), which is an extension of the storyline between the two drawings.

In the *Ben Ten Fight* (*LS18*, Figure 4.1, Chapter 4), Luke began similarly, by drawing *Ben Ten* on the left and explaining, "This is *Ben Ten*. Now he becomes a monster … He is fighting the bad guys," he drew two video-cameras on the right. Introducing more characters to the story who entered into a confrontation with each other, Luke continued by drawing several straight lines across and radiating from the first *Ben Ten*, seemingly typifying the blades of a helicopter, to "make him fly" while dramatising his narrative:

> The guns are firing from *Ben Ten*'s pocket. His guns are firing at the video cameras … because they are naughty … Now they are firing. "Pcho! Pcho! … They are firing at each other … Pum! Pum! Pum! Oooh! Get them! Eeennn. On the motorway. Wragh! Bvummm! Bvummm! Wragh! Wragh! Bvumm! Bvumm! Dish! Pum! Pum! Pum! … Pum! Look! This one is shooting at *Ben Ten* and *Ben Ten* is shooting at this one, and at this and this. Dish!

Using fantasy characters where superheroes fight villains, Luke created an "allegoric fantasy on paper" (Wright, 2007, p. 22), experiencing and mediating feelings, concepts, conflicts, and tensions that he ascribed to *Ben Ten*. Dyson (1997) argued that children appropriate superheroes' narratives of war and weapons to create their own good and evil guys as role models whose experiences overcome human nature. Marsh (2000) suggested that manipulating superhero characters gives children a sense of control over disorder and evil, assuming the role of *Ben Ten* perhaps empowered Luke to face his challenges. In the *Ben Ten* drawings, Luke conveyed mixed experiences of "active violence" (Nicolopoulou et al., 1994, p. 114), with elements of fighting for power, killing, and destruction, from which he simultaneously derived satisfaction in protecting the vulnerable and fighting the evil guys to make the world better – as do all superheroes.

As Thea, Bertly, and Luke have shown through their drawings, themes of love, power, good, and evil intermingle. Emotions and identities are played out in universally understood scenarios. Drawings show how love and protection can be found when powerful characters use their power to overcome evil and protect the vulnerable. Young children's drawings explore these complex weaves of eternal themes.

### Note

1 Eeyore is a fictional character from the Winnie the Pooh books; Diego is an action-adventure hero cartoon character from the series, *Go, Diego, Go!* (Viacom International Incorporation, 2015), who rescues animals and which Luke watched on TV.

# 11 Drawing, talk, narrative and collaboration

*Figure 11.1* In the Garden 2 – Talking Animals (LH30) – by Luke.

## The role of talk and narrative in creating meaning

This chapter discusses how children use talk and narrative as a supportive mode to create meaning while they draw and the place of copying in collaboration and interaction around drawing.

The meanings of children's drawings are often obscure to adult eyes. Recognising this challenge leads to an acknowledgment of the importance of conversation and narrative to enhance the meanings children attribute to their drawings. Informal conversations, before, during, and after the drawings are made, offer opportunities to ask children questions and seek clarification of their intentions. This creates a space for children to voice their thoughts, maintaining control over the pace and direction of conversations and shaping and refining their intended meanings. A more profound understanding of drawings can arise from talking with and listening to children's drawing-narratives. Conversational interactions between the children and Jo and between the children themselves while drawing next to each other generated further drawing insights. Talk was crucial to the semiotic process; it being a catalyst to help children extend their static drawing into a drawing-narrative that aided their articulation and uncovered layered meanings. Subjective interpretation of finished drawings, without the children's voiced perspectives and the insights of their parents, limits the depth of understanding and significance for the children. Informal, improvised, and *ad hoc* conversations and narratives were developed as needed across the drawing process and were integral to shaping meanings, providing deeper, more coherent understanding. Luke, Thea, and Bertly used their talk and narrative powerfully to effectively construct and represent their meanings with fluidity.

The children's use and level of talk during the drawing process varied. They drew silently, engaged in intermittent dialogue, maintained continuous monologues, or had conversations with nearby peers and adults. The nature of their talk depended on many factors: personalities, moods, subject matter, media available, ambiance, and dynamics at that particular time. Talk was multifaceted, serving as a tool for children variously to develop a drawing: to share and describe the content, articulate the drawing process, or seek advice regarding technical aspects. Talk facilitated children's efforts to internalise and verbalise their intentions and engagement in "complex dialogues which encapsulated a completely remembered experience" (Coates & Coates, 2011, p. 99). Talk included the elaboration or attribution of meaning to a drawing. Children used "word play" (Wright, 2007, p. 17) to include a playful and amusing twist to their narrative, and talk was also a "narrative function" (Hopperstad, 2008b, p. 136), signifying a transformation in their drawings or a shift in meaning. Talk enabled children to create engaging stories and fostered social interaction.

Luke's, Thea's, and Bertly's interactions with their peers contributed to their use of talk as a conceptual tool, the processing of abstract ideas, and the development of knowledge (Coates, 2002; Anning & Ring, 2004; Ahn & Filipenko, 2007; Wright, 2011). The children talked with an adult (their parents and/or Jo) to share their plans, convey the subject matter, request assistance, seek encouragement, or gain a fresh perspective. Ultimately, talk and narratives became integral to the children's process of self-construction, mediation, and authoring of self (Edmiston, 2008; Wright, 2010b). They variously narrated stories about who they were, their emotions, wishes, dreams, and interests, providing insights into the individuals they aspired to be. Most of these functions of talk and narratives have been incorporated in our interpretations of the drawings throughout the book; here we use one drawing to spotlight the value of talk in the process of drawing and the interpretation of meaning.

Luke's *In the Garden 2 – Talking Animals* (LH30, Figure 11.1) features a playful narrative with a humorous storyline. This drawing, adorned with vibrant and appealing cut-out stickers, created an unusual enthusiasm in Luke to draw and inspired a comical tale. The drawing appears to be an ordinary garden scene featuring animals, a flower, a tree, a skyline, and a grass line. Only Luke's accompanying narrative, with its whimsical storyline, brings the drawing to life.

After attaching some stickers, Luke paused to share with his mother and Jo his intention to create a story involving animals. He silently continued his drawing, then seamlessly transitioned between the roles of the different characters in his drawing, immersing himself in their personas. Using a variety of voices, he skilfully acted out, narrated, and animated the different characters, as if he were producing a puppet show. Using direct speech integral to his drawing-narrative, Luke weaved a cohesive, intricate narrative, giving depth and complexity to his drawing's meaning:

> Once there was a rubber duck that was walking, and she met a worm. [changing intonation trying to imitate the voice of a duck] "Look what a worm! Can I eat you?" [changing to a soft intonation for the worm] "No, otherwise I will throw you up into the sky and the wind will eat you up. [changing intonation to imitate the bee] "Bzzzzzzzzzz," bee. [changing intonation to voice the snail] "Oh, man!" said the snail to this [the bee].

Luke stopped his narrative, saying:

> Let me draw the tree's mouth … Oh man! All of them have a mouth now! … Oh man! Oh man! Now the buzz buzz. Now the flower. … Oh man! Everyone is saying "Bla, bla, bla, bla."

His mother asked him if the story continued. Luke replied, "The story has finished," but continued his narrative by saying:

> "Oh man! Bzzzzzz. Who is this? Is this a buzz bee? Oh man! What is your name?" [changing intonation to imitate the bee] "My name is Bee Bufuvva, Snaily Kevin" said the bee [Luke laughed]. "Bzzzzzz."

The full transcript[1] emphasises four important elements of the narrative: humour-infused, improvised, and animated; seamless transition and fluidity; and an articulated plan.

Throughout the drawing-narrative, several instances added a playful and amusing dimension. From the opening sentence, Luke injected humour designed to create a hilarious scenario, given its inherent impossibility. How could a tiny worm, much smaller than a duck, toss it into the sky, and how could the wind eat it up? Children's drawings are not always rationally understandable, and their narrative, like Luke's, sometimes goes beyond the visual and the confinement of reality. Other amusing instances occurred when Luke invented Bee Bufuvva, and his playful intonation while uttering the name, the alliteration inherent in it (the repeated B, U, and V sounds), his infectious laughter, and the gleeful expression on his face all indicated that Luke found this character amusing and eagerly anticipated his mother and Jo laughing too. In the same sentence, he mentioned "Snaily Kevin," adding another layer of humour by using his father's name. The repeated exclamation, "Oh man!" delivered with exaggerated mockery added another layer of levity to the narrative.

Luke's dialogue between the animals vividly showcases his ability to craft improvised and animated narrative, which effectively transformed the drawing into a *narrative scene*, where the narrative was inspired by and evolved from the drawing itself. Luke skilfully assumed the roles of illustrator, scriptwriter, narrator, and producer of his imaginative tale. Weaving an intricate and mythical plot about fictional characters, he broke the confines of his drawing, creating a fluid, spontaneous narrative where the plot evolved according to his interest and his audience. Luke's drawing transcended the limitations of product and content and assumed an emergent nature, guided by his own prevailing humour and inclinations at that moment.

Luke's narrative demonstrated his capacity to articulate his plan and his readiness to embrace fluidity in the unfolding plot. This narrative development involved "authorial agency" (Dyson, 1997, p. 396) as Luke actively shaped his characters and story, guided by his thought-in-action and spontaneous imagination. In his character-based drawing, Luke seamlessly moved between drawing and narrative, stopping occasionally to explain his actions, such as drawing mouths on the tree, flower, and mushroom, so that they could talk. These pauses served as opportunities for Luke to order his thoughts, introduce additional detail, elaborate his ideas, and provide clarification, all within the fluid narrative and process of meaning-making. Luke frequently revisited and expanded previous aspects of his drawing, refining his thoughts as the narrative unfolded. This allowed Luke to develop his drawing-narrative with a coherence vital to a compelling storyline.

Luke's drawing and narrative may have had other purposes. At the time of the drawing, Luke had been using challenging behaviour, towards his mother. Luke knew that his mother did not accept nonsensical behaviour and he did not like it when she ignored him because of his behaviour. Creating a comical drawing-narrative, Luke was perhaps seeking to ease tension, lighten the atmosphere, and re-establish the usual warm relationship between them. Luke was perhaps using his drawing-narrative to convey the importance for him of having a voice, being allowed the space and time to have his say, justify his behaviour, and be listened to. The drawing-narrative enlivened Luke's drawing, enabling him to transform a static image into an animated and comic storyline.

## Talking and copying

Children's drawings frequently incorporate some form of copying. They draw what other children are drawing; others' ideas are transformed; and they borrow from various sources, including storybooks, television, film, and events. Earlier, we discussed instances where Luke, Thea, and Bertly copied from each other or other children when they drew. Here we consider how, when children draw, they copy for different reasons and frequently talk while copying.

Copying is regularly regarded as "an offence" (Mavers, 2011, p. 13), "illegal" (Dyson, 2010, p. 8), "ethically 'wrong' or educationally unacceptable" (Mavers, 2011, p. 2), a form of cheating, not to be emulated. Copying is usually seen as a passive activity without creativity or imagination, where children have no ideas of their own. However, scholars challenge this negative perspective and argue that copying is integral to the semiotic process (Dyson, 2010; Hopperstad, 2010; Ring, 2010; Mavers, 2011). Looking at the drawing habits of Luke, Thea, and Bertly, we see that copying is not a 'mere' replication, explicitly drawing on others' work, but often involves a "remix" (Mavers, 2011, p. 12), where children selectively borrow ideas and inspiration from others to reinterpret into their new drawings. Children connect their knowledge with what they borrow to create new meanings in their drawings. Drawing involves processes of reselecting, redesigning and reproducing meanings, as children change their drawings into something new. Viewed this way, two drawings may appear similar but may differ significantly in meaning. In the act of copying, children continue to exercise their agency in shaping and designing their drawings with personal meaning. Sanctioned copying occurs when the "copier" has full approval of the "copied" and is not "stealing," or "cheating" but collegial collaboration. Luke, Thea and Bertly copied, often sharing ideas while sitting next to and interacting with others; they copied form, content, and materials, sometimes developing and maintaining friendships in the process.

### Luke's ways of copying

Luke copied the use of *complex modes* from his peers. His preferred semiotic style was a *simple mode* (Chapter 5), where he mostly used drawing and mark-making with crayons and/or gem markers. Luke watched his peers using a multiplicity of modes and media that were novel to him: cutting paper, glueing lollipop sticks, tracing, and attaching stickers. The similarity in the use of *complex modes* between Luke's drawing and his peers was distinctly observable.

When Luke drew *Two Diamonds in the Sky* (*LH36*, Figure 11.2), his main aim seemed experimental: to try out the mode of dabbing glitter and their effects, as he often saw Thea and Sandra do. Luke first used glue, glitter, and sequins at home; perhaps he felt safer trying new modes and materials away from his more experienced peers. The shimmering materiality of the glitter and sequins inspired him to typify the stars as diamonds. Following Kress'

*Drawing, talk, narrative and collaboration* 179

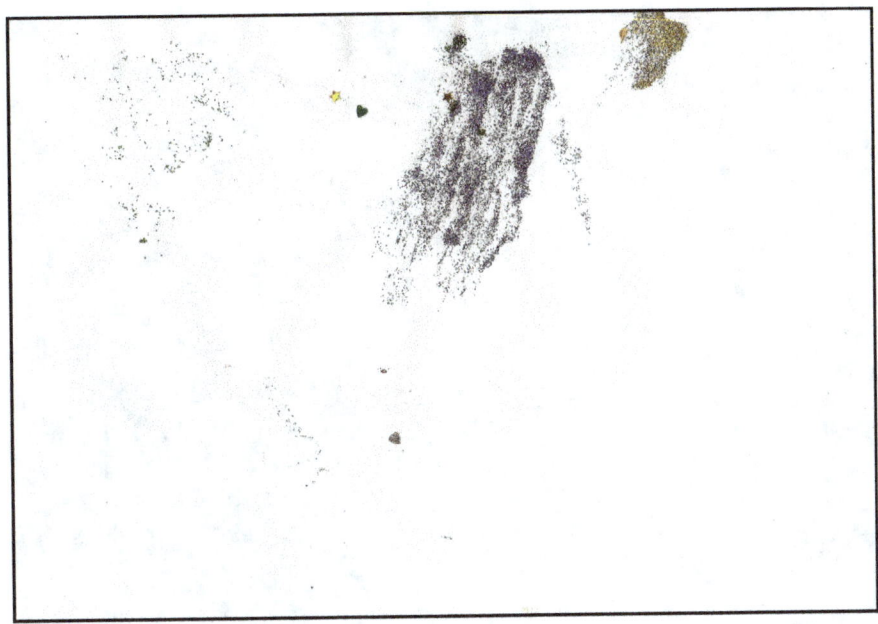

*Figure 11.2* *Two Diamonds in the Sky (LH36)* – by Luke.

(1997, p. 29) notion of "successive transitions," Luke, like his peers, moved between modes, contexts, ideas, and meanings, first exploring the modes of dabbing and spreading glitter, then experimenting with unfamiliar modes and media at home.

Luke was sitting next to Martina, watching her glueing and taping paper to her drawing, and began to copy her use of these modes. He selected two pieces of corrugated paper, which he cut into small portions and glued them to the centre of his drawing; this resulted in *A Worm* (*LS16*, Figure 5.7, Chapter 5). After outlining a worm, Luke again copied Martina and others using sticky-tape (another new medium to him) and secured the glued brown paper with tape. Luke used the mode of dabbing that he had previously watched others using to dab and spread some glitter glue to signify the worm food, working with a distinctively different medium from his usual paper and pen repertoire. Copying can bring change to the content and transform meaning as new skills are acquired.

Luke was sitting next to Thea, who was drawing *Romina's Aeroplane* (*TS30*, Figure 9.14, Image 2, Chapter 9) when he drew *An Aeroplane 2* (*LS23*, Figure 2.1, Chapter 2). Luke followed Thea, who was skilled in using different media, and copied what she did. The form and content of the drawings are similar but also distinct. Thea began drawing, and Luke followed, copying her use of modes, as they each drew an aeroplane. Luke probably copied the g modes and semiotic resources (the glueing paper, sticks, and

180　*Children making meaning*

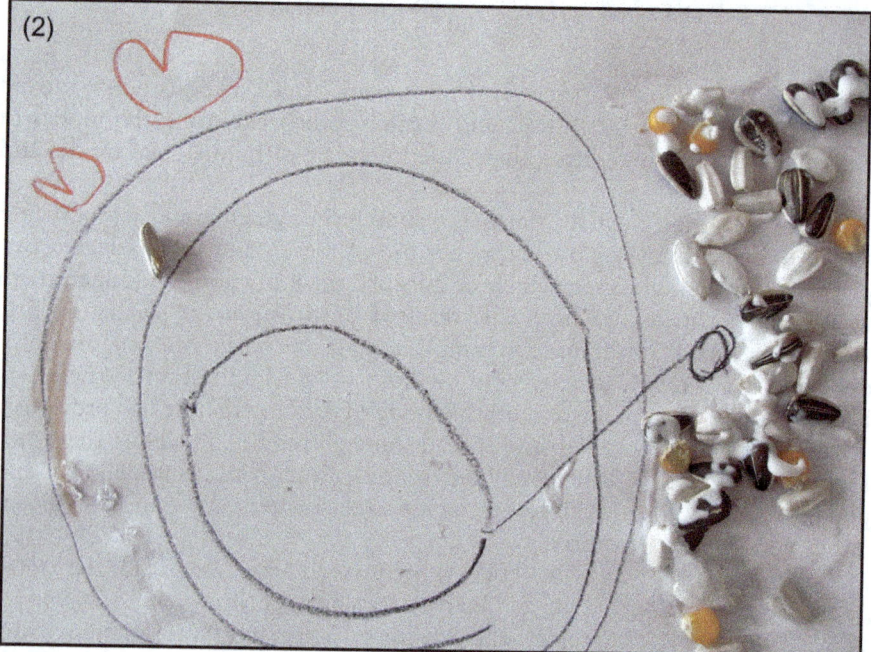

*Figure 11.3* The Snail (LS10) [1] – by Luke; The Snail (TS12) [2] – by Thea.

dabbing glitter) used by Thea and represented similar content to Thea (an aeroplane). Luke used his agency to selectively reshape and design his drawing with his original combinations and meaning-making processes, making it different from Thea's. While Thea's rectangular shapes were blue and made of paper, Luke's were green and made of foam, and Thea secured her wooden sticks with glue only, but Luke added sticky tape. Luke, like Thea, drew an aeroplane, but their meanings differed: Luke's drawing represented a fighter jet from the outside, with the wooden sticks signifying combat equipment; Thea drew the inside of a passenger aeroplane, the wooden sticks being wings. Thus, the *form* and *content* of both drawings were similar, but the meanings were different.

Luke, again sitting next to Thea, drew *The Snail* (*LS10*, Figure 11.3, Image 1), copying Thea's drawing in *form* (circular drawing and glued seeds), *content* (a snail), title (*The Snail*), and narrative. Thea said that she was going to draw *The Snail* (*TS12*, Figure 11.3, Image 2), saying that her snail "is like this" as she drew circles, perhaps the snail's shell. Questioning the subject of her drawing, Luke copied Thea's idea to draw a snail, declaring "Mine is longer." A comparison of the drawings shows that Luke's snail is more elongated over the paper. Picking on the seeds, Thea claimed, "The snail is going to eat them all ... he is out already (referring to the antennae) ... it is eating," as Luke copied her idea, adding, "Even mine ... I gave him a lot of food to eat ... mine is out already too"; like Thea, Luke glued seeds to his paper. Thea attached the seeds in front of the snail, next to the antennae, where his mouth was, and Luke attached his seeds beneath the snail. Luke and Thea continued to engage in playful social talk, teasing each other and seemingly trying to outdo each other while contentedly copying one another's ideas:

LUKE: Mine [the snail] got out before Thea's. Mine gets out in the rain, in the sun. And in the wind.

THEA: Even mine comes out in the rain too.

LUKE: [attached a blue sticker rhinoceros, and some olive leaves]. He is going to eat the food as well. I think he has enough food," [making his drawing different from Thea's].

THEA: [Thea then drew two hearts] Because I love him. [It wasn't clear whether she was referring to the snail or Luke].

### Thea's ways of copying

Thea rarely copied from others, being usually very confident in drawing and familiar with using different media. Thus, she frequently became a leader when drawing with others, who often copied her skills and use of modes and media, and sometimes the *form* and *content*. Occasionally, Thea copied from other children, usually as a form of friendship rather than out of a need for help or ideas; she seemed to enjoy sharing collegial interests and developing relationships with her peers in playful reciprocity (see Chapter 6).

Thea, sitting next to Sandra with Shaun close by, drew *A Ship* (TS38, Figure 9.5, Image 3, Chapter 9). She began before communicating with them, seemingly focused on what she wanted to draw. Beginning with the outline of what to her appeared to be "a butterfly," she described the middle section as the centre of the butterfly, with the red square on top as the head, and the rectangular sides as "the wings. Small. Small. Small." Meanwhile, taking the cue from Thea, Sandra began to draw a butterfly, which she filled with glitter glue. Thea seemed to like Sandra's idea and immediately filled her outlined butterfly drawing with a mixture of multi-coloured glitter glue. The children appeared to enjoy being in synchrony: Sandra copied Thea's idea of drawing a butterfly, and Thea copied Sandra's use of glitter glue. This example of strong collaboration shows their enjoyment of amicably copied ideas while fostering and sustaining their friendship. Shaun asked if Thea had drawn a ship, which she initially denied. Thea listened to Shaun's persistent assertion that "It looks like a ship," and she agreed, "Yes, it is a ship. This is a ship. No, it is not going to be a butterfly anymore." Thea colluded with Shaun, engaging in a negotiation of the subject matter and its original intended meaning, just as she might negotiate her role during pretend play, adapting the meaning of her drawing to fit Shaun's perspective. Thea attributed the meaning of a ship to her shape and continued to develop her drawing thus. Shaun's critical feedback led Thea to consider another "possible meaning" (Hopperstad, 2008b, p. 145), as she concurred with his idea and transformed the subject of her drawing from a butterfly to a ship. The reading, interpretation, and meaning attributed to the sign (the ship) were fluid and socially constructed in the interaction between Shaun and Thea.

Using tracing paper, Sandra next traced a photo of herself. Thea immediately copied this technique, stating, "I am going to trace myself" as she traced her photograph, wrote her name in pencil, then cut and glued the image to the top left of her drawing, labelling it "the captain of the ship." The messy interplay of the coloured glitters, the pale colour of the tracing paper, and the pencil make it difficult to define the cut-out of the tracing paper. Using scissors, Sandra then cut out the bottom of her drawing because a crocodile was going to eat the girl. Listening to Sandra's narrative, Thea again copied Sandra, cutting off the bottom part of her drawing, which represented the sea, because "Sandra's crocodile came to my picture and cut off my drawing as well." This created a sense of reciprocity and collaboration between the two, who used their drawings as a stage for narration (Wright, 2007). Thea made an intentional shift into imagination to connect her drawing to Sandra's as the two proceeded with smiles and non-verbal gestures, indicating their enjoyment.

Thea's drawing *Travelling in a Car or Aeroplane* (TS40, Figure 6.5, Image 1, Chapter 6) was briefly discussed as an example of drawing as social play. Thea, sitting beside Neil, developed her drawing by copying his choice of subject, modes, and media (Figure 6.5, Image 2, Chapter 6). Their shared endeavour centred on depicting similar vehicles capable of being transformed into a car, boat, or aeroplane as the situation demanded and driven by a superhero. Thea and Neil were slowly becoming friends, enjoying spending more time together each day. Neil initiated the drawing, and Thea declared that she was copying his car:

JO: What are you drawing, Thea?
THEA: It is like Neil's.
JO: What are you drawing, Neil?
NEIL: It is a car. It is our car.
JO: And what is yours, Thea?
THEA: A car too. It is our car. I am going to draw like Neil. I am copying Neil exactly.
(*to Neil*) I am drawing exactly like you.

In their "playing *at* drawing" (Wood & Hall, 2011, p. 274), Thea and Neil copied from each other, interacting playfully as they entered in and out of play to share colours, ideas, humorous anecdotes, and concerted discussions while each creating a similar vehicle. This helped them develop their drawing into a "socially meaningful activity" (Cox, 2005a, p. 123), simultaneously shaping their friendship through mutual interaction (Coates, 2002; Coates & Coates, 2006; Hopperstad, 2008a; Dyson, 2010). The resemblance between the two drawings is striking. Thea copied Neil in drawing the vehicle (initially a car), the colours he used, the gas pedals, the characters, and the name-writing.[2] Children are likely to influence the content and direction of each other's work when they collaborate and how they interact and use materials (Coates & Coates, 2006). When, for example, Neil pointed out that "mine [my car] has a gas pedal," Thea responded, "Even I have one like it," pointing to the protruding oval shape at the bottom of her drawing (Figure 6.6, Image 5, Chapter 6). Similarly, Thea and Neil compared their cars:

NEIL: This car is fifty-ten years old.
THEA: And this car is sixty-eight years old.
NEIL: So yours is older than mine ... but mine is bigger than yours.

And later:

NEIL: Sonic and I will stay in the car.
THEA: I am going to stay in the car as well.

These conversations highlight a composing of playful reciprocity. A similarly mutual exchange occurred when Neil described Sonic the Hedgehog (Sega Corporation, 2013), a powerful Play Station hero, which he drew in the middle of his illustration, with three knives on his head, presumably instead of spikes on his back. Neil said, "I am going to be Sonic ... because I love Sonic. A knife ... another knife here ... and another one here." Thea may not have known who Sonic was or what his superpowers were, yet she continued copying Neil's character, which she then labelled as "Fuel," stating, "I am going to draw a knife on his head. I am going to draw it up here" (Figure 6.6, Image 6, Chapter 6). Far from being a passive copier, Thea was actively evaluating Neil's drawings and comments and borrowing his ideas, which she transformed and adapted through a process of decision-making to create her unique character. Their two drawings appear similar, yet divergences are apparent (Figure 6.5, Images 1 and 2, Chapter 6). There is a clear difference between the two drawings in the organisation of colours, the finished drawings, and the meanings attributed to them. Thea's vertical strokes contrast Neil's horizontal ones; at one point, Neil opted to colour in dark blue while Thea decided to use a lighter shade (Figure 6.6, Image 6, Chapter 6), declaring, "I too am going to draw it in blue. But I am going to draw it in light blue. Our pictures are the same except for the blue." From there on, the differences between the drawings increased, with Thea beginning a process of "re-design(ing)" (Mavers, 2011, p. 21) where she changed the forms she copied, bringing significant change to the meanings, albeit in subtle ways. Thea drew her vehicle tilted on a rock, quite different from Neil's, explaining that being stuck on a rock, the car "is going to reach the sky." Neil explained that his car "can start and drive." Thea drew herself with a helmet, which Neil did not approve of. This shows that while Thea 'copied' Neil's idea of drawing herself next to Fuel, the fantasy character, she decided to add the helmet, thereby relating it to her experience when she "saw people wearing helmets driving by on a motorcycle ... so that if they fall off the motorcycle, they will not hurt themselves." During the process of drawing, Thea mostly chose to copy Neil, appropriating his ideas. Yet she was not passively and meaninglessly replicating his image; but actively noticing and interpreting his ideas, trying to make sense of them. Clearly, Thea was influenced by Neil, copying him with "stated intention" (Coates, 2002, p. 35), while agentively reconfiguring her drawing by constantly negotiating what forms to copy, what to modify or omit, and what to substitute, amend, or add. Thus, confirming Mavers's (2011, p. 16) suggestion that "there is no such thing as a copy because copying is an agentive process of remaking afresh," Thea acted as an interpreter of Neil's drawing and producer of her own, "connecting form and meaning in the production of the copy ... [which] is also a process of sign making" (Mavers, 2011, p. 15).

While they drew, Thea and Neil enjoyed light-hearted conversations as they entered in and out of play with an aura of well-being. Their drawings were tools for their socialisation as they shared ideas and jokes, created associations and new knowledge, and developed meanings. In their process of "co-authoring" (Edmiston, 2008, p. 35), Thea and Neil were "playing *at* drawing" (Wood & Hall, 2011, p. 274), using playful social interactions to enter each other's social worlds and maintaining their friendship. Both seemed to behave differently from their usual selves: Thea, usually a leader, became a follower, and Neil, who was often temperamental and antagonistic, was convivial, jolly, and warm towards Thea. The most significant aspect of the two drawings was that through their shared processes, collaborative interaction, and similarly constructed drawings, the children gave their drawing a social value, using drawing to playfully access, establish, and reflect their "social relations and contextual conditions" (Frish, 2006, p. 81).

### Bertly's ways of copying

The children frequently copied each other's use of modes and modalities. Bertly preferred to use a *simple mode* when he drew, only making drawings in *complex mode* at school. Perhaps Bertly was trying to imitate his peers, who were also experimenting with different media. When using *complex modes*, Bertly first watched his peers as they used different media, assimilating their ideas, skills, and techniques and then copying their use of materials, media, and modes to create a personally significant and meaningful drawing. Sometimes, the visual similarity between Bertly's drawing and those of his peers was clear.

Sandra's idea (Figure 11.4, Image 3) of taping a lollipop stick protruding from her drawing was copied by Bertly (*BS7: An Octopus*, Figure 11.4, Image 2) and Thea (*TS20: A Fan*, Figure 11.4, Image 1). Using the same medium, Thea and Bertly created different drawings with different meanings. As they drew, Bertly occasionally looked at Thea, who was sitting next to him, watching what she was doing while he drew silently, intermittently using the same modes. Thea began attaching lollipop sticks to the top of her paper (Figure 11.4, Image 1). Halfway through, she claimed that her drawing looked like Sandra's hanger drawing (Figure 11.4, Image 3). Using the same concept, Thea attached more lollipop sticks. Simultaneously, Bertly conscientiously glued two lollipop sticks in a slating position on each side of the red mark-making he had just done on his drawing. He made a separate red mark on one of the sticks, just like Thea, and then attached five lollipop sticks at the top. Bertly's drawing looked similar to Thea's, but he gave it a different meaning: "That is an octopus ... These are its legs (the five sticks on top) and these are its hands (pointing to the two sticks in the middle of the page)." Thea interpreted her attached lollipop sticks as a fan (*TS20*, Figure 11.4, Image 1).

These lollipop stick drawings confirm that children are influenced by their peers and learn to draw by observing and copying each other (Frisch, 2006). Hope (2008, p. 79) suggests that "once a technique appears within a group or class of children, the others quickly copy, and the new technique is tried out and explored by all." The modes and media available and used by Sandra were a catalyst for Bertly and Thea, enabling them to encode Sandra's concept of the lollipop-sticks-transformed-into-a-hanger and reinterpret it to signify "an octopus" and "a fan." Although the modes (glueing and taping), the media (lollipop sticks), and the *form* of the drawings shared similarities, each child engaged in redesigning and transforming their drawing to make novel meanings. Each drawing bore the distinctive imprint of their authors' unique interest and significance. In copying Sandra, Bertly and Thea used her influence to create unique drawings. Each child exercised their agency to bestow distinct

186  *Children making meaning*

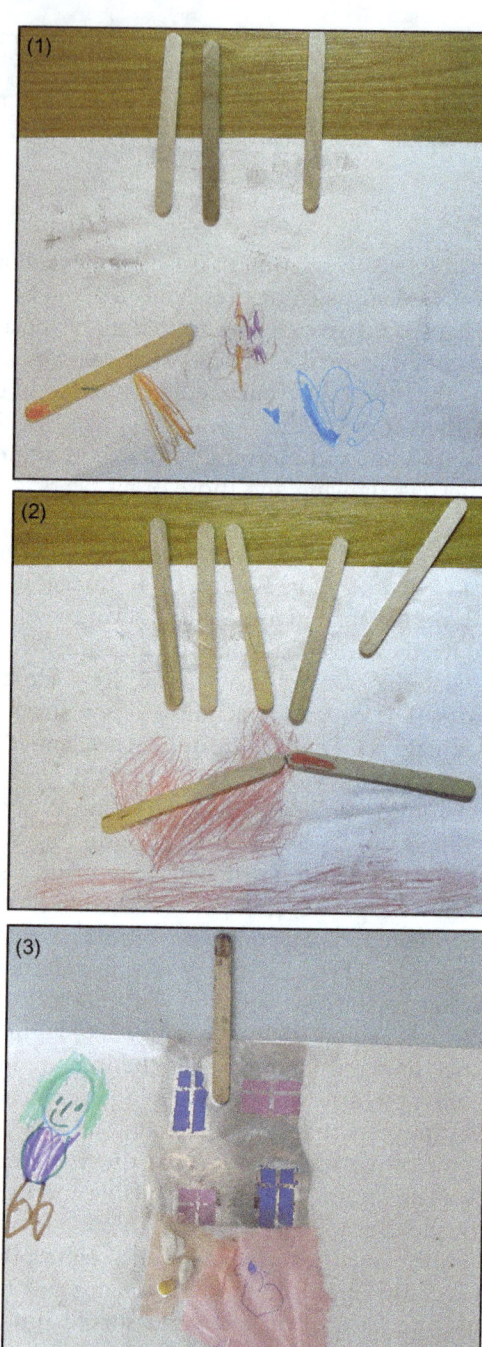

*Figure 11.4* A Fan (TS20) [1] – by Thea, *An Octopus (BS7)* [2] – by Bertly, *A Hanger for Presents for my Friends* [3] – by Sandra.

form and meaning to their drawing, where existing modes and themes were reconfigured to accommodate personal expression. Bertly and Thea used their immediate context, including their peers' use of modes, descriptions, and the development of their drawings, to create drawings with an original meaning and narrative.

In *A Party at Sea* (*BS11*, Figure 11.5, Image 1), which Bertly did at school whilst sitting beside Sandra (Figure 11.5, Image 2), he unusually used *complex modes* of drawing, scattering and dabbing of glitter, and glueing of sequences, as Sandra did. This difference in style was perhaps influenced by Bertly's penchant for occasionally talking to Sandra and watching her techniques and ideas. When Sandra said, "I want to use the glue," Bertly replied, "Even I want to use the glue" and did so. Children's interactions with their peers are likely to influence the use of modes that otherwise might have been excluded (Stein, 2008). As she drew, Sandra initiated occasional conversations with Bertly, though they worked mostly in silence.

After silently observing Sandra for a while, Bertly began drawing by emulating her technique of glueing a narrow strip of blue corrugated paper and securing it with tape to the middle of the sheet to represent the sky. This did not work for Bertly, who swiftly removed it and opted for his preferred mode and medium: drawing in pencil colours. Using different modes, Bertly and Sandra each found distinct avenues for making the sky. Sandra glued glitter to her picture. Bertly again attempted to copy her, but realised that Sandra had used almost all of the glitter, so she used sequins instead, effectively and skilfully, demonstrating flexibility in using various materials. Bertly was now constantly making decisions about what he could and could not achieve with available resources, and the meanings he aimed to convey, and the content of Bertly's and Sandra's drawings bore similarities. Sandra depicted miniature, toy-like people flying in the sky, which, according to her, were *en route* to people's homes to play. Hearing Sandra's narration, Bertly contributed to her description, likening the people to Tinker Bell in *Peter Pan's* film. Bertly described his drawing, explaining his use of glitter and sequins to signify people partying at sea, a description that shared commonalities with Sandra's analogy of toy-like figures. Bertly seemed inspired by Sandra, copying her while continually making choices about the meanings he made and how to make them. Infusing his thoughts and ideas into the drawing, he negotiated, interpreted, and challenged what Sandra was doing to produce his unique representation, resulting in two drawings bearing significant differences and distinctive contributions. As many semiotic theorists (Stein, 2008; Jewitt, 2009a; Kress, 2010; Mavers, 2011) argue, through their active choices and interests, meaning-makers re-use existing conventions and representational resources available, engaging in constant reinterpretation and reconfiguration of their signs and meanings through "symbolic reworking" (Nicolopoulou, 2008, p. 311). Influenced by his context, knowledge, and cultural background, Bertly made subtle changes to the meaning of his drawings. His apparent shortcoming in creating a drawing using a *complex mode* was overcome by his ability to copy Sandra's use of

188  *Children making meaning*

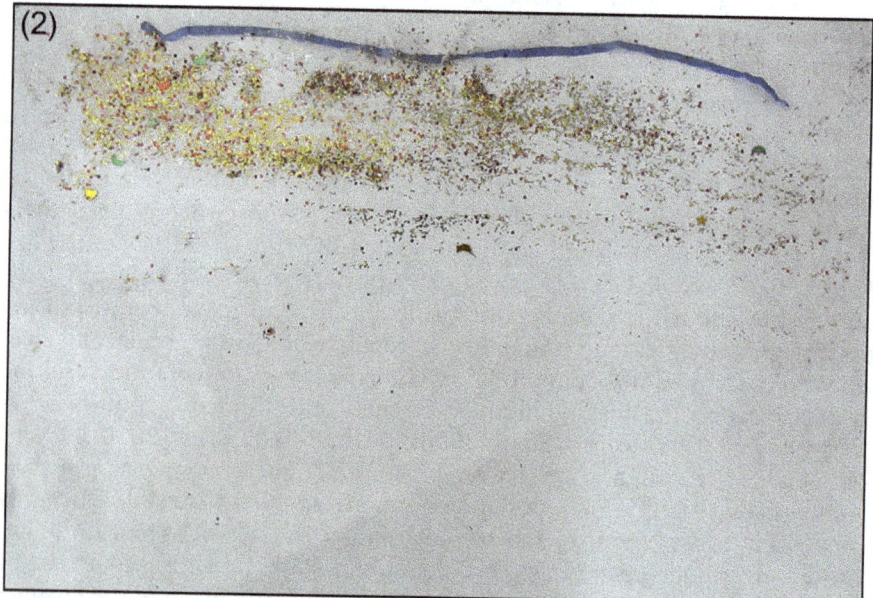

*Figure 11.5* *A Party at Sea (BS11)* [1] – by Bertly, *People Flying in the Sky* [2] – by Sandra.

different modes, giving him confidence to experiment. Through these personalised adjustments, however inconspicuous, he actively constructed his drawing to make a personalised and meaningful drawing rooted in his contextualised experiences.

Copying involves a blend of change, modification and originality, driven by the specific purpose of a drawing (Mavers, 2011). Bertly made choices to select, omit, and substitute forms and meanings in his drawings. Through this process, he established new connections and constructed a different, and distinctive drawing that reflected his interpretation. Copying is a way of trying out new modes that offer children additional affordances to make meaning. When Bertly followed Sandra's use of modes and meanings, he was transcending mere imitation to a higher level of meaning-making (Kress, 2000a; Jewitt, 2009a). Children's interests and social interactions with their peers are ways of shaping their use of unfamiliar modes and media to represent objects differently. As Bertly shows, this process involves a dynamic interplay between interacting with others and expressing internal meanings on paper. Like his peers, Bertly aspired to create more drawings with *complex modes*. Through peer-to-peer learning, Bertly emulated Sandra's use of different modes and learned how to employ them to create his own meaning. With Sandra's help as a model and the more knowledgeable other, the gap between what he could accomplish independently and what he could achieve with Sandra was narrowed (Vygotsky, 1978). Multimodal interactions between children, including verbal inquiries, suggestions, articulation, and observing others, influence what they do and how (Mavers, 2011). From a social semiotics perspective, Bertly was using the resources available to him at school and drawing inspiration from Sandra's ideas, as he chose. In selecting the most fitting resource, he was exercising his agency to express his unique meaning. Children learn to create meaning by observing others and by using a wide variety of resources (Mavers, 2011); thus, through copying Sandra, Bertly ventured beyond his preferred use of *simple mode* to experiment with new media and *complex modes*, acquiring the skills and confidence to "signifying meaning visually" (Hopperstad, 2008b, p. 148) in new and innovative ways.

Children engage in various forms of copying, each driven by distinct motivations or influenced by different ideological frames (Mavers, 2011). Luke, Bertly, and Thea copied in different forms, and the uses of copying varied:

- They copied each other's use of novel modes, media, and materials available (lollipop sticks in *BS7* and glitter in *BS11*).
- Copying enabled the development of friendships (Thea's *TS40* and Neil's cars).
- At times, copying included both replicating form and content of each other's drawings (Luke's *LS23* and Thea's *TS30* aeroplanes).

These three elements of copying often intertwine within the same drawing, making the distinctions less linear. Reflecting on the children's use of copying here, we suggest we can talk about *copying with* others rather than *copying from* others.

### Notes

1 A film clip of Luke drawing *In the Garden 2 – Talking Animals* (*LH30*, Chapter 11, Video 1) is available at https://sites.google.com/view/childrenmakingmeaning
2 Neil's name is a pseudonym to protect his identity.

# 12 Children's funds of knowledge
## Pedagogical considerations

*Figure 12.1* A MacDonald's Box (TH26) – by Thea.

### Knowledge, culture, and meaning

Children's drawings are inherently situated and influenced by the knowledge they acquire through their socio-cultural contexts. Meanings in children's drawings are not stand-alone products but co-constructed through interactions between children, significant people in their lives, and the cultural values that surround them. Their daily experiences, family routines, diverse backgrounds, lifestyles, values, social relationships, attitudes, popular culture, digital technologies, artefacts, and living environments contribute to children's funds of knowledge. Such personally acquired knowledge essentially shapes meaning in children's drawings (Vygotsky, 1978; Rogoff, 1990; Lave & Wenger, 1991; Hedges, 2011;

DOI: 10.4324/9781003427582-12

Chesworth, 2016; Moll, 2019). Children's homes and communities are "repositories of knowledge" (Gonzalez, 2005, p. 26) and rich sources of cultural capital (Moll et al., 1992). This chapter examines how drawings, as socio-cultural artefacts, are profoundly influenced by context, relationships, and experiences.

This chapter considers how viewing drawings through theoretical lenses can help influence drawing pedagogy. Here we consider how children's funds of knowledge acquired through experience in home and community strongly influence their drawings.

## Funds of knowledge: home influences

Children's family life influenced their drawings; here we reflect on the influence of Luke's, Thea's, and Bertly's fathers' hobbies, family routines, and celebrations.

### *Fathers' hobbies*

Many of Thea's and Bertly's drawings featured fish, stimulated by both fathers' interest in fish and the sea (Bertly's *An Octopus: BS7*, Figure 7.7; *A Shark: BH14*, Figure 7.13, Chapter 7; *A Shark in the Sea: BH21*, Figure 9.9; *An Octopus for You: BH28*, Figure 9.19, Chapter 9; Thea's *Dad Coming Home: TH20*, Figure 8.4, Image 2, Chapter 8; *The Aquarium Shop: TH23*, Figure 9.18, Chapter 9). Bertly's father owned a boat and frequently went fishing with his brothers; Bertly actively engaged in conversations about such trips and saw and ate the fish he brought home. Bertly's father also watched fish documentaries with his son, including television documentaries about sharks. Chapters 7 and 9 discussed Bertly's drawings featuring sharks and octopuses (*BS7, BH14, BH21, BH28*).

Thea's father grew up by the sea, swam, and kept aquatic fish. Thea and her father shared this interest, and Thea's drawings showed the wealth of knowledge she accrued through her observations, conversations, activities, and experiences rooted in her father's passion for fish. In her drawings of aquaria (*TH23; TH20*), Thea communicated her unique funds of knowledge. In *The Aquarium Shop* (*TH23*, Figure 9.18, Chapter 9), Thea drew two adjacent aquaria, mirroring what she had seen "in the aquarium shop next to her grandma's house." Thea conveyed what she knew about aquaria, including the necessity of providing light and seaweed ("grass"). In *Dad Coming Home* (*TH20*, Figure 8.4, Image 2, Chapter 8), which represents her father's return from work, Thea included the shrimp aquarium in their kitchen, the primary gathering place for them. Upon arriving home from work, Thea's father always spent time attending to the shrimp in the aquarium.

### *Family life, routines, and practices*

The three children's drawings reflect aspects of their family's lives. Luke made several drawings depicting quality family time, vividly conveying family enjoyment of relaxed outdoor activities: eating ice cream (*LH15*, Figure 5.10, Image 2, Chapter 5), leisurely walks (*LH18*, Figure 5.11, Image 1, Chapter 5), picnicking (*LH38*, Figure 5.11, Image 2, Chapter 5), and play-fighting with his mum (*LH54*, Figure 5.11, Image 3, Chapter 5). *Luke and Mum Play-fighting on a Picnic* (*LH54*) emerged as Luke initially wondered what to draw. His mother gently prompted: "Can we draw something of what we have done this weekend? What did we do? Where did we go?" Luke decided to draw their picnic, describing how their picnics involved "eating, drinking while seated on the grass under the shade of the trees," playing, and running around." What began as a calm scene of their picnic outing, soon evolved into a playful confrontation between Luke and his mother. Luke, who enjoyed play-fighting using imaginary guns, drew his mother as "a mama monster" engaging in a gunfight with him – an interest his mother did not share. This drawing, along with the accompanying narrative, mirrors a recurring disagreement between Luke and his mother as he sought to involve her in his imaginative play drawing:

LUKE: This is a mama monster. Ping. Ping. Ping. Pong.
MOTHER: A mama monster? Ok. What is this mama monster doing?
LUKE: Prrrrr. Playing guns.
MOTHER: Playing with guns?
LUKE: Playing guns. It is you.
MOTHER: It is me? Playing with the guns? … What is Luke doing? Is this you?
LUKE: Yes, that is me … I am firing guns. I fire you. You fire me.
MOTHER: Is that the story? I fire you and you fire me?
LUKE: Together.
MOTHER: Do you think we are having fun?
LUKE: Yes.
MOTHER: Do you think I am having fun?
LUKE: Yes.

The interaction between Luke and his mother offers a glimpse into his home experiences and ways of discipline (Riojas-Cortez, 2001). At surface level, it portrays an ordinary family picnic; it also encapsulates Luke's recurring debates with his mother about guns and shooting and his mother's ways of interrupting him to communicate her disapproval of his words and behaviour. It also shows Luke's deep appreciation for family togetherness, reinforcing the notion that children's drawings are profoundly influenced by their desire to connect (Chesworth, 2021).

*Tying the Blue Lady* (*LH24*, Figure 10.13) was discussed in Chapter 10 from the perspective of drawing as an arena for imaginative play where real-life experiences, fantasy, and myth converge. Here, we consider this drawing a reflection of how the family valued educational tours. Luke's mother explained that the cultural tour of the grand Verdala palace was intended to help their children develop an appreciation of local heritage. The history of the Verdala

## 194   Children making meaning

Palace is video-animated by the story of the *Blue Lady*, a young lady who refused to marry the man she was forced to spend her life with. Imprisoned in her room, wearing her blue wedding dress, she jumped to her death from a palace window instead of entering a loveless marriage. According to legend, the *Blue Lady* still roams the palace halls. This story fuelled Luke's imagination of fighting the *Blue Lady* to protect his family by *Tying a Blue Lady* (*LH24*, Figure 10.13). Family visits to cultural buildings enhance children's funds of knowledge (Hedges et al., 2011; Volman & Gilde, 2021).

Thea's drawings of *Me in a Muddy Puddle and Lots of Birds* (*TH14*, Figure 10.7, Chapter 10) and *Me in the Rain* (*TH15*, Figure 12.6, Image 1) reflected family outings in the countryside. Walking after rainfall, Thea and her sister enjoyed jumping in puddles; their parents understood the experiential learning gained through messy physical movement and the sense of well-being their children gained. *A McDonald's Box* (*TH26*, Figure 12.1) reflects a family outing to McDonald's after watching their father run a marathon. Thea's delight in the rare pleasure of a Happy Meal with her family and the lunchbox they received with their food is captured here, demonstrating Thea's funds of knowledge from that experience and usual family life. It symbolises a health-conscious family that seldom eats fast food and emphasises physical activity and sports, reflecting their mutual support of the father in his race. Thea's *A Wine Bottle and an Ice-cream* (*TH17*, Figure 12.2) represents "wine bottles ... and ice-cream." Thea clarified that the wine is for

*Figure 12.2* *A Wine Bottle and an Ice-cream (TH17)* – by Thea.

# Children's funds of knowledge: pedagogical considerations 195

*Figure 12.3* Grass in our Field (BH30) [1], Pizza (BH1) [2], My Mum Driving (BH37) [3] – by Bertly.

her father because "mummy does not really like it." Her mother explained that dinner guests the previous weekend brought wine and ice-cream as gifts (common gifts that people in Malta bring when invited to dinner). Thea's drawing reflects her funds of knowledge gained through this family event. Thea's drawings reflect some socio-cultural dynamics around dinner guests and the practice of gift-giving.

Bertly's family life and experiences show his interest in the weather, such as in *The Storm* (*BH16*, Figure 9.20, Chapter 9), which stems from his father's need to be aware of the weather forecast for his job. Bertly's mother monitored weather forecasts, especially during the winter, to plan her children's clothes for the next day. The weather is often featured in Bertly's drawings. Other drawings, for example, *Grass in our Field* (*BH30*, Figure 12.3, Image 1) show how Bertly's family spent weekends together, frequently featuring family time in "daddy's field" (Chapter 7).

Bertly's drawings also feature his family at home. In *Pizza* (*BH1*, Figure 12.3, Image 2), Bertly referred to the family baking pizza together, conveying stretching the dough and adding toppings typically used for making his favourite pizza, Capricciosa. The drawing sparked a conversation about the family's shared enthusiasm for cooking and the smell of their home when they baked and cooked.

*My Mum Driving* (*BH37*, Figure 12.3, Image 3) features Bertly and his sister in their car with their mother driving, depicting their weekday school run where "the three of us, myself, Jael and mum, are driving in our car ... because my father would be at work." Bertly shared this drawing with his father, who inquired, "Why didn't you draw me as well?" Bertly added his father. Bertly skilfully amalgamated his knowledge and experiences from family life and conversations into his drawings, which tangibly reflect his unique funds of knowledge built up from *his* family life (González et al., 2005).

Bertly's drawings of the family's preparations for his grandmother's birthday (*BH33*, *BH34*, and *BH35* Figure 9.15, Chapter 9), include balloons and a birthday card. Bertly, his mother, and his sister talked about the upcoming birthday celebrations, the food they would prepare, and the gift they would give their grandmother. These drawings illustrate Bertly's knowledge domain, rooted in his familiarity with his family's rituals around birthday celebrations. Such family-based drawings are indicative of the children's unique experiences of family lives and mark key moments, capturing family interests, traditions, and cultural traits, values, and beliefs (Riojas-Cortez, 2001; González et al., 2005; Hedges et al., 2011).

## Funds of knowledge: community-based influences

Richly varied community-based experiences – often instigated by families – frequently influenced children's drawings. Children's community-acquired knowledge of their geo-cultural contexts, national and international celebrations, and popular culture are reflected in their drawings.

### Geo-cultural contexts

The term "geo-cultural context" (De Rosa et al., 2018, p. 13) refers to the geographic location and characteristics of a country or region, its population, and associated social and cultural attributes, national history, landscapes, ideologies, languages, rituals, traditions, religions, food, and festivities, all of which feed into children's funds of knowledge. Geo-cultural influences emphasise that what may seem evident within one region may not hold true for others, and what carries significance in one country might appear inconsequential to another. Emblematic of the geo-cultural context of the Maltese islands, the children's drawings featured: fireworks, churches and religious statues, religious and traditional summer festas, customary cuisine, aeroplanes and boats, sunshine, and heavy rainfall. Notable events and the strong feelings stemming from the micro and macro contexts of the children's worlds are often expressed in drawings (Anning & Ring, 2004).

### Fireworks

Capturing the essence of the Maltese geo-cultural context was Bertly's *Fireworks* (*BS16*, Figure 7.1), discussed in Chapter 7. Fireworks are integral to Maltese summers. Each weekend, one or more villages or towns celebrate their patron saint in a religious feast intertwined with traditional and cultural Maltese celebrations. Each festa spans an entire week, featuring lively band marches and street food, climaxing in a religious procession of the statue of the patron saint on Sunday. Throughout the week, fireworks illuminate the skies, creating a summer-long spectacle. Bertly's community-inspired funds of knowledge were acquired from his experiences of Maltese summer festas, especially fireworks. These feed his home-acquired funds of knowledge – specifically about detonating fireworks.

Bertly's funds of knowledge acquired from his home and community included fireworks, gunshots, and the chimney in the story of *The Three Little Pigs* in his drawing-narrative of *Fireworks*. Bertly drew upon media, societal conversations, and a familiar story, blending them with communal and personal experiences, to construct an understanding of his cultural framework of fireworks, gunshots, fires, and chimneys. His depiction was imbued with a distinctive, personal hallmark infused with individualised meanings.

Tracing such meaning-making across various modes, timeframes, and spaces demonstrates that children seamlessly blend their personal, conventional, and cultural experiences – with some imagination – to construct and convey their distinct meanings (Albers, 2007), unbound by convention and fact. Children generate and refashion their ideas, developing complex chains of meaning that they express through images and narratives. Bertly entwined his personal experiences and social conventions in a drawing that provided a glimpse of his accumulated knowledge from his home and community realities. Such interplay between a child's home and community provides the tools to connect with and make meaning of their socio-cultural environments (Chesworth, 2016).

*Religious statues*

Religion plays a vital role in Maltese culture. Thea's *The Holy Mary* (*TH2*, Figure 12.4) provides some insights into her family's religious beliefs, which add depth to the interpretation of this drawing. Thea's geo-cultural context includes statues of holy and religious figures, including the Holy Mary. Maltese homes, schools, niches in streets, churches, buses, and roadside shrines hold the statues, and during religious feasts and processions, they are carried out of the churches through the streets. The statues are integral to the Maltese landscape, heritage, and traditions. Thea's drawing of the Holy Mary conveyed her understanding of her family's connection with the statue, formed from home and community influences of Catholicism.

The significance of Thea's depiction of the Holy Mary deepens when we consider her reference to a pair of statues, Saint Joseph and the Holy Mary, at the entrance to their home. Thea's mother had put the statues away sometime before, and Thea's reference to missing them suggests they meant more to her than her mother supposed. The drawing became a way for Thea to express her desire for the family's statues to be reinstated. Even though the drawing

*Figure 12.4* The Holy Mary (TH2) – by Thea.

does not feature any heart symbols, Thea's words, "I love Holy Mary. I pray to the Holy Mary," further express her love and devotional connection with the Holy Mary. Her mother was surprised that Thea drew the Holy Mary, stating, "I wouldn't have dreamt that she would ever draw them." This drawing opened a window into Thea's world, capturing something of the religious context of her home and community, and Thea's connection with religious symbolism adds depth to the interpretation of her drawing.

*Traditional and summer festas*

Summer in Malta is full of festivities. In addition to the weekly village feasts, other traditional festas, preserve traditions and promote local produce. The annual Strawberry Feast known in Maltese as "Festa Frawli," celebrating the strawberry harvest takes place near Thea's home. The festa offers opportunities to purchase fresh produce and enjoy strawberry-themed food and drinks. Traditional musical and folk dance performances entertain people while they explore stalls filled with traditional Maltese delicacies and talk with local craftspeople showcasing and selling their work. Much of this vibrant scene is

# Children's funds of knowledge: pedagogical considerations 199

captured in Thea's drawing, *A Snail Playing a Guitar* (*TH39*, Figure 9.14, Image 6, Chapter 9). The Strawberry Feast provided Thea with a rich source of information about Maltese traditions. Describing her illustration as "a male snail playing the guitar softy," Thea explained that she "thought of strawberries when I was drawing this," even though there was no strawberry in her drawing. Her description seems to be a merging of watching a male guitarist playing traditional folk music with a customary snail delicacy being eaten at the feast. This family outing immersed Thea in local community culture, and through her drawing, she processed and interpreted her experience, blending fiction and reality in her *Festa Frawli*. Thea said, "One day I will try snails. I will eat real snails," suggesting her understanding of the food eaten at the strawberry feast. Thea's community-derived funds of knowledge became "funds of identity" (Esteban-Guitart & Moll, 2014) and strengthened her sense of cultural heritage.

### Aeroplanes and boats

Several of Thea's drawings featured aeroplanes (*TS23: An Aeroplane that Flies*, Figure 6.8, Chapter 6; *TS30: Romina's plane*, Figure 9.14, Image 2; *TS18: An Aeroplane*, Figure 9.14, Image 3; *TS26: Daddy's Aeroplane*, Figure 9.21, Chapter 9) and boats (*TH8: Erica and Mum before I was Born*, Figure 6.7, Chapter 6; *TS38: A Ship*, Figure 9.5, Chapter 9; *TH15: Me in the Rain*, Figure 12.6, Image 1). In these drawings, Thea discussed family members travelling on planes or boats; her fascination with them was no doubt influenced by family travel by air and sea and the geo-cultural fabric of Malta, where planes fly daily and boats of all types and sizes sail in the harbours and surrounding sea.

Luke's *On the Gozo Ship* (*LH2*, Figure 12.5) also shows how drawing can reflect children's geo-cultural contexts. The Maltese archipelago consists of

*Figure 12.5* **On the Gozo Ship (LH2)** – by Luke.

five islands, with Malta and Gozo being the two main islands. Maltese families often visit Gozo for day trips or short breaks, while Gozitans frequently make the 20-minute journey on the 24-hour Gozo Channel ferry to Malta for work or study. The weekend prior to drawing *On the Gozo Ship*, Luke's extended family travelled by ferry to Gozo. Luke captured this experience in his drawing, which included family members looking out of portholes. While portraying a family event, this also conveys an experience that enriched Luke's understanding of the vessels he saw during the journey – a mode of transportation vital to the islands. Luke learned about the ship itself, its construction, its amenities, the noise, and the role of the captain, as well as about Gozo and its distinct characteristics. Home- and community-influenced funds of knowledge inform and enrich one another (Hedges, 2014), uniquely blended and processed with the richness of the children's active participation in multigenerational activities (González et al., 2005).

*Typical rainy weather*

Bertly's drawings often included weather (*BH16: The Storm*, Figure 9.20, Chapter 9), often highlighting daily weather conditions. Thea depicted her experiences of rainy days (*TH14: Me in a muddy puddle*, Figure 10.7; *TH15: Me in the rain*, Figure 12.6, Image 1). These and others, particularly Bertly's *Heavy Rain* (*BS12*, Figure 12.6, Image 2), are quintessential representations of rainfall in Malta. Despite being a relatively arid country known for sunshine, when it rains in Malta, it often pours heavily. As Bertly described in *Heavy Rain*, "It is the rain pouring. It is pouring heavily." During such downpours, life comes to a halt. Roads get flooded, and people rush, sometimes in a state of panic, to get home, avoiding flood-prone areas. The experience of sudden, heavy rain and strong winds depicted in Thea's drawing *My Family* (*TH22*, Figure 8.5, Image 1, Chapter 8) and Bertly's *Tank in the Wind* (*BH9*, Figure 12.6, Image 3), and the scorching sun (depicted in many of the children's drawings), are strong elements of the children's funds of knowledge.

*Maps and mapping*

Travel interests all three children. Thea seemed fascinated with journeys where roads, bridges, and tunnels connected places, mirroring the road network in Malta and how her family commuted. Thea's *A Tunnel to the Farm* (*TS29*, Figure 12.7, Image 1) illustrates a journey from Thea's home to a farm. The green corrugated paper symbolises a tunnel, vividly capturing her experience of driving through it. She explained, "This is a tunnel so that people will walk under the tunnel and will come to the farm … Once we were going to the farm and we drove under the tunnel. And we got to the farm." Thea created a road map of the journey, emphasising the importance of the tunnel in her narrative. Such drawings are boldly schematic, reflecting the dynamic movements

# Children's funds of knowledge: pedagogical considerations 201

Figure 12.6 *Me in the Rain (TH15)* [1] – by Thea; *Heavy Rain (BS12)* [2], *Tank in the Wind (BH9)* [3] – by Bertly.

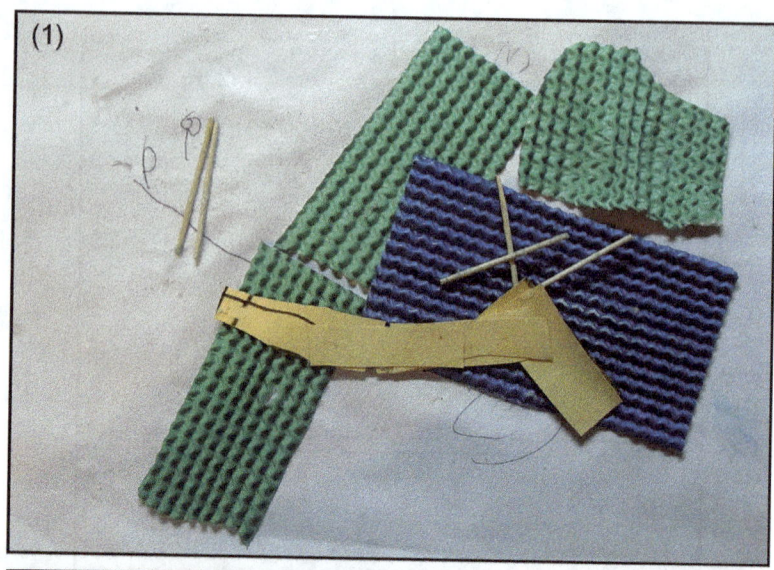

*Figure 12.7 A tunnel to the farm (TS29) [1]; Two churches, a roundabout and a swimming pool (TH33) [2] – by Thea.*

and positions that often feature in children's schematic development (Athey, 2007; Nutbrown, 2011). In *Two Churches, a Roundabout, and a Swimming Pool* (*TH33*: Figure 12.7, Image 2), Thea drew a map of the area outside her house. It featured a van driving along a "Road (that) takes you to the church. Here (green glitter glue) is a church and here (red glitter glue) is another church. This is the St Joseph chapel and this is the bigger church." In Malta, where churches are often situated in close proximity, this representation made perfect sense. Thea was referring to the small church near her home and the large church in the town where she attended school. She further elaborated on the road, saying, "The pink is the roundabout … Next to the church there is going to be a pool." Her mother clarified, "I know why you drew the swimming pool on the church square … because when it rains that area collects a lot of water and I tell them, 'The swimming pool is full.'"

Thea's unconventional maps indicate her knowledge of her surroundings – her hamlet, town, and community – and her unique perspective on her world.

*Celebrations*

Drawings made at home and school were infused with celebratory, communal, and cultural influences, functioning as both "conservators and innovators of cultural traditions" (Dyson, 2001b, p. 13). Christmas was special for them all, and even though our data collection did not span Christmas, they continued to depict Christmas-themed scenes, especially at school. A Father Christmas sack in the role-play area and Christmas wrapping paper in the drawing area seemed to sustain this interest. At home, drawing *Me Carrying a Bag Full of Candy* (*LH49*, Figure 5.1, Chapter 5), Luke portrayed himself carrying a bag full of candy, emulating Father Christmas distributing presents, a role they dramatised at school. Similarly, in *TS19: Presents or Fruit* (Figure 12.8, Image 1). Thea represented gifts exchanged during Christmas, and Bertly drew himself dressed as Father Christmas with Jael wearing a Carnival costume as Queen of Hearts (*BH24: Father Christmas and Jael Queen of Hearts*, Figure 7.11), celebrating Christmas and Carnival, respectively. Other drawings related to Carnival and Easter (both much celebrated in Malta) aligned with the timing of our study, as the children celebrated both at home and school. In a home drawing, *Jael the Witch* (*BH19*, Figure 12.8, Image 2), Bertly drew his sister Jael as an Easter witch. In *A Card for Bernadette* (*TH28*, Figure 9.16 – Images 3 & 4, Chapter 9), Thea drew herself as a flower, replicating her Carnival costume. Easter is also featured in home drawings. Bertly's *An Easter Egg* (*BH31*, Figure 12.8, Image 3) and Luke's *An Easter Egg for Me, Sausage Rolls for Mama* (*LH32*, Figure 12.8, Image 4). Bertly's *Mum and Dad* (*BH5*, Figure 10.8, Chapter 10) marks Valentine's Day (also highly celebrated in Malta), where he depicts his parents connected by a line, symbolising their love. Such drawings provided glimpses into the children's lived cultures of celebration and documented significant celebrations and memories that served as milestones in their lives (Coates & Coates, 2011).

*Figure 12.8* Presents and Fruit (TS19) [1] – by Thea; *Jael the Witch (BH19)* [2]; *An Easter Egg (BH31)* [3] – by Bertly; *An Easter Egg for Me, Sausage Rolls for Mama (LH32)* [4] – by Luke.

*Popular culture*

The influence of popular culture on children's drawings is well-established (Marsh & Millard, 2000; Coates & Coates, 2006, 2011; Marsh, 2006; Danesi, 2007; Hall, 2010b). Luke, Thea, and Bertly showed distinct knowledge of popular culture, memorising and depicting specific characters and storylines. Bertly's drawings were often influenced by Disney films such as *Jack and the Beanstalk* (*BH7*, Figure 12.9, Image 1), *Pinocchio* (*BH26*, Figure 12.9, Image 2), *Pink Panther* (MGM, 1969–1979) (*BH27*, Figure 12.9, Image 3), *Pink Panther for my Birthday* (*BH32*, Figure 7.9, Chapter 7), and *Fireman Sam* (Mattel TV, 1987) (*BH18*, Figure 7.14, Chapter 7).

Children's funds of knowledge: pedagogical considerations 205

*Figure 12.9* Jack and the Beanstalk *(BH7)* [1]; *Pinocchio (BH26)* [2]; *Pink Panther (BH27)* [3] – by Bertly.

Thea's drawings often featured witches (*TS21: The Wicked Witch*, Figure 9.8, Image 4, Chapter 9) and fairy tales imbued with magical elements like pixie dust, as in *Things Falling in my Dream* (*TS16*, Figure 9.3, Chapter 9) and *The Fairy Princess* (*TS10*, Figure 9.6, Image 6, Chapter 9). These themes appeared to be mainly influenced by traditional tales and animated cartoons, respectively.

Luke's drawings were teeming with his favourite superhero character, *Ben Ten* (e.g. *LS18: Ben Ten Fight*, Figure 4.1, Chapter 4; *LH23: I am Ben Ten*, Figure 10.14, Chapter 10). Some influences were evident when children directly drew characters or replicated scenes from related cartoons; other connections were more obscure, with children borrowing generic elements from cartoon themes, narratives, or characters to craft drawings with an original storyline.

The children's media-inspired drawings indicated how they interpreted and selectively absorbed imagery from television and books, making personally significant drawings. Engaged in a process of transformation (Ring, 2006), the children skilfully navigated between various sources, blending fact with popular culture and applying their acquired "internal structures and ideas" (Kress, 1997, p. 58) in unique drawings.

## A funds of knowledge pedagogy

Children's interests form unique funds of knowledge, acquired through their everyday encounters, wherever they are (Chesworth, 2016; Hedges, 2021). Their participation in everyday practices in their home and communities becomes pivotal in shaping their interests (Hedges, 2014), which are reconstructed in their drawings, and as the many examples in this book show, their interests are many and varied.

The children's funds of knowledge, shaped by their geo-cultural experiences and exposure to popular culture, supported how they processed and expressed their perspectives on their everyday lives and fictional worlds (Thompson, 1999; Barroqueiro, 2010; Wood & Hall, 2011). The composition and associations of drawings enabled them to use home- and community-informed funds of knowledge to show their continuities of thought, experiences, and learning across these domains. A theory of funds of knowledge that emphasises how children's interests are powerfully rooted in and shaped by their contexts is core to understanding children's meaning-making and hence, to developing child-led pedagogy in the early years (Fisher, 2024). Luke, Thea, and Bertly's rich funds of knowledge led to deeply informed drawings as they merged their contexts and experiences.

Using a funds of knowledge perspective in educational settings offers educators valuable insights into young children's cultural and cognitive understandings (Moll et al., 1992). The importance of them understanding children as individuals, knowing their families and their socio-cultural contexts cannot be overstated. Children's free drawing and drawing-narratives can give educators untold insights into the matters they are paying attention to. Such understanding is essential if early education is effectively to facilitate children's whole learning through a culturally responsive curriculum that values and embraces children's interests and the children themselves as individuals. In the context of children's socio-cultural practices, meaningful pedagogy can accordingly be built around and informed by every child's unique funds of knowledge.

What each child brings to their early education setting can be a jumping-off point for further learning. Young children are early experts in many things, having served as young apprentices to gardeners, drivers, cooks, and other adults in their lives; in their drawings, they have been pilots, engineers, animal rescuers, fairies, and rescuing superheroes! They are expert cataloguers of culture and compelling storytellers. They have shown their strong sense of social justice and humanity. They have much to offer their peers and their educators. Early years educators can craft pedagogy that respects the unique riches children bring, working with them to meaningfully enrich their learning. Educators who build on children's funds of knowledge build on firm foundations because their pedagogy will match their learners.

This means educators coming to an understanding that children must have control over their free drawings with rich, varied, and plentiful resources to create their multimodal meanings. Given space, time, and resources, children's drawings are richer and more reflective of their unique interests, critical commentary, and knowledge. Further, adult attempts to control children's drawing risks restriction of their ideas, limiting their ability to employ their funds of knowledge. Educators should resist the tendency to ask children to draw specific lesson content. This is not *drawing*, but *recording*, and whilst recording may have a place at times, this should not be regarded as - or replace - the uniqueness of free drawing.

Adopting a funds of knowledge perspective in early years settings calls for educators to be receptive and responsive to children's interests and experiences, which are rooted in their socio-cultural contexts and extend beyond school environments (Hedges et al., 2011; Volman & Gilde, 2021). Meaningful dialogues between educators, parents, and children offer educators a deeper understanding of the children's sociocultural experiences and their funds of knowledge, leading to more meaningful pedagogy (Chesworth, 2016). A funds of knowledge perspective respects children's rights as learners and enables their educators to better comprehend how children's perspectives are expressed through their drawings. They can better understand children's interests to inform their planned and spontaneous pedagogy. In early childhood settings, the development of culturally sensitive and culturally responsive curricula, shaped by the children's interests and capabilities, will enhance children's learning and engagement (Riojas-Cortez, 2001; González et al., 2005; Chesworth, 2016; Hedges, 2021). A funds of knowledge pedagogy that includes and values children's free drawing should be at the heart of early years practice.

# 13 Listening to children drawing

*Figure 13.1 Me (LS25)* – by Luke.

## Hearing the meaning-makers

Throughout this book, we have listened to three children drawing to understand more about their ways of meaning-making. Watching and listening to children as they draw is a great privilege, which provides a *portal* to their lives, their ways of thinking about their lives, and their worlds. Watching children draw helps to capture their here-and-now moments, value the importance of their drawing, and appreciate the remarkable ordinariness of their everyday experiences. As we listen to children draw, at home or in their group setting, we can better learn to believe in children, trust them more deeply, to more honestly respect their ideas, and to value - more highly - the significance of what they say and do. In our study with Luke, Thea, and Bertly, we saw their multiple modes and various ways of communicating their emotions as they represented many themes in their drawings, reflecting their lives and fantasies. We learned that children's drawings can sometimes be complex and deeply meaningful to them, and their words are often laden with sense-making, specific to their situations and contexts. Luke, Thea, and Bertly taught us how their social and cultural contexts are reflected in their drawings as we developed a deep appreciation for their ways of sign-making and came to understand meaning-making from their perspective. Time spent listening to the children as they draw can teach us how they use their drawings to create and recreate their identities, as they playfully and intently try on characters and behaviours that variously communicate and epitomise their unique lives.

In this book, we have seen the childhoods of three children through their drawings. They showed us how childhoods can be understood and communicated, from the perspective of children themselves – if we listen. We have shown that drawing is a valuable tool and a mode children use to create their unique meanings as they construct their present and imaginary identities and communicate something about themselves. If we listen sensitively to children's drawings, we can learn more about who they are, how they feel, where they belong in their communities, who their families are to them, and what is important to them. In our study, the children drew themselves into many identities: from their pasts, in relational identities of their present (e.g. *LS25: Me*, Figure 13.1), in the future, or as fantasy characters. In trying on and reflecting on their multiple identities, we see the children affirming who they have been, are, will be, and might be. In affirming their various identities, the children – as they drew – confirmed themselves as creators and curators of their worlds.

Focusing on three children over several months, at home and in their kindergarten class, has yielded a depth of perspective, homing in on the small, intricate, and intimate details of their meanings. This approach to studying young children's drawings offers new insights into how children's drawings might be perceived as a *portal* to their meaning-making. We have seen in the children's drawings the importance of drawing *in itself* and of the drawing process, with drawing-talk and narratives being crucially insightful in terms of uncovering otherwise hidden meanings and opening up a view of children's funds of knowledge.

We have also shown the importance of adults listening to children draw. Through drawing children find ways of communicating their meanings about all manner of things. Our three drawers have told some quite incredible tales in their drawings. Learning from them leads us to focus on the notion of adults as *active listeners* to drawers – adults who attend to the meanings that come through listening with their eyes and hearts, as they focus on the talk that children often use to accompany their drawing acts.

Not all children draw spontaneously and happily or feel at ease using drawings as a means of communication, meaning-making, or story-making. Some children more naturally communicate through their free play or other preferred modes. Adults need to maintain a sensitivity to individual children and be willing to listen to them in whichever modes they use, learning to listen to what each child is communicating and opening up drawing to them where possible.

Having shared the drawing lives of Luke, Thea, and Bertly, we conclude this book with some implications for all those responsible for the care, learning, and well-being of young children. In particular, we are thinking about how parents, educators, and policymakers might use what we have learned from studying the children's drawings. We offer some thoughts on drawing:

- at home
- in educational settings, and
- regarding professional development, leadership, and policy

## Nurturing identities through children's drawings

In exploring the children's meaning-making through their drawings, we witnessed the power of drawing to enhance children's self-expression, identity construction, and communication. Luke's, Thea's, and Bertly's drawings illuminated the profound reality that children are fundamentally drawers of their own identities.

Frequently, children's drawings are disregarded, misunderstood, overlooked, and underused in early childhood classrooms; especially when rigid curricula are imposed - and learning objectives are externally enforced - with little space for child-centred pedagogies or children's ideas and interests. The act of drawing is not something merely to keep children occupied between adult-directed sessions; it is how they often voice aspects of their lives. In drawing, children make sense of their experiences, relationships, and personal narratives and communicate their meanings to others. Luke, Thea, and Bertly used their drawings to articulate and represent intimate and complex personal narratives that conveyed aspects of themselves their familial connections - the things that mattered to them - the rich tapestries of their thoughts and emotions. For children, drawing can be a way of expressing both *simple* and *complex* ideas that might otherwise be left unsaid and, thus unheard. The journeys of self-discovery undertaken by Luke, Thea, and Bertly are potent and made real through their drawings. Adults (including parents, educators, researchers and psychologists) need sufficiently to understand what drawing *is* for children and the meanings they convey through their drawings.

## Drawing at home

When parents and other family members see the significance of children's drawings in understanding their worlds, the importance of spending time with children as they draw, listening to their drawing narratives, and appreciating the meanings they convey becomes clearer. Parents are perfectly placed to create a home environment that values and acknowledges their child's drawings and foster a sense of validation and exploration. Remembering that drawing is multimodal, parents can provide a space where children can draw with easy access to an array of resources such as:

- Drawing materials: different types of paper, pencils and pencil colours, pens, gel pens, markers, and crayons
- Craft materials: lollipop sticks, googly eyes, pipe cleaners, buttons, tape, scissors, stickers, ribbon, wool, glue sticks, glitter, pom poms, sequins, glue, tape and scissors
- Recycled material: cardboard, bottle caps, cork caps, packaging, fabric, buttons and magazines
- Natural materials: feathers, sand, leaves, flower petals and shells.

Such resources can be stored in a way that works for the family: on a low trolley, in a storage box, on a flat surface, on a shelf, or wherever they can be easily accessed and used. This requires that parents accept some mess from time to time and allow children control over what they want to draw and how they want to make their drawings. Parents, of course, will make their own decisions around what to provide for children and involve them in helping to clear up and tidy away after drawing. Parents can actively listen to their children as they draw, using their intimate knowledge of their children to talk with them as they respond to their drawings and engage in meaningful conversations about drawing. This active attending, with children when they draw, provides a platform for them to explore and articulate a range of themes, experiences, thoughts, and feelings and engenders a sense of validation and support. Parents who make a point of being near their children as they draw and become partners in their drawing will become increasingly attuned to their children as drawers, listening to their narratives and engaging in the process. Such parent engagement can move a drawing from an end product to be praised and possibly displayed to a deeply meaningful, active interaction through which insightful meanings are made. Parents and other family members can prompt, show interest, model, and draw alongside or with their children in an atmosphere of shared collaboration and meaning-making. Just as storytelling or reading creates a strong bond with children (Hall, 2023), closely observing them while drawing and collaborating with them can be a positive time for families. Parents who understand more about drawing as a meaning-making process can better value children's drawings, accept their children's preferred modes, and more fully enjoy their children's drawing processes, as they play an increasingly pivotal role in nurturing and affirming their children's developing identities.

## Drawing in educational settings

Like parents, educators are key influences in children's developmental journeys. When educators truly understand the value of drawing as a mode and language of communication and embrace drawing as one of Malaguzzi's "hundred languages" (Edwards et al., 1998, p. 12), they have acquired a vital pedagogical tool. Children need their educators to trust drawing as a vital and valuable process, requiring knowledge, understanding, sufficient time, and a designated space that is well-resourced, easily accessible, and comfortable for children to draw, free from distractions and interruptions. Educators who encourage children to express themselves through drawing alone or co-creating drawings with others are patient pedagogues who allow children time to think and plan their drawings, appreciate unfolding developments and changes, and let the children finish their drawing (if they wish to) at their own pace. When educators adopt a slow pedagogy around children's drawings, they can learn from engaging in unique and unfolding conversations as children develop their drawing-narratives. When drawing is an integrated element of a child-centred curriculum, educators provide children with a medium to express themselves that goes beyond expected forms of communication, and consider drawing as a significant mode for meaning-making. Where educators appreciate drawing as a social practice, they inspire the co-construction of meaning and shared understanding. Drawing affords children opportunities to engage in conversation as they construct and reconstruct the familiar and the strange, the ordinary and the extraordinary, to develop their new understandings, build shared interests, and make new meanings. When educators approach drawing in these ways, they learn more about the children they teach, their interests, and their funds of knowledge. They are also better positioned to support children's holistic development and build on what children already know and can do as they enable the next steps in learning to be taken in a socially constructed pedagogy. Recognising the diversity of identities that emerge through drawings can help educators develop their teaching strategies in ways that embrace individuality, nurture each child's emotional well-being, encourage inclusivity, and respect children's rights, so that all children can bring what they know to their drawing processes.[1]

## Professional development, leadership, and policy

Providers of initial training and continuing professional development for early childhood educators and setting leaders have a significant role in shaping the landscape of early childhood development, curriculum, and pedagogy. Recognising the intrinsic value of drawing calls for those responsible for the initial training of teachers and other educators, to consider the integration of drawing as a core focus (not a time-filling pastime) into educational curricula and pedagogy. Policymakers too, need to understand the importance of drawing to young children's learning and thus, to the training and development of educators. Such a move would be a powerful step towards acknowledging the multifaceted potential of drawing for children's cognitive, social, and emotional development. Reggio Emilia preschools value drawing to the point that every preschool has an atelierista and every teacher uses drawing as pedagogy (Vecchi, 2010). Taking Malta and England as examples, among many other countries, we see the prioritisation of formally taught literacy and numeracy early in children's lives, with their multimodal modes of communication sidelined, often un(der)valued, and misunderstood. If the importance of children's drawing were better understood, policymakers could perhaps give educators licence to use drawing as a pedagogical medium that promotes educational provision by listening to children's voices, truly understanding those voices, and creating pedagogic interactions that build on children's interests.

The importance of children's drawings requires collective responsibility. All adults responsible to children, for their living, their early education, and well-being, need to come to a point where they recognise and honour children's agency in communicating their ideas and constructing their identities. What we set out here can serve as guideposts for all adults in children's lives to acknowledge the vital role of drawing in children's early learning and development as a key means of communication for them. Providing drawing-conducive spaces at home and in group learning settings will enable children to flourish.

## Drawing is...

When adults are present during the process of drawing, comfortably attending with a child closely, in-depth, and at length from beginning to end, they can witness their movements and facial expressions and hear their accompanying dramatised vocalisations and sound effects that reflect their thinking process. This gives a multifaceted perspective on the activity, enhancing meaning. The many hours of being with Luke, Thea, and Bertly as they drew, prompted us to consider drawing from an insightful and personal perspective, as if looking through a kaleidoscope, whereby each drawing has unique patterns, symbolisations, and characteristics. New insights were gained by watching and talking with the children about their drawings, and new interpretations and meanings emerged. This leads us to view drawings through many lenses. We suggest that drawing is...

- *Meaningful*: Communicating a child's understanding of their experiences.
- *Fluid*: Children continuously change, shift, transform and edit to improve, clarify, articulate, and re-present their drawing and related emergent meaning more effectively.
- *A conversation*: Children, the available material, colour, mood, and thoughts are in constant conversation to create a visual representation. Drawing is a conversation between child-child and child-adult, who discuss the drawing and its evolving meaning and, in the process, inspire each other.

- *A narrative*: A story – what happened, what might happen – real, imagined, or an amalgam; a story of joy, sadness, fear, courage, pain, and hope.
- *A portal*: A window to self-thought, self-reflection, self-expression, and a child's perception of the world, of others, and of themselves; a gateway to what they know, what they think, and what they are feeling; an entry to their world, to issues of importance to them, to their experiences.
- *Identity*: A representation of a child's personality; who they are in the present, were in the past, or might be in the future, both real and imagined.
- *Dynamic:* Action: movement, gestures, facial expressions, vocalisations, sound effects, narratives, and silence communicate meaning more effectively.

## Identifying young drawers…

Seeing young drawers individually, respects their rights to unique and respected personhood. Through closely attending to children when they draw and studying how they develop and interact with their drawings, we suggest nuanced perspectives on children as drawers, whereby young drawers can be identified as many different types of drawers:

- *Conductor:* As a conductor of an orchestra who unifies performers, sets the tempo, and shapes the sound of the music while controlling its interpretation and pace, a child draws with rhythm, unifying the objects and figures through a theme or story, shaping the drawing with a unique and distinctive identity while controlling its representation and interpretation.
- *Film director:* As a film director who casts actors, interprets scripts, and identifies a location while ensuring a cohesive and visually appealing final production, a child selects and draws the characters, sets a background and context to create a story or a text that is cohesive and visually appealing and which can be interpreted by others.
- *Set designer:* As a set designer who designs the scenery and creates the environment for a drama, including props and special effects, and communicates ideas to other designers, a child draws the scenery of their illustration, creating the background, while communicating their ideas to other drawers and supporting their narration with sound effects and vocalisations.
- *Novelist:* As a novelist who chooses a topic and writes fiction, a child chooses the topic of their drawing and draws stories, bringing what they know from their experience or imagination to the drawing.
- *Structural engineer:* As a structural engineer who breaks down difficult problems into smaller, more manageable parts to find a solution, a child works out a solution to the problems they encounter in their drawings, identifying the best material to signify their meaning, solving a problem in their drawing by drawing an alternative escape route or using their drawings as a platform for conflict resolution, and finding a peaceful solution to a disagreement between characters they draw.

- *Inventor:* As an inventor designs or produces new creations, a child invents real and imaginary worlds and innovative objects in drawings.
- *Artist:* As an artist strives to communicate ideas or feelings through art, working with different materials to embellish their art, a child communicates thoughts and emotions through drawing, decorating it to include detail and embellishment.
- *Scriptwriter or narrator:* As a scriptwriter or narrator creates storylines, a child supports a drawing with elaborate narratives, stories of events and experiences, or periods of silence, that bring detail and a deeper understanding of the drawing.
- *Performer:* As a performer entertains their audience with acting, singing, or dancing, a child supports their drawing with movement, acting, and dramatisation to engage them while giving more meaning to the drawing.

Whichever role might best fit a child, according to their drawer behaviours and traits we observe, we can see children creating improvised and complex stories full of personal thoughts, feelings and universal moral qualities. Children often draw themselves a solution to the problem they have drawn themselves into: objects are given mouths to speak, a rope falls from the sky, a ghost is tied up, and a button makes a plane land. Children bring their personal theories to their drawing stories.

## Finally…

The study reported in this book, investigated the multiple layers of meaning-making that young children create and communicate through their drawings. It contributes to understanding the richness of young children's unique meaning-making processes. We have listened to Luke's, Thea's, and Bertly's narratives, subjective interpretations, poignant silences, and ways of meaning-making. In so doing, we have uncovered insights into how they used drawing as a meaningful space. We have seen how, in drawing, they voiced their emotions and ideas and communicated their knowledge and theories. We better understand the transformative and agentive processes that they used to construct and mediate their identities. We urge everyone privileged to spend time in young children's company to listen to them as they draw their meanings and share their lives.

# References

Adams, E. (2003). Power drawing. *International Journal of Art and Design Education* 21(3), 220–233. https://doi.org/10.1111/1468-5949.00319

Adams, E. (2004). *Power drawing: Space and place*. The Campaign for Drawing.

Adams, E. (2012). The Campaign for Drawing. In H. Barbosa & J. Quental (Eds.), *Proceedings of the 2nd International Conference of Art, Illustration and Visual Culture in Infant and Primary Education* (p. 26–32). Blucher. https://doi.org/10.5151/edupro-aivcipe-06

Ahmad, J. F. (2018). Children's drawings in different cultures: An analysis of five-year-old Jordanian children's drawings. *International Journal of Early Years Education* 26(3), 249–258. https://doi.org/10.1080/09669760.2018.1444587

Ahn, J. (2006). *Learning through representation: Young children's meaning-making via narratives*. [Doctoral dissertation, University of British Columbia, Vancouver, Canada]. https://circle.ubc.ca/handle/2429/18227

Ahn, J., & Filipenko, M. (2007). Narrative, imaginary play, art and self: Intersecting worlds. *Early Childhood Education Journal* 34(4), 279–289.

Aiello, G. (2020). Inventorising, situating, transforming: Social semiotics and data visualisation. In M. Engebretsen & H. Kennedy (Eds.), *Data visualisation in society* (pp. 49–62). Amsterdam University Press. https://doi.org/10.1515/9789048543137-007 https://library.oapen.org/bitstream/id/da811a79-99fd-4ad7-b52e-45076a32beb4/9789048543137.pdf

Albers, P. (2007). *Finding the artist within: Creating and reading visual texts in the English language arts classroom*. International Reading Association.

Alderson, P., & Morrow, V. (2011). *The ethics of research with children and young people: A practical handbook*. Sage Publications.

Allen, G. (2005). Research ethics in a culture of risk. In A. Farrell (Ed.), *Ethical research with children* (pp. 15–26). Open University.

Amanti, C. (2005). Beyond a beads and feathers approach. In N. Gonzalez, C. L. Moll, & C. Amanti (Eds.), *Funds of knowledge: Theorising practices in households, communities and classrooms* (pp. 131–142). Lawrence Erlbaum Associates.

Anderson, J. K., Ellis, J. P., & Jones, A. M. (2014). Understanding early elementary children's conceptual knowledge of plant structure and function through drawings. *CBE - Life Sciences Education 13*, 375–386.

Anning, A. (2002). Conversations around young children's drawing: The impact of the beliefs of significant others at home and school. *International Journal of Art & Design in Education 21*(3), 197–208.

Anning, A., & Ring, K. (2004). *Making sense of children's drawings*. Open University.

Archer, A., & Newfield, D. (2013). Challenges and opportunities of multimodal approaches to education in South Africa. In A. Archer & D. Newfield (Eds.), *Multimodal approaches to research and pedagogy: Recognition, resources and access* (pp. 1–18). Routledge.

Athey, C. (1990). *Extending thought in young children*. Paul Chapman.

Athey, C. (2007). *Extending thought in young children* (2nd ed.). Paul Chapman.

Atkinson, D. (2002). *Arts in education: Identity and practice. Landscapes: The arts, aesthetics, and education*. Kluwer Academic Publishers.

Atkinson, D. (2009). How children use drawing. In S. Hearne, S. Cox, & R. Watts (Eds.), *Readings in primary art education* (pp. 139–152). Intellect Books.

Bakhtin, M. M. (1981). *The dialogic imagination: Four essays* (C. Emerson & M. Holquist, Trans.). In M. Holquist (Ed.), University of Texas Press.

Bakr, F. S. (2019). How children express their happiness through drawing. *Multi-knowledge Electronic Comprehensive Journal for Education and Science Publications 26*, 1–10.

Banks, M. (2001). *Visual methods in social research*. Sage.

Barroqueiro, R. (2010). Language and art in early childhood: An examination of form, content and social context. *International Art in Early Childhood 2(1)*, 1–16.

Bateman, J., Wildfeuer, J., & Hiippala, T. (2017). *Multimodality: Foundations, research and analysis – A problem-oriented introduction*. De Gruyter.

Bearne, E. (2009). Multimodality, literacy and texts: Developing a discourse. *Journal of Early Childhood Literacy 9(2)*, 156-187.

Berthelsen, D. (2009). Participatory learning: Issues for research and practice. In D. Berthelsen, J. Brownlee, & E. Johansson (Eds.), *Participatory learning in the early years: Research and pedagogy* (pp. 1–11). Routledge Taylor & Francis.

Bezemer, J. (2021). Social semiotics: Theorising meaning-making. In D. Nestel, G. Reedy, L. McKenna, & S. Gough (Eds.), *Clinical education for the health professions: Theory and practice* (pp. 1–18). Springer. https://doi.org/10.1007/978-981-13-6106-7_26-1

Bezemer, J., & Cowan, K. (2021). Exploring reading in social semiotics: Theory and methods. *International Journal of Primary, Elementary and Early Years Education 49(1)*, 107.

Bezemer, J., & Kress, G. (2008). Writing in multimodal texts: A social semiotic account of designs for learning. *Written Communication 25(2)*, 166–195. https://doi.org/10.1177/0741088307313177

Bezemer, J., & Kress, G. (2016). *Multimodality, learning and communication: A social semiotic frame*. Routledge.

Bissex, G. L. (1980). *GNYS AT WRK: A child learns to write and read*. Harvard University.

Blagdanic, S., Kadijevic, G. M., & Kovacevic, Z. (2019). Gender stereotypes in preschoolers' image of scientists. *European Early Childhood Education Research Journal 27(2)*, 272–284. https://doi.org/10.1080/1350293X.2019.1579551

Bland, D. (2018). Using drawing in research with children: Lessons from practice. *International Journal of Method in Education 41(3)*, 342–352. https://doi.org/10.1080/1743727X.2017.1307957

Bleiker, C. A. (1999). The development of self through art: A case for early art education. *Art Education 52(3)*, 48–53.

Blunden, A. (2014). *Notes on perezhivanie.* https://www.ethicalpolitics.org/seminars/perezhivanie.htm

Blunden, A. (2016). Perezhivanie: From the dictionary of psychology. *Mind, Culture and Activity 23*(4), 272–273. https://doi.org/10.1080/10749039.2016.1225310

Bock, Z. (2016). Multimodality, creativity and children's meaning-making: Drawings, writings, imaginings. *Stellenbosch Papers in Linguistics Plus 49*, 1–21. https://doi.org/10.5842/49-0-669

Bourne, J., & Jewitt, C. (2003). Orchestrating debate: A multimodal analysis of classroom interaction. *Reading: Literacy and Language 37*(2), 64–72.

Boyatzis, C., & Albertini, G. (2000). A naturalistic observation of children drawing: Peer collaboration processes and influences in children's art. *New Directions for Child and Adolescent Development 90*, 31–48. https://doi.org/10.1002/cd.23220009003

Brechet, C. (2015). Representation of romantic love in children's drawings: Age and gender differences. *Social Development 24*(3), 640–658. https://doi.org/10.1111/sode.12113

British Educational Research Association, BERA. (2018). *Ethical guidelines for educational research* (4th ed.). https://study.sagepub.com/sites/default/files/bera_ethical_guidelines_2018_4th_ed.pdf

Brockmeier, J. (2001). Texts and other symbolic spaces. *Mind, Culture, and Activity 8*(3), 215–232.

Brooks, M. (2004). Drawing: The social construction of knowledge. *Australian Journal of Early Childhood 29*(2), 41–49.

Brooks, M. (2005). Drawing to learn. Drawing as a unique mental development tool for young children: Interpersonal and intrapersonal dialogues. *Contemporary Issues in Early Childhood 6*(1), 80–91.

Brooks, M. (2009a). Drawing to learn. In M. Narey (Ed.), *Making meaning: Constructing multimodal perspective of language, literacy and learning through arts-based early childhood education* (pp. 9–30). Springer.

Brooks, M. (2009b). Drawing, visualisation and young children's exploration of "big ideas." *International Journal of Science Education 31*(3), 319–341.

Brooks, M. (2009c). What Vygotsky can teach us about young children's drawing. *International Art in Early Childhood Research Journal 1*(1), 1–13.

Bruner, J. (1986). *Actual minds, possible worlds.* Harvard College.

Bruner, J. (1996). *The culture of education.* Harvard University.

Bucknall, S. (2014). Doing qualitative research with children and young people. In A. Clark, R. Flewitt, M. Hammersley, & M. Robb (Eds.), *Understanding research with children and young people* (pp. 69–84). Sage.

Burkitt, E., Watling, D., & Message, H. (2019). Expressivity in children's drawings of themselves for adult audiences with varied authority and familiarity. *British Journal of Developmental Psychology 37*, 354–368. https://psycnet.apa.org/doi/10.1111/bjdp.12278

Capruso, M., Buratta, L., & Mazzeschi, C. (2022). Primary and middle-school children's drawings of lockdown in Italy. *Frontier Psychology 13*. https://doi.org/10.3389/fpsyg.2022.982654

Capurso, M., di Castelbianco, F. B., & Di Renzo, M. (2021). "My life in the hospital": Narratives of children with a medical condition. *Continuity in Education 2*, 4–25. https://doi.org/10.5334/cie.12

Cartoon Network. (2013). *Cartoonito.* Turner Sports & Entertainment digital network. https://cartoonito.cartoonnetwork.com.au/

Chandler, D. (2007). *Semiotics: The basics* (2nd ed.). Routledge.

Chesworth, L. (2016). A funds of knowledge approach to examining play interests: Listening to children's and parents' perspectives. *International Journal of Early Years Education 24*(3), 294–308. https://doi.org/10.1080/09669760.2016.1188370

Chesworth, L. (2021). Observing, recognising and responding to children's funds of knowledge and interests. In Early Years Coalition. *Birth to five matters: Non-statutory guidance for the early years foundation stage: Early education.* https://birthto5matters.org.uk/wp-content/uploads/2021/03/Observing-recognising-and-responding-to-Childrens-funds-of-knowledge-and-intrests.pdf

Christmann, G. B. (2008). The power of photographs of buildings in the Dresden urban discourse. Towards a visual discourse analysis. *Qualitative Social Research 9*(3), Art 11, 1–18. https://www.qualitative-research.net/fqs/

Christodoulakis, N., Vidal Carulla, C., & Adbo, K. (2021). *Perezhivanie* and its application within early childhood science education research. *Education Science 11*, 813. https://doi.org/10.3390/educsci11120813

Clark, A. (2005). Listening to and involving young children: A review of research and practice. *Early Child Development and Care 175*(6), 489–505.

Clark, A. (2007). A hundred ways of listening: Gathering children's perspectives of their early childhood environment. *Young Children 62*(3), 76–81.

Clark, A., & Moss, P. (2001). *Listening to young children: The Mosaic Approach.* National Children's Bureau and Joseph Rowntree Foundation.

Coates, E. (2002). 'I forgot the Sky!' Children's stories contained within their drawings. *International Journal of Early Years Education 10*(1), 21–35.

Coates, E., & Coates, A. (2006). Young children talking and drawing. *International Journal of Early Years Education 14*(3), 221–241. https://doi.org/10.1080/09669760600879961

Coates, E., & Coates, A. (2011). The subjects and meanings of young children's drawings. In D. Faulkner & E. Coates (Eds.), *Exploring children's creative narratives* (pp. 86–110). Routledge.

Coates, E., & Coates, A. (2020). Images in words and pictures: Issues arising from a shared experience of talking and drawing. *Children & Society 35*, 244–258. https://doi.org/10.1111/chso.12423

Cope, B., & Kalantzis, M. (2000). Introduction. Multiliteracies: The beginnings of an idea. In B. Cope & M. Kalantzis (Eds.), *Multiliteracies: Literacy learning and the design of social futures* (pp. 3–8). Routledge, Taylor & Francis.

Cox, M. (1997). *Drawings of people by the under-5s.* Falmer Press.

Cox, M. (2005a). Intention and meaning in young children's drawing. *International Journal of Art & Design Education 24*(2), 115–125.

Cox, M. (2005b). *The pictorial world of the child.* Cambridge University.

Craft, A. R., & Chappell, K. A. (2016). Possibility thinking and social change in primary schools. *Education 3-13, 44*(4), 407–425. https://doi.org/10.1080/03004279.2014.961947

D'warte, J., & Woodrow, C. (2023). Engaging methods for exploring 'Funds of identity' in early childhood contexts. *Education Science 13*(4), 1–13. https://doi.org/10.3390/educsci13010004

Danesi, M. (2007). *The quest for meaning: A guide to semiotic theory and practice.* University of Toronto.

Danielsson, K., & Selander, S. (2021). *Multimodal texts in disciplinary education: A comprehensive framework.* Springer. https://link.springer.com/book/10.1007/978-3-030-63960-0

David, M., Edwards, R., & Alldred, P. (2001). Children and school-based research: 'Informed consent' or 'educated consent'? *British Educational Research Journal 27*(3), 347–365.

Davis, J. H. (2005). *Framing education as art: The octopus has a good day*. Teachers' College.

De Rosa, A. S., Dryjanska, L., & Bocci, E. (2018). Evaluative dimensions of urban tourism in capital cities by first-time visitors. In M. Khosrow-Pour (Ed.), *Encyclopedia of information science and technology* (4th ed.). https://doi.org/10.4018/978-1-5225-2255-3.

De Ruyter, D., & Conroy, J. (2002). The formation of identity: The importance of ideals. *Oxford Review of Education 28*(4), 509–522.

Deguara, J. (2015). *Meaning-making in young children's drawings* (Ethos ID: uk.bl.ethos.707067). [Doctoral dissertation, University of Sheffield, UK]. White Rose eTheses Online https://etheses.whiterose.ac.uk/9980/

Deguara, J. (2019). Young children's drawings: A methodological tool for data analysis. *Journal of Early Childhood Research, 17*(2), 157–174. https://doi.org/10.1177%2F1476718X18818203

Disney. (1940). *Pinocchio*. https://www.disneyplus.com/en-mt/movies/pinocchio/3awzEJp1S6xg

Disney. (2005–2010). *Little Einsteins*. https://www.disneyplus.com/en-mt/series/little-einsteins/1G9YmlC37TnO

Disney. (2011). *Imagination movers*. https://www.disneyplus.com/en-mt/series/imagination-movers/24omOqtoud5P

Disney. (2014). *The new adventures of Winnie the Pooh*. https://www.disney.co.uk/winnie-the-pooh/characters/

Disney. (2015). *Jake and the never land pirates*. https://www.disney.co.uk/disney-junior/jake-and-the-never-land-pirates/index.jsp

Djonov, E., & Zhao, S. (2017). Social semiotics: A Theorists and a theory in retrospect and prospect. In S. Zhao, E. Djonov, A., Björkvall, & M. Boeriis (Eds.), *Advancing multimodal and critical discourse studies* (pp. 1–7). Routledge. https://doi.org/10.4324/9781315521015

Drake, J. E. (2023). How children can use drawing to regulate their emotions. *Theory into Practice 62*(2), 181–192. 1080/00405841.2023.2202132

Drake, J. E., & Winner, E. (2013). How children use drawing to regulate their emotions. *Cognition and Emotion 27*(3), 512–520. https://doi.org/10.1080/02699931.2012.720567

Dressman, M. (2020). Multimodality and language learning. In M. Dressman & R. W. Sadler (Eds.). *The handbook of informal language learning* (pp. 39–55). Wiley.

Driessnack, M. (2006). Draw-and-tell conversation with children about fear. *Qualitative Health Research 16*(10), 1414–1435. https://doi.org/10.1177/1049732306294127

Dyson, A. H. (1986). Transitions and tensions: Interrelationships between the drawing, talking and dictating of young children. *Research into the Teaching of English 20*(4), 379–409.

Dyson, A. H. (1989). *Multiple worlds of child writers: Friends learning to write*. Teachers' College.

Dyson, A. H. (1993a). From prop to mediator: The changing role of written language in children's symbolic repertoires. In B. Spodek & O. N. Saracho (Eds.), *Yearbook in early childhood education Volume 4: Language and literacy in early childhood education* (pp. 21–41). Teachers' College.

Dyson, A. H. (1993b). *Social worlds of children learning to write in an urban primary school*. Teachers College, Columbia University.

Dyson, A. H. (1995). Writing children: Reinventing the development of childhood literacy. *Written Communication 12*(1), 4–46. https://doi.org/10.1177/0741088395012001002

Dyson, A. H. (1997). *Writing superheroes, contemporary childhood, popular culture and classroom literacy*. Teachers College.

Dyson, A. H. (2001a). Donkey Kong in Little Bear country: A first grader's composing developing m the media spotlight. *The Elementary School Journal 101*(4), 417–433.

Dyson, A. H. (2001b). Where are the childhoods in childhood literacy? An exploration in outer (school) space. *Journal of Early Childhood Literacy 1*(1), 9–39. https://doi.org/10.1177/14687984010011002

Dyson, A. H. (2002). The drinking God factor: A writing development remix for "all" children. *Written Communication 19*(4), 545–577. https://doi.org/10.1177/074108802238009

Dyson, A. H. (2003). "Welcome to the jam" popular culture, school literacy, and the making of childhoods. *Harvard Educational Review 73*(3), 328–361. https://doi.org/10.17763/haer.73.3.d262234083374665

Dyson, A. H. (2010). Writing childhoods under construction: Re-visioning 'copying' in early childhood. *Journal of Early Childhood Literacy 10*(1), 7–31.

Eckhoff, A. (2019). *Participatory research with young children*. Springer.

Eckhoff, A., & Urbach, J. (2008). Understanding imaginative thinking during childhood: Sociocultural conceptions of creativity and imaginative thought. *Early Childhood Education Journal 36*, 179–185.

Edmiston, B. (2008). *Forming ethical identities in early childhood play*. Routledge, Taylor & Francis.

Edmiston, B. (2010). Playing with children, answering with our lives: A Bakhtinian approach to coauthoring ethical identities in early childhood. *British Journal of Educational Studies 58*(2), 197–211. https://doi.org/10.1080/00071000903522484

Edwards, C., Gandini, L., & Forman, G. (1998). Introduction: Background and starting points. In C. Edwards, L. Gandini, & G. Forman (Eds.), *The hundred languages of children: The Reggio Emilia approach –advanced reflections* (2nd ed., pp. 5–25). Ablex.

Egan, B. A. (1995). How do children perceive the activity of drawing? Some initial observations of children in an infant school. *IDATER: International conference on design and technology educational research and curriculum development*. https://dspace.lboro.ac.uk/dspace-jspui/bitstream/2134/1505/3/egan95.pdf

Egan, K. (1998). *The educated mind: How cognitive tools shape our understanding*. University of Chicago.

Einarsdottir, J., Dockett, S., & Perry, B. (2009). Making meaning: Children's perspectives expressed through drawings. *Early Child Development and Care 179*(2), 217.

Eisner, E. W. (2013). Forward: The development of graphic representation. In A. Machón (Ed.), *Children's drawings: The genesis and nature of graphic representation. A developmental study* (pp. 13–15). Fibulas.

Esteban-Guitart, M., & Moll, L. C. (2014). Funds of identity: A new concept based on the Funds of Knowledge approach. *Culture & Psychology 20*(1), 31–48. https://doi.org/10.1177/1354067X13515934

Fargas-Malet, M., McSherry, D., Larkin, E., & Robinson, C. (2010). Research with children: Methodological issues and innovative techniques. *Journal of Early Childhood Research 8*(2), 175–192. https://doi.org/10.1177/1476718X09345412

Farokhi, M., & Hashemi, M. (2011). The analysis of children's drawings: Social, emotional, physical and psychological aspects. *Procedia – Social and Behavioral Science 30*, 2219–2224. https://doi.org/10.1016/j.sbspro.2011.10.433

Ferholt, B. (2009). *The development of cognition, emotion, imagination and creativity as made visible through adult-child joint play: Perezhivanie through playworlds* (ProQuest ID: Ferholt_ucsd_0033D_10316. Merrit ID: ark:/20775/bb48134289). [Doctoral dissertation, University of California, San Diego]. ProQuest Dissertation Publishing https://escholarship.org/uc/item/0w22g2jd

Ferreiro, E., & Teberosky, A. (1982). Literacy before schooling. Heinemann.

Fisher, J. (2024). *Starting from the Child?: Teaching and learning fom 3-7* (5th ed.). Open University.

Flewitt, R. (2005). Is every child's voice heard? Researching the different ways 3-year-old children communicate and make meaning at home and in a preschool playgroup. *Early Years 25*(3), 207–222. 1080/09575140500251558

Flewitt, R. (2006). Using video to investigate preschool classroom interaction: Education research assumptions and methodological practices. *Visual Communication 5*(1), 25–50.

Flewitt, R. (2008). Multimodal literacies. In J. Marsh & E. Hallet (Eds.), *Desirable literacies: Approaches to language & literacy in the early years* (2nd ed.,) (pp. 122–139). Sage.

Fourie, J. S. (2020). *Using drawings to understand the causes of anger in young children* [Masters dissertation, University of Pretoria]. https://repository.up.ac.za/bitstream/handle/2263/78453/Fourie_Using_2020.pdf?sequence=1&isAllowed=y

Frisch, N. S. (2006). Drawing in preschools: A didactic experience. *International Journal of Art & Design Education 25*(1), 74–85.

Fulková, M., & Tipton, T. M. (2011). Diversifying discourse: The influence of visual culture on children's perception and creation of art. In D. Faulkner & E. Coates (Eds.), *Exploring children's creative narratives* (pp. 132–156). Routledge.

Gallacher, L. A., & Gallagher, M. (2008). Methodological immaturity in childhood research? Thinking through 'participatory methods.' *Childhood 15*(4), 499–516. https://doi.org/10.1177/0907568208091672

Gardner, H. (1980). *Artful scribbles: The significance of children's drawings*. Basic Books.

Gardner, H. (1982). *Art, mind and brain: A cognitive approach to creativity*. Basic Books.

Golomb, C. (2002). *Child art in context: A cultural and comparative perspective*. American Psychological Association.

Golomb, C. (2004). *The child's creation of a pictorial world*. Lawrence Erlbaum.

González, N. (2005). Beyond culture: The hybridity of funds of knowledge. In N. Gonzalez, C. L. Moll, & C. Amanti (Eds.), *Funds of knowledge: Theorising practices in households, communities and classrooms* (pp. 29–46). Lawrence Erlbaum.

González, N., Moll, L. C., & Amanti, C. (Eds.). (2005). *Funds of knowledge: Theorising practices in households, communities and classrooms*. Lawrence Erlbaum.

Goodman, M. J. S. (2018). *Children draw: A guide to why, when and how children draw*. Reaktion Books.

Graham, M. S., & Benson, S. (2010). A springboard rather than a bridge: Diving into multimodal literacy. *English Journal 100*(2), 93–97.

Groundwater-Smith, S., Dockett, S., & Bottrell, D. (2015). *Participatory research with children and oung people*. Sage.

Hagood, M. C. (2008). Intersections of popular culture, identities and new literacies research. In J. Cairo, M. Knobel, C. Lankshear, & D. J. Leu (Eds.), *Handbook of research on new literacies* (pp. 531–551). Lawrence Erlbaum.

Hall, E. (2008, September). *"My brain printed it out!" Drawing, communication, and young children: A discussion.* Paper presented at the British Educational Research Association Annual Conference 2008, Heriot-Watt University, Edinburgh.

Hall, E. (2009). Mixed messages: The role and value of drawing in early education. *International Journal of Early Years Education 17*(3), 179–190.

Hall, E. (2010a). Identity and young children's drawings: Power, agency, control and transformation. In P. Broadhead, J. Howard, & E. Wood (Eds.), *Play and learning in the early years* (pp. 95–111). Sage.

Hall, E. (2010b). *The communicative potential of young children's drawings* [Doctoral dissertation, University of Exeter, United Kingdom]. https://ore.exeter.ac.uk/repository/handle/10036/105041

Hall, E. (2011). Identity and young children's drawings: Power, agency, control and transformation. In P. Broadhead, J. Howard, & E. Wood (Eds.), *Play and learning in the early years* (pp. 95–112). Sage.

Hall, M. (2023). 'That was our little five minutes of shush … a kiss and a cuddle and have our books': Sensory affinities among families during shared reading with children. *Sociology.* https://doi.org/10.1177/00380385231217627

Halliday, M. A. K. (1978). *Language as social semiotic: The social interpretation of language and meaning.* Edward Arnold.

Halliday, M. A. K. (1994). Language as social semiotic. In J. Maybin (Ed.), *Language and literacy in social practice.* The Open University.

Han, S. (2011). Education, semiotics, and the virtual world of second life. *The International Journal of Arts Education 9*(2), pp. 53–73. https://ed.arte.gov.tw/uploadfile/periodical/3054_9-2-p.53-73.pdf

Harcourt, D. (2011). A phased approach to researching with young children: Lessons from Singapore and beyond. *Early education and development 22*(5), 818–838. https://doi.org/10.1080/10409289.2011.596462

Harcourt, D., & Conroy, H. (2011). Informed consent: Processes and procedures seeking research partnerships with young children. In D. Harcourt, B. Perry, & T. Waller (Eds.), *Researching young children's perspectives: Debating the ethics and dilemmas of educational research with children* (pp. 38–51). Routledge Taylor & Frances.

Harcourt, D., & Sargeant, J. (2011). The challenges of conducting ethical research with children. *Education Inquiry 2*(3), 421–436.

Hartle, L., & Jaruszewicz, C. (2009). Rewiring and networking language, literacy and learning through the arts: Developing fluencies in technology. In M. Narey (Ed.), *Making meaning: Constructing multimodal perspectives of language, literacy and learning through arts-based early childhood education* (pp. 187–206). Springer.

Hawkins, B. (2002). Children's drawing, self-expression, identity and imagination. *International Journal of Art and Design Education 21*(3), 209–219.

Hedges, H. (2011). Rethinking Sponge Bon and Ninja Turtles: Popular culture as funds of knowledge for curriculum co-construction. *Australasian Journal of Early Childhood 36*(1), 25–29.

Hedges, H. (2014). Young children's 'working theories': Building and connecting understandings. *Journal of Early Childhood Research 12*(1), 35–49. https://doi.org/10.1177/1476718X13515417

Hedges, H. (2021). Children's interests: Challenging taken-for-granted understandings. *Early Education Journal* 93.
Editor By Cathy Nutbrown: https://app.sheepcrm.com/early-education/journal/93/

Hedges, H. (2021). Children's interests: Challenging taken-for-granted understandings. *Early Education Journal*, (Children's Interest, Spring 2021), Issue 93, pp. 4–6.

Hedges, H., Cullen, J., & Jordan, B. (2011). Early years curriculum: Funds of knowledge as a conceptual framework for children's interest. *Journal of Curriculum Studies* 43(2), 185–205. https://doi.org/10.1080/00220272.2010.511275

Hedges, H., & Jones, A. (2012). Children's working theories: The neglected sibling of Te Whāriki's learning outcomes. *Early Childhood Folio* 16(1), 34–39.

Hibbert, M. (2013). Video production and multimodal play. In L. Vasudevan & T. Dejaynes, (Eds.), *Arts, media, and justice: Multimodal explorations with youth*. Peter Lang.

Higgins, L. T. (2004). Cultural effects on the expression of some fears by Chinese and British female students. *The Journal of Genetic Psychology* 165(1), 37–50. https://doi.org/10.3200/GNTP.165.1.37-50

Holland, D., Lachicotte, W., Skinner, D., & Cain, C. (1998). *Identity and agency in cultural worlds*. Harvard University.

Holliday, R. (2004). Reflecting the self. In C. Knowles & P. Sweetman (Eds.), *Picturing the social landscape: Visual methods and the sociological imagination* (pp. 49–64). Routledge, Taylor & Francis.

Hope, G. (2008). *Thinking and learning through drawing in primary classrooms*. Sage.

Hopperstad, M. H. (2008a). How children make meaning through drawing and play. *Visual Communication* 7(1), 77–96.

Hopperstad, M. H. (2008b). Relationships between children's drawing and accompanying peer interaction in teacher-initiated drawing sessions. *International Journal of Early Years Education* 16(2), 133–150.

Hopperstad, M. H. (2010). Studying meaning in children's drawings. *Journal of Early Childhood Literacy* 10(4), 430–452. https://doi.org/10.1177/1468798410383251

Hull, G. A., & Nelson, M. E. (2005). Locating the semiotic power of multimodality. *Written Communication* 22(2), 224–261.

International Management Group. (IMG). (2014). *The world's strongest man*. https://www.theworldsstrongestman.com/results/

Ivashkevich, O. (2009). Children's drawing as a sociocultural practice: Remaking gender and popular culture. *Studies in Art Education: A Journal of Issues and Research* 51(1), 50–63. https://www.academia.edu/2551828/Childrens_Drawing_as_a_Sociocultural_Practice_Remaking_Gender_and_Popular_Culture

James, A., & Prout, A. (2015). Introduction. In A. James & A. Prout (Eds.), *Constructing and reconstructing childhood: Contemporary issues in the sociological study of childhood* (3rd ed., pp. 1–6). Routledge Falmer.

Jenkins, A. J. (2010). *The rainbow colours song*. https://www.youtube.com/watch?v=tRNy2i75tCc

Jewitt, C. (2002). The move from page to screen: The multimodal reshaping of school English. *Visual Communication* 1(2), 171–195.

Jewitt, C. (2008). Multimodality and literacy in school classrooms. *Review or Research in Education* 32, 241–267.

Jewitt, C. (2009a). An introduction to multimodality. In C. Jewitt (Ed.), *The Routledge handbook of multimodal analysis* (pp. 14–27). Routledge, Taylor & Francis.

Jewitt, C. (2009b). Different approaches to multimodality. In C. Jewitt (Ed.), *The Routledge handbook of multimodal analysis* (pp. 28–39). Routledge, Taylor & Francis.

Jewitt, C., Bezemer, J., & O'Halloran, K. (2016). *Introducing multimodality*. Routledge.

Jewitt, C., & Forceville, C. (2021). *Metaphor. Glossary of multimodal terms*. MODE. National Centre for Research Methods. https://multimodalityglossary.wordpress.com/metaphor/

Jewitt, C., Kress, G., Ogborn, J., & C. Tsatsarelis, (2000). Teaching and learning: Beyond language. *Teaching Education 11*(3), 327–341. https://doi.org/10.1080/713698977

Jewitt, C., & Oyama, R. (2001). Visual social semiotics. In T. Van Leeuwen & C. Jewitt, (Eds.), *A handbook of visual analysis* (pp. 134–156). Sage.

Jolley, R. P. (2009). *Children and pictures: Drawing and understanding*. Wiley-Blackwell.

Jones, G., & Ponton, L. (2002). *Killing monsters: Why children need fantasy, super heroes, and make-believe violence*. Perseus Books.

Jones, S. (n.d.). *Superheroes and children's culture*. https://wordandimage.files.wordpress.com/2007/08/jones-superheroes-and-children.pdf

Jordan, B. (2004). Scaffolding learning and co-constructing understandings. In A. Anning, J. Cullen, & M. Fleer (Eds.), *Early childhood education: Society and culture* (pp. 31–42). Sage.

Kampeza, M., & Delserieys, A. (2020). Acknowledging drawing as a mediating system for young children's ideas concerning change of state of matter. *Review of Science, Mathematics and ICT Education 14*(2), 105–124.

Kangas, M., Kultima, A., & Ruokamo, H. (2011). Children's creative collaboration – a view of narrativity. In D. Faulkner & E. Coates (Eds.), *Exploring children's creative narratives* (pp. 63–85). Routledge.

Kaplun, C. (2019). Children's drawings speak a thousand words in their transition to school. *Australasian Journal of Early Childhood 44*(4), 392–407. https://doi.org/10.1177/1836939119870887

Kellogg, R. (1959). *What children scribble and why*. N. P. Publications.

Kellogg, R. (1969). *Analyzing children's art*. Mayfield Publishing.

Kellogg, R. (1979). *Children's drawings / Children's minds*. Avon.

Kellogg, R., & Plaskow, D. (1972). *The crucial years*. Society for Education through Art.

Kendrick, M., & McKay, R. (2004). Drawings as an alternative way of understanding young children's constructions of literacy. *Journal of Early Childhood Literacy 4*(1), 109–128. https://psycnet.apa.org/doi/10.1177/1468798404041458

Kessler, M. (2022). Multimodality. *ELT Journal 76*(4), 551–554. https://doi.org/10.1093/elt/ccac028

Kim, H., & Han, T. I. (2022). "What kind of person do you want to become?": Analyzing young children's drawings on gender ideals. *Early Childhood Education Journal*. https://doi.org/10.1007/s10643-022-01437-9

Kjørholt, A. T., Moss, P., & Clark, A. (2005). Beyond listening: Future prospects. In A. Clark, A. T. Kjørholt, & P. Moss (Eds.), *Beyond listening: Children's perspectives on early childhood services* (pp. 175–187). Policy Press.

Knight, L. (2009). Dreaming of other spaces: What do we think about when we draw? *The Psychology of Educational Review 33*(1), 10–17.

Konleczna, E. J., & Talu, E. (2023). The symbolism of fear-themed drawings of Turkish and Polish Children. *Original Research Projects 40*(2), 111–138. https://doi.org/10.12775/PBE.2022.021

Kozulin, A., Gindis, B., Ageyev, V., & Miller, S. (2003). Introduction: Sociocultural theory and education – students, teachers, and knowledge. In A. Kozulin, B. Gindis, V. Ageyev, & S. Miller (Eds.), *Vygotsky's educational theory in a cultural context* (pp. 1–14). Cambridge University Press.

Krauss, S. E. (2005). Research paradigms and meaning making: A primer. *The Qualitative Report 10*(4), 758–770.
Kress, G. (1997). *Before writing: Rethinking the paths to literacy*. Routledge.
Kress, G. (2000a). Design and transformation: New theories of meaning. In B. Cope & M. Kalantzis (Eds.), *Multiliteracies: Literacy learning and the design of social futures* (pp. 153–161). Routledge, Taylor & Francis.
Kress, G. (2000b). Multimodality. In B. Cope & M. Kalantzis (Eds.), *Multiliteracies: Literacy learning and the design of social futures* (pp. 182–202). Routledge Taylor & Francis.
Kress, G. (2003a). *Literacy in the new media age*. Routledge, Taylor & Francis.
Kress, G. (2003b). Perspectives on making meaning: The differential principles and means of adults and children. In N. Hall, J. Larson, & J. Marsh (Eds.), *Handbook of early childhood literacy* (pp. 154–166). Sage.
Kress, G. (2004). *Reading images: Multimodality, representation and the New Media. Information Design Journal 12*(2), 110–119. https://doi.org/10.1075/idjdd.12.2.03kre
Kress, G. (2005). Gains and losses: New forms of texts, knowledge, and learning. *Computers and Composition 22*, 5–22.
Kress, G. (2008). "Literacy" in a multimodal environment of communication. In J. Flood, S. B. Heath, & D. Lapp (Eds.), *Handbook of research on teaching literacy through the communicative and visual arts, Volume II* (pp. 91–100). Lawrence Erlbaum Associates, Taylor & Francis, International Reading Association.
Kress, G. (2010). *Multimodality: A social semiotic approach to contemporary communication*. Routledge.
Kress, G. (2013). Recognising learning: A perspective from a social semiotic theory of multimodality. In I. De Saint-Georges & J. J. Weber (Eds.), *Multilingualism and multimodality: Current challenges for educational studies* (pp. 119–140). Sense Publishers.
Kress, G., & Jewitt, C. (2003). Introduction. In C. Jewitt & G. Kress (Eds.), *Multimodal literacy* (New Literacies and Digital Epistemologies, 4) (pp. 1–18). Peter Lang.
Kress, G., Jewitt, C., Ogborn, J., & Tsatsarelis, C. (2001). *Multimodal teaching and learning: The rhetorics of the science classroom*. Continuum.
Kress, G., & Van Leeuwen, T. (1996). *Reading images: A grammar of visual design*. Routledge.
Kress, G., & Van Leeuwen, T. (2001). *Multimodal discourse: The modes and media of contemporary communication*. Hodder Education.
Kress, G., & Van Leeuwen, T. (2006). *Reading images: A grammar of visual design*. Routledge.
Lähdesmäki, T. Baranova, J., Ylönen, S. C., Koistinen, A-K., Mäkinen, K., Juškiene et al., (2022). A sociocultural approach to children's visual creations. In T. Lähdesmäki, J. Baranova, S. Ylönin, A. Koistinen, K. Mäkinen, V. Juškiene, & I. Zaleskiene (Eds.), *Learning cultural literacy through creative practices in schools* (pp. 17–30). Springer.
Lamm, B., Gernhardt, A., & Rübeling, H. (2019). How societal changes have influenced German children's gender representations as expressed in human figure drawings in 1977 and 2015. *Sex Roles 81*, 118–125. https://doi.org/10.1007/s11199-018-0978-5
Lancaster, L. (2003). Moving into literacy: How it all begins. In N. Hall, J. Larson, & J. Marsh (Eds.), *Handbook of early childhood literacy* (pp. 145–153). Sage.
Lancaster, L. (2007). Representing the ways of the world: How children under three start to use syntax in graphic signs. *Journal of Early Childhood Literacy 7*(2), 123–154. https://doi.org/10.1177/1468798407079284

Lancaster, L. (2013). Opening it all up: Using multimodal analysis to investigate early literacy. *International Journal of Qualitative Research* 6(3), 395–423.

Lancaster, L., & Roberts, R. (2006). *Grammaticisation in early mark making: A multimodal investigation* (RES-000-22-0599). Economic and Social Research Council. https://www.esrc.ac.uk/my-esrc/grants/RES-000-22-0599/read

Lave, J., & Wenger, E. (1991). *Situated learning: Legitimate peripheral participation*. Cambridge University.

Leigh, R. S., & Heid, K. A. (2008). First graders constructing meaning through drawing and writing. *Journal for Learning through the Arts* 4(1), 1–12.

Loizos, P. (2000). Video, film and photographs as research documents. In Bauer, M. & G. Gaskell (Eds.), *Qualitative researching with text, image and sound: A practical handbook*, (pp. 93–107). Sage.

Long, J., & He, J. (2021). Social semiotics and the related interpretation. Advances in Social Science, Education and Humanities Research, 571. *Proceedings of the 2021 5th International Seminar on Education, Management and Social Sciences* (ISEMSS 2021). Atlantis.

Longobardi, C., Quaglia, R., & Iotti, N. O. (2015). Reconsidering the scribbling stage of drawing: A new perspective on toddlers' representational processes. *Frontier Psychology* 6(1227), 1–9. https://doi.org/10.3389/fpsyg.2015.01227

Lowenfeld, V., & Brittain, L. (1987). *Creative and mental growth* (8th ed.). Prentice Hall.

Luquet, G. H. (2001). *Children's drawings [Le dessin enfantin]*. (A. Vostall, Trans.). (1927). Free Associations Press.

Lyon, P. (2020). Using drawing in visual research: Materializing the invisible. In L. Pauwels & D. Mannay (Eds.), *The Sage handbook of visual research method* (2nd ed., pp. 297–308). Sage.

Machón, A. (2013). *Children's drawings: The genesis and nature of graphic representation. A developmental study*. Fibulas.

MacNaughton, G. (2004). Exploring critical constructivist perspectives on learning. In A. Anning, J. Cullen, & M. Fleer (Eds.), *Early childhood education: Society and culture* (pp. 43–54). Sage.

MacNaughton, G., & Smith, K. (2005). Transforming research ethics: The choices and challenges of researching with children. In A. Farrell (Ed.), *Ethical research with children* (pp. 112–123). Open University.

Malchiodi, C. A. (1998). *Understanding children's drawings*. The Guilford Press.

Malin, H. (2013). Making meaningful: Intention in children's art making. *International Journal of Art & Design* 32(1), 6–17.

Marsh, J. (2000). 'But I want to fly too!': Girls and superhero play in the infant classroom. *Gender and Education* 12(2), 209–220.

Marsh, J. (2003). Early childhood literacy and popular culture. In N. Hall, J. Larson, & J. Marsh (Eds.), *Handbook of early childhood literacy* (pp. 112–125). Sage.

Marsh, J. (2006). Global, local/public, private: Young children's engagement in digital literacy practices in the home. In J. Rowsell & K. Pahl (Eds.), *Travel notes from the new literacy studies: Case studies in practice* (pp. 19–38). Multilingual Matters.

Marsh, J. (2010). Young children's play in online virtual worlds. *Journal of Early Childhood Research* 8(1), 23–39. https://doi.org/10.1177/1476718X09345406

Marsh, J., & Millard, E. (2000). *Literacy and popular culture: Using children's culture in the classroom*. Paul Chapman.

Marsh, J., Wood, E., Chesworth, L., Nisha, B., Nutbrown, B., & Olney, B. (2019). Makerspaces in early childhood education: Principles of pedagogy and practice.

*Mind, Culture and Activity* 26(3), 221–233. https://doi.org/10.1080/10749039.2019.1655651

Marvel Comics. (2015). *Iron man.* https://www.marvel.com/comics/series/20476/invincible_iron_man_(2015_-_2016)

Mattel Television. (1987). *Fireman Sam.* https://firemansam.fandom.com/wiki/The_Official_Website

Matthews, J. (1997). The 4 dimensional language of infancy: The interpersonal basis of art practice. *International Journal of Art & Design* 16(3), 285–293.

Matthews, J. (1999). *The art of childhood and adolescence: The construction of meaning.* Falmer Press, Taylor & Francis Group.

Matthews, J. (2003). *Drawing and painting: Children and visual representation* (2nd ed.). Sage.

Mavers, D. (2007a). Investigating how children make meaning in multimodal maps. *Reflecting Education* 3(1), 24–28.

Mavers, D. (2007b). Semiotic resourcefulness: A young child's email exchange as design. *Journal of Early Childhood Literacy* 7(2), 155–176.

Mavers, D. (2011). *Children's drawing and writing: The remarkable in the unremarkable.* Routledge, Taylor & Francis.

Mavers, D., & Newfield, D. (2012). Transduction. Glossary of multimodal terms. MODE. https://multimodalityglossary.wordpress.com/

Mehawesh, M. I. (2014). The socio-semiotic theory of language and translation: An overview. *International Journal of Humanities and Social Science* 4(8), 87–96.

Metro-Goldwyn Mayer [MGM]. (1969–1979). *The Pink Panther show.* https://ondemand.spectrum.net/tv/mgm/8679796/the-pink-panther-show/

Mills, K. A. (2009). Multiliteracies: Interrogating competing discourses. *Language and Education* 23(2), 103–116.

Moll, L. C. (2000). Inspired by Vygotsky: Ethnographic experiments in education. In C. D. Lee & P. Smagorinsky (Eds.), *Vygotskian perspectives on literacy research: Constructing meaning through collaborative inquiry* (pp. 256–268). Cambridge University.

Moll, L. C. (2019). Elaborating funds of knowledge: Community-oriented practices in international contexts. *Literacy research: Theory, method, and practice* 68, 130–138. https://doi.org/10.1177/2381336919870805

Moll, L. C., Amanti, C., Neff, D., & González, N. (1992). Funds of knowledge for teaching: Using a qualitative approach to connect homes and classrooms. *Theory into Practice* 31(2), 132–141.

Moula, Z., Walshe, N., & Lee, E. (2021). Making nature explicit in children's drawings of wellbeing and happy spaces. *Child Indicators Research* 14, 1653–1675. https://doi.org/10.1007/s12187-021-09811-6

Mukherji, P., & Albon, D. (2010). *Research methods in early childhood: An introductory guide.* Sage.

Ngwenya, N., Malherbe, N., & Seedat, M. (2022). Multimodality, cultural production and the protest event: Considerations of space, politics, and affect in South Africa. *Multimodality & Society* 2(2), 114–130. https://doi.org/10.1177/26349795221099903

Nicolopoulou, A. (1997). Worldmaking and identity formation in children's narrative play-acting. In B. D. Cox & C. Lightfoot (Eds.), *Sociogenetic perspective on internalisation* (pp. 157–187). Lawrence Elbraum Associates.

Nicolopoulou, A. (2008). The elementary forms of narrative coherence in young children's storytelling. *Narrative Inquiry* 18, 299–325.

Nicolopoulou, A., Scales, B., & Weintraub, J. (1994). Gender differences and symbolic imagination in the stories of four-year-olds. In A. H. Dyson & C. Genishi (Eds.), *The need for story: Cultural diversity in classroom and community* (pp. 102–123). National Council of Teachers of English.

Nielsen, C. S. (2009). Children's embodied voices: Approaching children's experiences through multi-modal interviewing. *Phenomenology & Practice 3*(1), 80–93.

Norris, S. (2004). *Analysing multimodal interaction: A methodological framework.* Routledge, Taylor & Francis.

Nutbrown, C. (1996). Wide eyes and open minds – observing, assessing and respecting children's early achievements. In C. Nutbrown (Ed.), *Children's rights and early education: Respectful educators: Capable learners* (pp. 44–55). Paul Chapman.

Nutbrown, C. (2006). *Threads of thinking: Young children learning and the role of early education* (3rd ed.). Sage.

Nutbrown, C. (2011). Naked by the pool? Blurring the image? Ethical issues in the portrayal of young children in arts-based educational research. *Qualitative Inquiry 17*(3), 3–14.

Nutbrown, C. (2021). Analysing and interpreting data from research with young children: Faithfulness, integrity and trustworthiness in eliciting meaning. In L. Arnott & K. Wall (Eds.), *Research through play: Participatory methods in early childhood* (pp. 83–95). Sage.

Nyland, B. (2009). The guiding principles of participation: Infant, toddler groups and the United Nations Convention on the rights of the child. In D. Berthelsen, J. Brownlee, & E. Johansson (Eds.), *Participatory learning in the early years: Research and pedagogy* (pp. 26–43). Routledge, Taylor & Francis.

O'Halloran, K. L. (2009). Historical changes in the semiotic landscape: From calculation to computation. In C. Jewitt (Ed.), *The Routledge handbook of multimodal analysis* (pp. 98–113). Routledge, Taylor & Francis.

Oksanen, U. (2008). Picturing the landscape of the knowledge society: A semiotic point of view on adolescents' pictorial metaphors. In L. Unsworth (Ed.), *Multimodal semiotics: Functional analysis in contexts of education* (pp. 237–252). Continuum.

Ormerod, F., & Ivanic, R. (2002). Materiality in children's meaning-making practices. *Visual Communication 1*, 65. https://doi.org/10.1177/147035720200100106

Pahl, K. (1999). *Transformations: Meaning-making in nursery education.* Trentham Books.

Pahl, K. (2001). Texts as artefacts crossing sites: Map making at home and at school. *Reading: Literacy and language 35*(3), 120–125.

Pahl, K. (2009). Interactions, intersections and improvisations: Studying the multimodal texts and classroom talk of six- to seven-year-old. *Journal of Early Childhood Literacy 9*(2), 188–210. https://doi.org/10.1177/1468798409105586

Pahl, K., & Rowsell, J. (2010). *Artifactual literacies: Every object tells a story.* Teachers College Press.

Paine, S. (1981). Introduction. In S. Paine (Ed.), *Six children draw* (pp. 1–8). Academic Press.

Paine, S. (1997). Early obsessive drawings and personal development. *Journal of Art & Design Education 16*(2), 147–156.

Paley, V. G. (1988). *Bad Guys don't have birthdays: Fantasy play at four.* University of Chicago.

Palvan, S., Zareii, K., Hoseini, A. S. S., Haghani, H. (2021). The effect of exchanging drawings with peers on the happiness of children with cancer, aged 7-11 years: A clinical trial. *PLoS One 16*(10), e0257867. https://doi.org/10.1371/journal.pone.0257867

Pariser, D. (1995). Not under the Lamppost: Piagetian and Neo-Piagetian research in the arts. *Journal of Aesthetic Education 29*(3), 93–108.

Penn, G. (2000). Semiotic analysis of still images. In M. W. Bauer & G. Gaskell (Eds.), *Qualitative researching with text, image and sound: A practical handbook* (pp. 227–245). Sage.

Pinto, G., Tosi, F., & Incognito, O. (2021). Drawing places, recreating spaces: Visual voices from at-risk children. *Humanities & Social Sciences Communications 8*(196), 1–7. https://doi.org/10.1057/s41599-021-00872-0

Podobnik, U., Jerman, J., & Selan, J. (2021). Understanding analytical drawings of preschool children: The importance of a dialog with a child. *International Journal of Early Years Education 32*(1), 189–203. https://doi.org/10.1080/09669760.2021.1960802

Price, S., Björkvall, A., & Kress, G. (2012). Materiality. Glossary of multimodal terms. MODE. https://multimodalityglossary.wordpress.com/materiality/

Punch, K. F. (2005). *Introduction to social research: Quantitative and qualitative approaches* (2nd ed.). Sage.

Ring, K. (2006). What mothers do: Everyday routines and rituals and their impact upon young children's use of drawing for meaning making. *International Journal of Early Years Education 14*(1), 63–84. https://doi.org/10.1080/09669760500446416

Ring, K. (2010). Drawing with seven-year olds: Assuming the role of teacher. *International Art in Early Childhood Research Journal 2*(1), 1–19. https://artinearlychildhood.org/content/uploads/2022/03/ARTEC_2010_Research_Journal_1_Article_3.pdf

Ring, K., & Anning, A. (2004, Sept). Early childhood narratives through drawing. *Tracey: Drawing and visual research.* Loughborough University. https://ray.yorksj.ac.uk/id/eprint/87/

Riojas-Cortez, M. (2001). Preschoolers' funds of knowledge displayed through sociodramatic play episodes in a bilingual classroom. *Early Childhood Education Journal 29*(1), 35–40.

Rogoff, B. (1990). *Apprenticeship in thinking: Cognitive development in social context.* Oxford University.

Rose, G. (2012). *Visual methodologies: An introduction to researching with visual materials* (3rd ed.). Sage.

Rose, S. E., Jolley, R. P., & Burkitt, E. (2006). A review of children's teachers' and parents' influences on children's drawing experiences. *International Journal of Art & Design Education 25*(3), 341–349.

Rudolph, S. (2014). Theorising through visual and verbal metaphors: Challenging narrow depictions of children and learning. *Art & Early Childhood: Personal Narratives & Social Practices 31*, 93–106. https://doi.org/10.58295/2375-3668.1030

Sawyer, R. K. (2002). *Improvised dialogues: Emergence and creativity in conversation.* Greenwood.

Sawyer, R. K. (2011). "Improvisation and narrative." In D. Faulkner & E. Coates (Eds.), *Exploring children's creative narratives* (pp. 11–38). Routledge.

Schaffer, H. R. (1992). Joint involvement episodes as contexts for cognitive development. In H. McGurk (Ed.), *Childhood and social development: Contemporary perspective* (pp. 99–130). Lawrence Erlbaum.

Schirrmacher, R. (2002). *Art and creative development for young children* (4th ed.). Delmar Thomson Learning.

Schulz, R., Schroeder, D., & Brody, C. M. (1997). Collaborative narrative inquiry: Fidelity and the ethics of caring in teacher research. *International Journal of Qualitative Studies in Education 10*(4), 473–485. https://doi.org/10.1080/095183997237052

Sega Corporation. (2013). *Sonic the Hedgehog*. https://info.sonicretro.org/Sonic_the_Hedgehog_(2013_game)

Seizov, O., & Wildfeuer, J. (2017). Introduction: Rethinking multimodality in the twenty-first century. In O. Seizov & J. Wildfeuer (Eds.), *New studies in multimodality: Conceptual and methodological elaborations* (pp. 1–14). Bloomsbury.

Semali, L. M. (2002). Transmediation: Why study the semiotics of representation? In L. M. Semali (Ed.), *Transmediation in the classroom: A semiotics-based media literacy framework* (pp. 1–20). Peter Lang.

Senzaki, S., Masuda, T., & Ishii, K. (2014). When is perception top–down and when is it not? Culture, narrative, and attention. *Cognitive Science 38*, 1493–1506. 10.1111/cogs.12118

Short, K. G., Kaufman, G., & Kahn, L. H. (2000). "I just need to draw": Responding to literature across multiple sign systems. *The Reading Teacher 54*(2), 160–171.

Siegel, M. (2006). Rereading the signs: Multimodal transformation in the field of literacy education. *Language Arts 84*(1), 65–77.

Siegel, M., Kontovourki, S., Schmier, S., & Enriquez, G. (2008). Literacy in motion: A case study of a shape-shifting kindergartener. *Language Arts 86*(2), 89–98.

Skattebol, J. (2006). Playing boys: The body, identity and belonging in the early years. *Gender and Education 18*(5), 507–522.

Smith, A. B. (2007). Children's rights and early childhood education: Links to theory and advocacy. *Australian Journal of Early Childhood 32*(3). https://doi.org/10.1177/183693910703200302

Smith, A. B. (2011). Respecting children's rights and agency: Theoretical insights into ethical research procedures. In D. Harcourt, B. Perry, & T. Waller (Eds.), *Research young children's perspectives: Debating the ethics and dilemmas of educational research with children* (pp. 11–25). Routledge.

Solomon, C., & Grimley, M. (2011). Metaphors used by Year 5 and Year 6 children to depict their beliefs about Maths. *Mathematics: Traditions and [New] practices*. https://ir.canterbury.ac.nz/server/api/core/bitstreams/12e308c9-bd2f-4fa5-981e-ee7e1be90079/content

Soundy, C. S. (2015). Making sense of children's drawings and semiotic explorations. *Dimensions of Early Childhood 43*(3), 39–46. https://files.eric.ed.gov/fulltext/EJ1150453.pdf

Souzandehfar, M., & Soozandehfar, S. M. A. (2020). The meaning-making of the children's drawings as a manifestation of their visual literacy competence. *Journal of Language Horizons 4*(1), 227–245. https://doi.org/10.22051/lghor.2020.27164.1158

Stein, P. (2008). *Multimodal pedagogies in diverse classrooms: Representation, rights and resources*. Routledge, Taylor & Francis.

Sunday, K. E. (2015). Relational making: Re/Imagining theories of child art. *Studies in Art Education 56*(3), 228–240.

Sunday, K. E. (2017). Drawing as a relational event: Making meaning through talk, collaboration and image production. In M. J. Narey (Ed.), *Multimodal perspectives of language, literacy and learning in early childhood: The creative and critical "art" of making meaning* (pp. 87–105). https://doi.org/10.1007/978-3-319-44297-6_5

Talu, E. (2019). Reflections of fears of children to drawings. *European Journal of Educational Researcher 8*(3), 763–779.

Tang, K. S., Jeppsson, F., Danielsson, K., & Nestlog, E. B. (2022). Affordances of physical objects as a material mode of representation: A social semiotics perspective of hands-on meaning-making. *International Journal of Science Education 44*(2), 179–200. https://doi.org/10.1080/09500693.2021.2021313

Tay-Lim, J., & Lim, S. (2013). Privileging young children's voices in research: Use of drawings and a co-construction process. *International Journal of Qualitative Methods 12,* 65–83.

Tembo, S., & Benham, F. (2023). Gender and LGBTQ+ inclusive practice in early childhood. In C. Nutbrown (Eds.), *Early childhood education: Current realities and future priorities.* Sage.

The New London Group (Cazden, C., Cope, B., Fairclough, N., Gee, J., Kress, G., Luke, A. et al.). (1996). A Pedagogy of Multiliteracies: Designing Social Futures. *Harvard Educational Review 66*(1), 60–92.

The New London Group. (2000). A pedagogy of multiliteracies: Designing social futures. In B. Cope & M. Kalantzis (Eds.), *Multiliteracies: Literacy learning and the design of social futures* (pp. 9–38). Routledge, Taylor & Francis.

Thomas, N., & O'Kane, C. (1998). The ethics of participatory research with children. *Children & Society 12*(5), 336–348. https://doi.org/10.1111/j.1099-0860.1998.tb00090.x

Thompson, C. M. (1995). "What should I draw today?" Sketchbooks in early childhood. *Art Education 48*(5), 6–11.

Thompson, C. M. (1999). Action, autobiography and aesthetics in young children's self-initiated drawings. *International Journal of Art & Design Education 18*(2), 155–161.

Thompson, C. M. (2017). Listening for stories: Childhood studies and art education. *Studies in Art Education 58*(1), 7–16.

Thompson, C. M., & Schulte, C. M. (2019). Repositioning the visual arts in early childhood education. In O. N. Saracho (Ed.), *Handbook of research on the education of young children* (4th ed., pp. 133–148). Routledge.

Timonen, K. (2023). Making meaning of an artwork: Promoting expression of thoughts through artwork for patients with eating disorders. *Social semiotics.* https://doi.org/10.1080/10350330.2023.2194523

Türkcan, B. (2013). Semiotic approach to the analysis of children's drawings. *Educational Sciences: Theory & Practice 13*(1), 600–607.

TV Tropes Foundation. (n.d.). *Western animation: Ben 10.* https://tvtropes.org/pmwiki/pmwiki.php/WesternAnimation/Ben10

United Nations. (1989). *United Nations Convention no the Rights of the Child. Treaty no, 27531.* United Nations Treaty Series, 1577, pp. 3–178. https://treaties.un.org/doc/Treaties/1990/09/19900902%2003-14%20AM/Ch_IV_11p.pdf

Unsworth, L. (2001). *Teaching multiliteracies across the curriculum: Changing contexts of text and image in classroom practice.* Open University.

Van Leeuwen, T. (2005). *Introducing social semiotics.* Routledge Taylor & Francis.

Vasquez, V. (2005). Resistance, power-tricky and colorless energy. In J. Marsh (Ed.), *Popular culture, new media and digital literacy in early childhood* (pp. 201–217). Routledge Falmer, Taylor & Francis.

Vasudevan, L. (2011). Re-imagining pedagogies for multimodal selves. *Society for the Study of Education 110*(1), 88–108.

Vecchi, V. (2010). *Art and creativity in Reggio Emilia: Exploring the role and potential of ateliers in early childhood education.* Routledge: Taylor & Francis Group.

Viacom International Incorporation. (2015). *Go Diego, Go!* Nick Junior. https://www.nickjr.com/go-diego-go/

Villarroel, J. D., Antón, A., Zuazagoitia, D., & Nuño, T. (2018). A study on spontaneous representation of animals in young children's drawings of plant life. *Sustainability 10*(1000), 1–11. https://doi.org/10.3390/su10041000

Volman, M., & Gilde, J. (2021). The effects of using students' funds of knowledge on educational outcomes in the social and personal domain. *Learning, Culture and Social Interaction 28*, 100472. https://doi.org/10.1016/j.lcsi.2020.100472

Vygotsky, L. S. (1978). *Mind in society: The development of higher psychological processes*. Harvard University Press.

Vygotsky, L. S. (1994). The problem of the Environment. In R. Van der Veer & J. Van Valsiner (Eds.), *The Vygotsky Reader* (pp. 338–354). Blackwell (Original work published 1934).

Vygotsky, L. S. (1997). *The collected works of L. S. Vygotsky, Vol. 4: The history of the development of higher mental functions*, R. W. Rieber (Ed.), (M. J. Hall, Trans.). (1941). Plenum Press.

Vygotsky, L. S. (1998). *The collected works of L. S. Vygotsky, Vol. 5: Child psychology*. Plenum Press.

Vygotsky, L. S. (2012). *Thought and language* (A. Kozulin, Trans.). (1962) The Massachusetts Institute of Technology.

Walker, K. (2007). Review of research: Children and their purple crayons: Understanding their worlds through their drawings. *Childhood Education 84*(96). https://doi.org/10.1080/00094056.2008.10522983

Wang, Z., & Brown, G. (2019). *Analysing students' free response drawings: Perceptions of assessment*. Sage. https://doi.org/10.4135/9781526487674

Watson, M. W., & Schwartz, S. N. (2000). The development of individual styles in children's drawing. *New Directions for Child and Adolescent Development 90*, 49–63. https://doi.org/10.1002/cd.23220009005

Wiles, R., Crow, G., Heath, S., & Charles, V. (2008a). The management of confidentiality and anonymity in social research. *International Journal of Social Research Methodology 11*(5), 417–428. https://doi.org/10.1080/13645570701622231

Wiles, R., Prosser, J., Bagnoli, A., Clark, A., Davies, K., Holland, S., & Renold, E. (2008b). *Visual ethics: Ethical issues in visual research. ESRC National Centre for Research Methods Review Paper*. National Centre for Research Methods, NCRM/011. https://eprints.ncrm.ac.uk/421/1/MethodsReviewPaperNCRM-011.pdf

Wohlwend, K. (2008). Play as a literacy of possibilities: Expanding meanings in practices, materials, and spaces. *Language Arts 86*(2), 127–136.

Wohlwend, K. (2009). Early adopters: Playing new literacies and pretending new technologies in print-centric classrooms. *Journal of Early Childhood Literacy 9*(2), 117–140.

Wood, E., & Hall, E. (2011). Drawings as spaces for intellectual play. *International Journal of Early Years Education 19*(3–4), 267–281.

Woolford, J., Patterson, T., Macleod, E., Hobbs, L., & Hayne, H. (2015). Drawing helps children to talk about their presenting problems during a mental health assessment. *Clinical Child Psychology & Psychiatry 20*(1), 68–83. https://doi.org/10.1177/1359104513496261

Wright, S. (2003). Ways of knowing in the arts. In S. Wright (Ed.), *Children, meaning-making and the arts* (pp. 1–31). Pearson Education.

Wright, S. (2005). Young children's meaning-making through drawing and 'telling': Analogies to filmic textual features. *Australasian Journal of Early Childhood 32*(4), 1–20.

Wright, S. (2006). *Graphic-narrative play: Authoring through multiple texts*. Paper presented at the American Educational Research Association Annual Conference, San Francisco. Project Number: CRP 9/04 SW. https://www.researchgate.net/publication/289130325_Graphic-narrative_play_Authoring_through_multiple_texts

Wright, S. (2007). Graphic-narrative play: Young children's authoring through drawing and telling. *International Journal of Education and the Arts 8*(8), 1–27.

Wright, S. (2008). Young children's meaning-making through drawing and 'telling': Analogies to filmic textual features. *Australian Journal of Early Childhood 32*(4). https://www.earlychildhoodaustralia.org.au

Wright, S. (2010a). *Children's meaning-making through graphic-narrative play. Arts-based research in early childhood education forum* (11th May, 2010). Unesco—National Institute of Education, Singapore: Centre for Arts Research in Education.

Wright, S. (2010b). *Understanding creativity in early childhood: Meaning-making and children's drawings*. Sage.

Wright, S. (2011). Meaning, mediation and mythology. In D. Faulkner & E. Coates (Eds.), *Exploring children's creative narratives* (pp. 157–176). Routledge Taylor & Francis.

Zlateva, A. (2019). *How to read children's drawings*. Centre for Resilience and Socio-Emotional Health, University of Malta. https://www.um.edu.mt/library/oar/bitstream/123456789/48957/1/How%20to%20Read%20Childrens%20Drawings%20final.pdf

# Index of Authors

Adams, E. 3, 20–22, 27, 50, 83, 120, 123, 131, 148, 217
Ahmad, J. F. 21, 28, 29, 217
Ahn, J. 2, 22, 24–27, 50, 90, 132, 175, 217
Aiello, G. 13, 127
Albers, P. 3, 21, 197, 217
Albertini, G. 30, 105, 219
Albon, D. 33, 229
Alderson, P. 39, 217
Allen, G. 38, 217
Amanti, C. 28, 217, 223, 229
Anderson, J. K. 152, 217
Anning, A. 3, 16, 18, 19, 21, 25, 29, 88, 175, 196, 217, 218, 226, 228, 231
Archer, A. 15, 16, 218
Athey, C. 77, 203, 218
Atkinson, D. 21, 23, 218

Bakhtin, M. M. 14, 218
Bakr, F. S. 148, 218
Banks, M. 39, 218
Barroqueiro, R. 208, 218
Bearne, E. 12, 218
Benham, F. 34, 233
Benson, S. 10, 223
Berthelsen, D. 6, 218, 230
Bezemer, J. 10–17, 74, 218, 225
Bissex, G. L. 20, 218
Blagdanic, S. 4, 218
Bland, D. 4, 218
Bleiker, C. A. 26, 218
Blunden, A. 6, 219
Bock, Z. 20, 219
Bourne, J. 12, 219
Boyatzis, C. 30, 105, 219
Brechet, C. 162, 219

British Educational Research Association (BERA) 37, 219, 224
Brittain, L. 19, 30, 228
Brockmeier, J. 26, 129, 219
Brooks, M. 6, 22, 25, 56, 219
Brown, G. 4, 234
Bruner, J. 4, 5, 24, 27, 219
Bucknall, S. 32, 219
Burkitt, E. 90, 219, 231

Capurso, M. 2, 4, 219
Cartoon Network 109, 219
Chandler, D. 14, 219
Chappell, K. A. 153, 220
Chesworth, L. 7, 17, 80, 192, 193, 206, 207, 220, 228
Christmann, G. B. 23, 220
Christodoulakis, N. 6, 220
Clark, A. 3, 33, 219, 220, 226, 234
Coates, A. 2, 3, 6, 19–21, 24, 25, 27, 29, 35, 64, 92, 93, 113, 115, 158, 165, 166, 184, 200
Coates, E. 2, 3, 6, 20, 21, 24, 25, 27, 29, 35, 69, 102, 126, 175, 183, 184, 203, 204, 220, 223, 226, 231, 235
Conroy, H. 37, 224
Conroy, J. 64, 90, 93, 110, 132, 164, 221, 224
Cope, B. 8, 220, 227, 233
Cowan, K. 12, 13, 16, 218
Cox, M. 3, 4, 19, 20, 22, 24, 25, 30, 74, 102, 154, 165, 183, 218, 220, 229
Craft, A. R. 153, 220

Danesi, M. 13, 204, 220
Danielsson, K. 12, 200, 233
David, M. 38, 221
Davis, J. H. 4, 22, 221

De Rosa, A. S. 196, 221
De Ruyter, D. 64, 90, 110, 132, 164, 221
Deguara, J. 8, 40, 221
Delserieys, A. 152, 226
Disney 29, 95, 204, 221
Djonov, E. 13, 221
Drake, J. E. 61, 136, 221
Dressman, M. 10, 221
Driessnack, M. 137, 221
D'warte, J. 7, 220
Dyson, A. H. 5, 15, 19–21, 23, 25, 26, 45, 52, 165, 169, 170, 173, 177, 178, 183, 203, 221, 222, 230

Eckhoff, A. 32, 222
Edmiston, B. 26, 28, 54, 80, 82, 129, 132, 135, 155, 165, 170, 175, 184, 222
Edwards, C. 2, 212, 221, 222
Egan, B. A. 25, 222
Egan, K. 24, 68, 222
Einarsdottir, J. 4, 8, 29, 222
Eisner, E. W. 3, 16, 222
Esteban-Guitart, M. 199, 222

Fargas-Malet, M. 33, 222
Farokhi, M. 1, 4, 223
Ferholt, B. 6, 223
Ferreiro, E. 20, 223
Filipenko, M. 2, 22, 25, 26, 50, 90, 132, 175, 217
Fisher, J. 206, 223
Flewitt, R. 23, 39, 41, 103, 219, 223
Fourie, J. S. 135, 136, 137, 148, 223
Frisch, N. S. 3, 19, 24, 30, 185, 223
Fulková, M. 13, 24, 223

Gallacher, L. A. 32, 223
Gallagher, M. 2, 223
Gardner, H. 26, 56, 111, 119–121, 124, 125, 165, 223
Gilde, J. 194, 207, 223
Golomb, C. 19, 27, 28, 223
González, N. 7, 28, 151, 192, 196, 200, 207, 217, 223, 229
Goodman, M. J. S. 2, 223
Graham, M. S. 10, 223
Grimley, M. 87, 232
Groundwater-Smith, S. 38, 223

Hagood, M.C. 27, 223
Hall, E. 2–4, 6, 9, 20, 21, 24–30, 49, 50, 52, 103, 121, 126, 129, 132, 154, 155, 165, 168, 171, 183, 185, 204, 211, 224, 227
Hall, M. 206, 234
Halliday, M. A. K. 13, 224
Han, T. I. 2, 4, 228
Han, S. 15, 224
Harcourt, D. 37, 38, 224, 232
Hartle, L. 15, 224
Hashemi, M. 1, 4, 223
Hawkins, B. 26, 80, 129, 224
He, J. 13, 14, 209
Hedges, H. 7, 80, 191, 194, 196, 200, 206, 207, 224, 225
Heid, K. A. 4, 228
Hibbert, M. 10, 225
Higgins, L. T. 140, 225
Holland, D. 26, 129, 225
Holliday, R. 39, 225
Hope, G. 3, 15, 22, 169, 170, 185, 214, 225
Hopperstad, M. H. 2, 22, 23, 25, 27, 30, 50, 80, 102, 118, 126, 175, 178, 182, 183, 189, 225
Hull, G.A. 82, 117, 225

International Management Group (IMG) 71, 225
Ivanic, R. 16, 230
Ivashkevich, O. 18, 225

James, A. 19, 225
Jaruszewicz, C. 15, 224
Jenkins, A. J. 69, 225
Jewitt, C. 3, 5, 10–13, 23, 24, 26, 41, 104, 187, 189, 219, 225–227, 230
Jolley, R. P. 21, 226, 231
Jones, A.M. 7, 217, 225
Jones, G. 28, 226
Jones, S. 28, 226
Jordan, B. 25, 225, 226

Kalantzis, M. 8, 220, 227, 233
Kampeza, M. 152, 226
Kangas, M. 25, 50, 226
Kaplun, C. 25, 226
Kellogg, R. 19, 30, 126, 226
Kendrick, M. 26, 64, 90, 110, 226
Kessler, M. 10, 226
Kim, H. 2, 4, 226
Kjørholt, A. T. 32, 226, 234
Knight, L. 153, 226
Konleczna, E. J. 137, 140, 226
Kozulin, A. 5, 226

Krauss, S. E. 15, 227
Kress, G. 3–5, 10–15, 17, 20–23, 41, 52, 68, 74, 90, 118, 119, 148, 169, 178, 187, 189, 206, 218, 226, 227, 231, 233

Lähdesmäki, T. 6, 8, 21, 227
Lamm, B. 4, 227
Lancaster, L. 20, 21, 29, 227, 228
Lave, J. 191, 228
Leigh, R. S. 4, 228
Lim, S. 24, 25, 233
Loizos, P. 33, 228
Long, J. 13, 14, 228
Longobardi, C. 20, 228
Lowenfeld, V. 19, 30, 228
Luquet, G. H. 18, 30, 228
Lyon, P. 1, 228

Machón, A. 3, 19, 126, 222, 228
MacNaughton, G. 28, 32, 228
Malaguzzi, l. 2, 19, 212
Malchiodi, C. A. 56, 228
Malin, H. 6, 228
Marsh, J. 21, 28, 29, 132, 173, 204, 223, 227, 228, 233
Marvel Comics 34, 52, 229
Mattel Television 34, 95, 110, 114, 204, 229
Matthews, J. 19, 20, 27, 102, 229
Mavers, D. 5, 13–16, 20–24, 28, 50, 80, 81, 105, 117, 126, 178, 184, 187, 189, 229
McKay, R. 26, 64, 90, 110, 226
Mehawesh, M. I. 12, 229
Metro-Goldwyn Mayer (MGM) 34, 229
Mills, K. A. 12, 229
Moll, L. C. 5, 7, 14, 117, 148, 192, 199, 206, 217, 222, 223, 229
Moss, P. 33, 220, 226
Moula, Z. 140, 229
Mukherji, P. 33, 229

Newfield, D. 15, 16, 117, 218, 229
Ngwenya, N. 14, 229
Nicolopoulou, A. 22, 24, 43, 168, 173, 187, 229, 230
Nielsen, C. S. 15, 24, 68, 230
Norris, S. 10, 12, 26, 230
Nutbrown, B. 228
Nutbrown, C. 23, 37, 39, 40, 43, 203, 224, 230, 233
Nyland, B. 32, 230

O'Halloran, K. L. 17, 225, 230
O'Kane, C. 37, 233
Oksanen, U. 169, 230
Ormerod, F. 16, 230

Pahl, K. 12, 71, 228, 230
Paine, S. 3, 21, 230
Paley, V. G. 169, 230
Palvan, S. 135, 230
Pariser, D. 19, 231
Penn, G. 40, 231
Pinto, G. 22, 231
Plaskow, D. 126, 226
Podobnik, U. 6, 24, 231
Ponton, L. 2. 8, 226
Price, S. 119, 231
Prout, A. 19, 225
Punch, K. F. 33, 231

Ring, K. 3, 16, 19, 21, 23, 29, 87, 175, 196, 218, 231
Riojas-Cortez, M. 7, 193, 196, 207, 231
Roberts, R. 20, 228
Rogoff, B. 191, 231
Rose, G. 39, 231
Rose, S. E. 6, 29, 90, 103, 231
Rudolph, S. 87, 231

Sargeant, J. 38, 224
Sawyer, R. K. 80, 231
Schaffer, H. R. 124, 231
Schirrmacher, R. 135, 231
Schulte, C. M. 19, 233
Schulz, R. 37, 232
Schwartz, S. N. 25, 234
Sega Corporation 80, 183, 232
Seizov, O. 10, 232
Selander, S. 12, 220
Semali, L. M. 15, 232
Senzaki, S. 21, 232
Short, K. G. 15, 233
Siegel, M. 13, 55, 232
Skattebol, J. 56, 164, 232
Smith, A. B. 6, 32, 33, 228, 232
Solomon, C. 87, 232
Soozandehfar, S. M. A. 5, 232
Soundy, C. S. 4, 5, 232
Souzandehfar, M. 5, 232
Stein, P. 10, 13–15, 41, 104, 197, 232
Sunday, K. E. 4, 19, 23–25, 232

Talu, E. 21, 135, 137, 140, 226, 232
Tang, K. S. 15, 233

Tay-Lim, J. 24, 25, 233
Teberosky, A. 2, 223
Tembo, S. 34, 233
The New London Group 8, 233
Thomas, N. 37, 233
Thompson, C. M. 4, 19, 21, 26, 121, 125, 206, 233
Timonen, K. 15, 233
Tipton, T. M. 13, 24, 223
Tűrkcan, B. 2, 4, 233
TV Tropes Foundation 34, 233

United Nations, 20, 37, 135, 230, 233
Unsworth, L. 8, 230, 233

Van Leeuwen, T. 5, 11, 68, 148, 224, 226, 227, 233
Vasquez, V. 12, 233
Vasudevan, L. 10, 225, 233
Vecchi, V. 213, 233
Viacom International Incorporation 173, 234

Villarroel, J. D. 84, 234
Volman, M. 194, 207, 234
Vygotsky, L. S. 2, 5, 6, 14, 16, 189, 191, 234

Walker, K. 4, 234
Wang, Z. 4, 234
Watson, M. W. 25, 234
Wenger, E. 191, 228
Wiles, R. 38, 39, 234
Winner, E. 136, 221
Wohlwend, K. 20, 234
Wood, E. 24, 27, 28, 48, 50, 52, 103, 121, 154, 155, 168, 171, 183, 184, 206, 224, 228, 234
Woodrow, C. 7, 220
Woolford, J. 90, 234
Wright, S. 2, 4, 13–16, 21–26, 28, 29, 48, 50, 106, 120, 125, 126, 159, 169–171, 173, 175, 182, 235

Zhao, S. 13, 221
Zlateva, A. 2, 92, 235

# Index of subjects

abstract: concepts/ knowledge 22, 24, 175; shapes/symbols 42; problems 154
action 19–21, 25–27, 34, 45, 48, 50, 56, 59, 69, 84, 102, 104, 114, 119, 120, 124, 139, 154, 164, 165, 168, 169, 171, 173, 177, 214
adult 2, 4, 7, 10, 13, 16–28, 32, 72, 86, 87, 95, 98, 100, 103, 110, 132, 137, 162, 174, 175, 207, 209, 210, 213, 219
affordances 11, 68, 189
agency: children's 13, 15, 16, 36, 37, 82, 178, 181, 185, 189, 213; authorial 177
analogy 170, 187
analysis 2, 3, 31, 39, 40, 42, 43, 119, 125, 126, 129
anger 61, 63, 64, 136, 137
animals 19, 34, 42, 68, 71, 76, 77, 80–86, 98, 104, 107, 112, 113, 119, 121, 124–127, 142–150, 154, 174, 176, 177, 190
anonymity 38, 39
art 2, 4, 15, 18, 215; artist 215
artefacts 3, 15, 21, 29, 32, 192
assent 37
atelierista 213
attuned 25, 37, 211; attunement 19, 124
authentic 32, 33, 35; 39; authenticity 38
authorial decisions 27; agency 117
authoring self 80, 132, 175; space 135; co-authoring 184, 222
autobiographical 104, 119, 124, 125

birth 90, 131
birthday 98, 109, 143, 145–148, 159, 196, 204
'bad-guys' 28, 52, 80, 120, 132, 136, 164, 165, 167, 169, 172

being ways of 2, 129; well-being 7, 13, 68, 111, 194, 210, 212, 213; human being 15, 17, 22, 24, 26, 132
beliefs family 7, 196; religious 197
*Ben Ten* 31, 34, 41, 42, 45, 50, 51, 69, 134, 135, 168, 169, 171–173, 206
Bertly's story 94–114
buildings 21, 42, 127, 194; castle 11, 42, 127, 134, 143, 154, 170; house 11, 21, 42, 44, 45, 71, 87, 92, 95, 121, 122, 127, 150, 158, 192, 203
butterflies 72, 76, 84, 87, 163

camera 32, 35, 36, 42, 50, 172; film 15, 29, 34–39, 45, 68, 69, 71, 93, 114, 170, 178, 187, 190, 204, 214; video 2, 32, 40, 42, 50, 69, 93, 95, 114, 172, 190, 194
Carnival 111, 148, 203
cartoon 29, 34, 45, 84, 95, 109, 114, 140, 169, 206; characters. 21, 69, 109, 114, 173
case study 36
categorisation 19, 126, 129
celebrate/celebration 29, 36, 88, 159, 163, 192, 196–198, 203
challenge 3, 17, 39, 174, 178
characteristics 34, 48, 55, 69, 92, 98, 105, 111, 121, 164, 196, 200, 213
child-centred 210, 212
children's rights 20, 32, 37, 38, 135, 207, 212, 214
choices 16, 32, 115, 165, 187, 189
collaboration 174–190, 211
communication 2–5, 10–26, 102, 135, 143, 210, 212, 213
community 2, 7, 13, 93, 192, 196–200, 203, 206

242  Index of subjects

complex mode 3, 40, 41, 46, 47, 49, 52, 54, 72–76, 80–83, 95–99, 104, 106, 115–119, 124, 125, 178, 185–189
complex theme 40, 41, 47–52, 72–80, 97–100, 104, 123
concepts 2, 4, 22, 24, 71, 132, 150, 153, 155, 164, 165, 170, 173
confidence 29, 74, 95–98, 148, 162, 171, 189
configuration styles 40, 48, 115–119, 125, 187
connection 2, 6–8, 11, 28, 90, 97, 100, 104, 123, 124, 126, 153, 158, 159, 163, 164, 189, 197, 198, 206, 210
consent 37, 39
construction: co-construction 27, 73, 103, 125, 172; of identity 26, 129, 210; of knowledge 138, 153; materials 45; of meaning 3, 192, 212; play 3; 3D 12; of self 22, 175; social construction 164, 192; toys 72, 95
constructivist 22, 25
content 3, 9, 14, 15, 19, 21, 24, 29, 30, 32, 34, 40, 48, 52, 55, 56, 68, 74, 76, 77, 80, 84, 90, 105, 107, 110, 115–27, 148, 175, 177–183, 187, 189; inventory of 40–43, 55, 84, 107, 126, 127
contextualised meaning/making 18, 19, 25, 30, 81, 172
control 20, 28, 33, 45, 64, 84, 133, 164, 165, 171, 173, 175, 207, 211, 214
conversations 2, 17, 24, 25, 27, 29, 32, 35, 39, 40, 71, 102, 151, 174, 175, 183, 184, 187, 189, 197, 211, 212
cooking 140, 145, 195
copying 23, 77, 80, 174, 178–190
creatures 42, 84, 87, 88, 106, 113, 127, 148, 150, 171
culture 7, 12–23, 29, 35, 43, 93, 101, 109, 110, 119, 126, 169, 191, 197, 199; popular 7, 21, 23, 29, 110, 119, 167–172, 191, 196, 204, 206
cultural capital 7, 133
curriculum 17, 207, 212
cutting 3, 11, 16, 41, 52–54, 74, 82, 97, 104, 134, 135, 169, 170, 178

data 32–48, 72–76, 95–98, 116–119, 125, 126, 203, 217
Data Cross-grid 41–43, 46–48, 72–76, 95–98, 116–119, 125, 203

death 28, 51, 52, 77, 174
definition: of drawing 3, 20, 117
denotation 41, 50, 62, 68, 104, 125, 152
description 3, 20, 41, 43, 50, 86, 105, 106, 120, 132, 151, 170, 187, 199
development: children's 5, 7, 12, 25, 90, 126, 203, 212, 213; in drawings 18, 19, 27, 30, 106, 168, 187; professional 210.
developmental stage theories 18, 19, 30, 192
dialogue 4, 25, 32, 64, 103, 120, 175, 177, 207
difference 19, 34, 46, 184, 187
digital 7, 12, 21, 29, 35, 36, 40, 42, 127, 191
discussion 17, 27, 32, 80, 101, 104, 183
Disney 29, 95, 204
dramatic play 27, 34, 119–126
drawer identities 117–154
drawer patterns 25, 115–126
drawing-conversations 2, 17, 24–29, 32, 35, 39, 40, 71, 102, 151, 174, 175, 183, 184, 187, 192, 211, 212
drawing-narrations 6, 27, 32, 121, 124

education 17, 20, 192; early childhood 24, 187, 207, 210, 212, 213; settings 27, 29, 206; systems 12; professionals 2, 8, 210, 212
educators 2, 7, 17, 29, 43, 206, 207, 210–213
emotion 2–6, 16, 21, 22, 28, 56, 61, 76, 86, 136, 148, 155–159, 162–164, 173, 175, 209, 212, 215
emotional self 129, 135
encouragement 26, 95, 121, 175, 212
engagement 7, 10, 37, 175, 211
environment 6, 14, 15, 28, 42, 71, 95, 117, 191, 197, 207, 211
ethics 23, 28, 31, 37, 39, 43, 54, 120, 155, 165, 178
events 6, 7, 14, 21, 26–28, 32, 48, 68, 69, 82, 84, 88, 111, 119, 124, 131, 132, 165, 178, 196, 215
everyday 6, 13, 15, 28, 29, 32, 42, 76, 92, 111, 127, 153, 154, 159, 206, 209
evil 28, 34, 54, 86, 134, 155–173
experimentation 15, 20, 23, 34, 47, 52, 68, 74, 81, 97, 98, 104, 106, 110, 117–119, 124, 172, 178, 179, 185, 189

## Index of subjects

expression 2, 3, 5, 10, 12, 15, 22, 72, 98, 156, 164, 177, 187, 210, 213, 214
extraordinary 3, 21, 114, 212

facilitation 17, 27, 32, 33, 175, 207
family brother 44, 52, 54, 56, 61–65, 131, 132, 136, 143, 163–165, 170, 171, 192; father/daddy 34, 37, 45, 48, 50, 56, 71, 77, 80, 82–84, 87, 90, 92, 93, 95, 98, 100, 111, 113, 131, 134–136, 140–159, 163, 177, 192–196; grandparents 71, 77, 84, 87, 92, 93, 98, 102, 103, 111, 145, 146, 150, 159, 161, 192; mother/mummy 17, 34, 37, 45–47, 52, 54–56, 60–63, 68–72, 77, 81–83, 86, 90–97, 101–105, 111, 124, 131, 134, 136, 138–145, 151–153, 158–160, 163, 165, 169, 176, 177, 193, 195–198, 203; parents 2, 17, 28, 34–39, 43, 45, 55, 56, 58, 65, 66, 79, 83, 86, 119, 130, 136, 146, 158, 175, 184, 186, 190–192, 195; siblings 38, 43, 45, 61, 71, 94; sisters 70, 71, 81–83, 92–95, 101, 104, 111, 131, 145, 194, 196, 203
fantasy 21, 26, 27, 29, 42, 48, 50, 52, 54, 56, 64, 69, 84, 90, 101, 107, 113, 114, 120, 124, 126, 127, 129, 131, 132, 134, 135, 165, 168, 169, 171, 173, 184, 193, 209
favourite 34, 72, 81, 92, 95, 109, 111, 195, 206
fear(s) 4, 52, 76, 84, 137–140, 164, 165, 171, 214
feelings 28, 32, 61, 64, 77, 84–87, 93, 131–137, 155, 158, 159, 163–165, 173, 196, 211, 215
fiction 21, 26, 27, 34, 54, 104, 106, 119, 120, 154, 165, 168, 171, 173, 177, 199, 206, 214
fighting 27, 34, 42, 54, 56, 60, 61, 64, 132, 134, 165, 168, 169, 171–173, 193, 194
film 15, 29, 34–39, 45, 68, 69, 71, 93, 114, 170, 178, 187, 190, 204, 214
*Film director* 214
fire 100, 127, 137; gun 42, 45, 50, 52, 64, 98, 100, 132, 168, 169, 171, 172, 193, 197
*Fireman Sam* 34, 95, 110, 114, 204

fireworks 94, 98, 100, 104, 124, 148, 196, 197
fish 71, 82, 84, 87, 88, 113, 139, 148, 150, 192; fishing: 82, 113, 192
flowers 34, 42, 76, 127, 156, 157, 163
fluidity 22–24, 50, 175–177
food 13, 42, 54, 55, 72, 86, 111, 127, 150, 179, 181, 194–199
*form* 9, 24, 26, 30, 32, 40, 41, 48, 50, 76, 81, 82, 97, 115–127, 169, 178, 179, 181, 184, 185, 187, 189
free drawing 2, 27, 29, 30, 206, 207
freedom 20, 29, 36, 72
friends/friendship 2, 6, 23, 25, 28, 30, 33, 34, 37, 42, 45, 56, 64, 66, 72, 86, 88, 90, 94, 103, 107, 127, 136, 142, 145, 158, 163, 165, 178–184, 186, 189
fun/funny 68, 71, 72, 193
*Funds of Knowledge* 5–8, 14, 17, 28, 40, 80, 100, 114, 117, 124, 126, 148, 191–207, 209, 212

games 7, 71, 72; digital 7, 12, 21, 29, 35, 36, 40, 42, 127, 191
geo: contexts 6;-cultural 105, 196, 197, 199, 206;-graphical 126
gesture/gesticulation 5, 10–12, 15, 22, 23, 27, 48, 98, 121, 164, 182, 214
gifts 145, 195, 203
glue/glueing 3, 11, 41, 47–55, 77, 80–83, 97, 104, 106, 110, 117, 120, 178, 179, 181, 182, 185, 187, 203, 211
good 28, 37, 45, 54, 64, 120, 134, 155–173
*good-guys* 28, 120, 165, 167, 169

happy/happiness 52, 68, 72, 76, 86, 140, 141, 145, 146
heritage 29, 105, 193, 197, 199
heroes 21, 34, 165, 173, 207
hierarchies: of relationships 26, 56, 92, 121; social 54
historical 14, 21, 29
home 2, 6, 7, 10, 15, 20, 28–30, 33–40, 45–48, 56, 62, 66, 69, 71–73, 76, 77, 86, 88, 90, 92, 94–96, 98, 101, 104, 109, 111, 113, 117, 119, 121, 122, 124, 138, 140, 145, 148, 158, 159, 162, 178, 179, 187, 192, 193, 195, 197, 198, 200, 203, 206, 209–211, 213
home visits 35, 36

## Index of subjects

house/household 7, 11, 21, 42, 44, 45, 71, 87, 92, 95, 121, 122, 127, 145, 150, 156, 158, 192, 203
human/humanity 12–15, 19, 28, 90, 132, 173, 207
humour 34, 71, 176, 177
"Hundred languages of children" 2, 212
hypotheses: children's 148, 154

identify/identifying 4, 23, 39, 46, 71, 92, 214
identities/ identity 2, 7, 20, 26, 27, 31, 52, 90, 92, 117–119, 125, 128–154, 173, 209–212, 215
imagination 2, 3, 5, 6, 8, 15, 22, 27, 28, 80, 90, 98, 101, 104, 111, 148, 170, 171, 177, 178, 182, 194, 197, 214
inclusion/inclusive 33–35, 169, 212
individual/individuality 6, 7, 12–17, 20, 25–27, 29, 34, 38, 126, 129, 175, 197, 206, 207, 210, 212, 214
influence/influential 2, 5, 6, 9, 11, 13–19, 21, 24, 27–30, 34, 40, 43, 54, 74, 80, 83, 88, 90, 93, 95, 97, 100, 106, 113, 117, 119, 126, 140, 162, 164, 165, 183–185, 187, 189, 191–193, 196–200, 203–206, 212, 219
informal 35, 174, 175
initial training 192
integrity 26, 54
interaction 2–4, 6, 8, 10, 13–15, 22, 25–29, 45, 68, 79, 95, 118, 167, 174, 175, 182–193, 211, 213
*interconnections* 6, 11, 28
interests: children's 2, 4, 11–14, 21–23, 25, 26, 34, 38, 39, 69, 76, 80, 105, 118, 175, 182, 187, 189, 200, 206, 207, 210, 212, 213; family 84, 100, 196
interpretation 3, 5, 7, 12–23, 32, 33, 36, 40, 43, 106, 126, 128, 129, 164, 175, 182, 187, 189, 197, 198, 213–215
intent/intentions 5, 6, 16–20, 23, 25–28, 68, 74, 80, 82, 102, 103, 106, 118, 128, 154, 171, 174–176, 184, 209
interpret/interpretation 3, 5–23, 32, 34, 36, 37, 39, 40, 43, 73, 84, 90, 96, 97, 112, 113, 116, 117, 126, 148, 158, 161, 164, 166, 167, 169, 170, 178–180, 184, 193–195

interrupt/interruption 32, 168, 193, 212
invention 3, 80, 123, 148, 153
*Inventory of content* 40, 42, 43, 55, 84, 107, 126, 127
*Iron Man* 34, 45, 52, 169, 171

joke 25, 45, 71, 184

kill/killing 52, 54, 64, 84, 86, 93, 100, 120, 134, 135, 137, 165–167, 169, 171–173
kinaesthetic 74, 103, 117, 119
kindergarten 2, 8, 31, 33–37, 43, 45, 72, 94, 95, 117

language: communication 4, 5, 12, 13, 17, 19, 22, 192, 212; home 7, 33, 35; spoken language(s) 33, 196; visual 3, 9, 19, 20
laptop/computer 34, 94, 95
layer(s): of meaning 3, 5, 9, 14, 16, 128, 170, 215; in drawing 76, 77
leadership 210, 212
life 19, 21, 28, 29, 48, 54, 76, 92, 98, 104, 114, 120, 121, 124, 131, 140, 153, 162, 165, 172, 176, 191–194, 198, 200;-cycle 148; experiences 14, 15, 77; sea-150, 151
listen/listening 6, 17, 24, 31, 32, 38, 42, 135, 137, 175, 177, 182, 208–215
literacy 8, 12, 17, 213; visual 5
love 34, 45, 56, 61, 68, 71, 72, 76, 87, 92, 93, 95, 105, 111, 117, 148, 155–165, 173, 181, 183, 194, 198, 203
Luke's story 44–69

Malta/ Maltese 2, 8, 31, 33, 43, 45, 71, 82, 98, 100, 152, 159, 163, 195–203, 213
manipulate/manipulation 16, 22, 27, 29, 45, 82, 118, 119, 148, 171
map/maps/mapping 200, 203
material/materiality 4, 10, 12, 15, 16, 20, 21, 25, 30, 33–36, 45, 47, 48, 54, 68, 71–74, 77, 81, 82, 96, 97, 106, 110, 117–119, 172, 178, 183, 185, 187, 189, 211, 213–215
*meaning-makers* 5, 15, 16, 187, 208
media 3, 11, 12, 15, 54, 104, 162, 175, 189, 194, 206; choice of 16, 17, 33–35, 47, 48, 52, 76, 77,

Index of subjects   245

96–98, 117–119, 185; combination of 29, 41, 74, 106, 178, 179, 181; digital-12, 29; popular-100, 109, 120; social-7
mediation/mediating 6, 25, 129, 175
metaphor 2, 10, 15, 24, 55, 66, 68, 86, 143, 169, 171
modal functioning 118, 119
mode/s 2–6, 9–23, 26, 29, 36, 40, 41, 46–54, 68, 72–83, 95–106, 115–119, 124, 125, 133, 159, 174, 178, 179, 181, 182, 185, 187, 189, 197, 209–213
monster/s 42, 76, 84, 86, 93, 121, 134, 137–139, 148, 149, 165, 172, 193
moral/morality 24, 26, 28, 39, 43, 54, 120, 155, 165, 215
movement 10–12, 15, 20, 27, 48, 103, 106, 132, 194, 200, 213–215
multimodal/ity 3–5, 9–17, 25, 28, 74, 81, 97, 104, 117, 129, 189, 207, 211, 213
music 28, 198, 199, 214
myth/mythical 21, 52, 69, 119, 120, 165, 168, 171, 177, 193

names 8, 31, 38, 42, 43, 127
narration 6, 11, 20, 27, 32, 50, 51, 74, 76, 77, 90, 101, 106, 120, 121, 124, 168, 182, 187, 214
narratives 2, 4, 5, 10, 11, 16, 17, 19, 21–24, 26, 27, 39, 41, 50, 52, 54, 64, 76, 77, 90, 100–106, 114, 119–125, 128, 131, 152, 165, 168, 175–190, 193, 197, 206, 209–215
nature 34, 71
negotiated 92, 106, 182, 187
night 60, 68, 71, 104, 105, 138, 159
novelist 214

object-centred 121
observation 2, 6, 35, 36, 39, 40, 97, 102, 104, 119, 124, 125, 192
opportunities 2, 6, 7, 33, 47, 118, 174, 177
ordinary 3, 16, 21, 28, 114, 159, 176, 193, 212
outdoors 34, 66, 79
ownership 32, 38, 132, 133

Pablo Picasso 19, 21
painting 2, 19, 71
participation 6, 33, 37, 200, 206
pedagogy 29, 192, 206, 207, 212, 213

peers 13, 24, 27, 28, 30, 45–47, 50, 54, 66, 68, 69, 72, 74, 76, 82, 94, 97, 101, 106, 117, 119, 175, 178, 179, 182, 185, 187, 189, 207
people 4, 6–8, 12–14, 21, 24, 26, 27, 29, 38, 42, 55–57, 68, 76, 81, 83, 84, 90, 91, 93, 94, 98, 103–108, 111, 119, 121, 124, 126, 127, 131, 137, 139, 148, 150, 158, 184, 187, 188, 191, 195, 198, 200
perception 4, 19–22, 25, 93, 131, 132, 165, 214
*perezhivanie* 5, 6, 8, 13, 14
performer 28, 121, 214, 215
person-centred 26, 56, 119, 121, 124, 125, 210
personal 7, 13–19, 21, 23, 26–29, 32, 35–39, 45, 50, 77, 80, 82, 92, 100, 106, 117–119, 121, 155, 164, 165, 178, 185, 187, 189, 197, 206, 210, 213–215
perspectives: children's 4, 21, 25, 32, 33, 129, 175, 206, 207, 214; cultural 14; individual 12; theoretical 3, 19, 30
photographs 29, 37–39, 45, 182
pink 42, 62, 63, 76, 88, 121, 127, 131, 136, 137, 145, 152, 159, 162, 169, 171, 203
*Pink Panther* 34, 95, 103, 107, 109, 204, 205
*Pinocchio* 95, 107, 109, 204, 205
pixilation 38, 39
place/s 7, 13, 16, 20, 21, 26, 34, 72, 90, 101, 109, 126, 132, 192, 198, 200
plan/ planning 16, 20, 21, 27, 56, 74, 102, 121, 175–177, 195, 207, 212
play 2, 4, 5, 7, 12, 16, 19–27, 34, 37, 41, 42, 45, 46, 48, 50–63, 66, 71, 72, 74, 77, 80, 86, 90, 94, 95, 100, 102, 103, 111, 118, 121, 123, 126, 127, 139, 140, 142, 145, 152, 155, 159, 165, 168–173, 175–177, 181–185, 187, 193, 199, 203, 210
pleasure 74, 119, 194
plot 27, 40–42, 46, 72, 95, 116, 119–121, 168, 177
policy 210, 212, 213
*portal* 6, 22, 208, 209, 214
possibility 50, 80, 140, 153, 176
potential 5, 11, 17, 38, 39, 82, 118, 148, 213
power 22, 26, 28, 32, 34–36, 45, 50, 52, 54, 56, 69, 80, 120, 132, 134,

136, 137, 155–175, 183, 184, 206, 210, 213
preference 30, 36, 37, 40, 74, 96, 116–119, 124, 126, 177
pretend 26, 52, 93, 120, 139, 182
product 3, 4, 17–19, 26, 80, 119, 177, 184, 191, 211, 214
prop 12, 19, 27, 103, 169, 214
protection 20, 37, 52, 87, 164, 165
pseudonyms 38, 43

questions 21, 27, 29, 32, 38, 140, 174

rain 66, 69, 90, 111, 127, 140, 151, 152, 181, 194, 196, 199–201, 203, 212
rainbow 42, 66, 69, 127, 140
re-configuration 22, 40, 48, 115, 116, 119, 125, 187
re-imagination 90
reading 11, 12, 14, 15, 29, 55, 68, 80, 182, 211
reality 5, 24, 26, 30, 69, 77, 101, 124, 165, 171, 177, 199, 210
relationships 3, 6, 7, 14, 19, 23–26, 29, 33, 35, 56, 92, 93, 119, 164, 191, 192, 210, 221
religion 33, 196, 197; Catholicism 197; church 42, 70, 127, 196, 197, 202, 203; niches 197; saints 197; shrines 197, statues 196, 197
remarkable 2, 16, 96, 209
repetition 6, 20, 36, 56, 63, 64, 72, 74, 177
replication 23, 31, 35, 176
representation 3–5, 8, 10, 11, 14, 16, 17, 19, 25–29, 33, 38, 39, 48, 86, 102, 116, 117, 132, 170, 187, 203, 213, 214
research 31–43
resources: full, 5, 7, 10, 13, 15–17, 26, 47, 50, 54, 71, 72, 74, 81–83, 97, 106, 117–119, 179, 187, 189, 207, 211
respect: two, 7, 25, 32, 33, 36–39, 45, 72, 81, 207, 209, 212, 214
roles 8, 28, 64, 90, 124, 129, 132–135, 171, 176, 177
routines 7, 28–30, 45, 191, 192

school 2, 6–8, 10, 15, 17, 21, 28–40, 44–50, 56, 61, 66, 68–73, 76, 77, 82, 84, 86, 88, 90, 94–98, 101, 104, 106, 110, 118, 121, 124, 136,-140,

165, 166, 169, 185, 187, 189, 195, 197, 203, 207, 213
scribble 18, 19, 95, 140, 148
scriptwriter 28, 121, 215
sea 82, 88, 104–106, 113, 127, 139, 148, 150, 151, 156, 157, 176, 177, 182, 187, 188, 192, 199
self 3, 6, 22, 24, 26, 42, 45, 52, 56, 64, 72, 80, 87, 90–95, 102, 106–111, 120, 121, 127, 129, 131–148, 158, 159, 162, 164, 165, 169, 171, 172, 175–177, 182, 184, 196, 203, 210, 214;-esteem 95, 148;-perception 93, 132, 165;-portrait 56, 64, 90, 106, 107, 109, 110;-starter. 26, 121;-reflexivity 16
set designer 214
sharks 76, 113, 137, 139, 150, 192
*sign-makers* 5, 10, 13–16
*sign-readers* 13, 14
signs 4, 5, 9–17, 28, 37, 74, 80, 182, 184, 187, 209
signify 6, 40, 50, 52, 55, 68, 118, 152, 173, 179, 185, 187, 214
silence 32, 95, 98, 121, 124, 175, 176, 185, 187
*Simple-complex modes* 40, 41, 46–52, 73–75, 95, 97, 99, 115–119, 125
*Simple-complex themes* 40–43, 46–50, 52, 54, 72–80, 82, 95–101, 106, 115, 116, 118, 119, 121, 124–127
size 56, 132, 150, 164, 199
skills: speaking 7, 12, 17, 25, 29, 30, 82, 95, 97, 117, 170, 179, 181, 185, 189
sky 42, 55, 66–68, 81, 98, 100, 105, 121, 126, 127, 140, 148, 151, 156–159, 176, 178, 179, 184, 187–191, 215
snails 76, 84, 145, 199
social: conventions 100, 197; drawers 27; justice 186; practice 19, 101, 212; relationships 7, 24, 191; semiotics 3–17, 189; talk 24, 181
socio-cultural 2, 5–9, 13, 14, 21, 23, 28–30, 34, 43, 100, 104, 114, 126, 129, 191, 192, 195, 197, 206, 207
*Sonic the Hedgehog* 80, 183, 184
spontaneity 3, 16, 25, 84, 100, 102, 121, 128, 177, 207, 210
stars 42, 66, 68, 105, 127, 159, 178
sticking 4, 97
stories/storytelling 4, 12, 15, 25–28, 33, 45, 76, 109, 114, 115, 118–121,

124, 126, 139, 140, 165, 168, 169, 175, 211, 214, 215
strong/strength 34, 45, 50, 52, 54, 62, 71, 82, 86, 88, 93, 120, 132, 134, 139, 150, 164, 165, 169, 171, 182, 196, 200, 207, 211
structural engineer 123, 207, 214
*subject matter generalist* 26, 121, 124, 125
sun 42, 66, 68, 69, 76, 77, 105, 127, 131, 140–142, 148, 151, 152, 157, 181, 196, 200
superheroes 21, 173, 207
superpowers 29, 34, 52, 54, 169, 170, 184
symbolism/symbols 4, 13–15, 19–22, 26, 42, 43, 54, 124, 127–129, 140, 156, 158, 163, 172, 187, 198, 200, 213

talk 2–5, 12, 20, 22–28, 32–36, 42, 43, 72, 74, 77, 86, 88, 94, 98, 100–104, 109, 117, 124, 136–139, 143, 174–190, 196, 198, 209–211, 213
teacher/s 8, 28–30, 43, 45, 71, 72, 94, 95, 137, 212, 213
technique 20, 23, 30, 52, 97, 104, 105, 182, 185, 187
television/TV 15, 21, 29, 34, 45, 55, 71, 72, 82, 84, 93–95, 107, 110, 150, 169, 173, 178, 192, 206
Thea's story 70–93
Theme/s 21, 29, 40–55, 68, 72–85, 90, 91, 95–101, 104–108, 113–121, 124–127, 155, 162, 164–169, 173, 187, 198, 203, 206, 209, 211, 214
theoretical principles 3, 5, 6, 8, 11, 192
theories 5–8, 18, 19, 22, 30, 154, 215
thinking 2–8, 11, 15, 16, 19, 22–25, 32, 39, 64, 80, 81, 83, 100, 102, 106, 110, 120, 129, 131, 139, 140, 148, 152–155, 163, 164, 208, 210, 213
transformation 11, 12, 20, 22, 23, 26, 52, 165, 175, 208
transitions 68, 82, 179
transport: aeroplane 9, 16, 42, 54, 71, 72, 76–78, 82–84, 92, 93, 104, 119, 123, 127, 132, 133, 145, 148, 152, 153, 179, 181–183, 189, 196, 199, 215; boats 42, 82, 90, 127, 145, 183, 192, 196, 199; bus 72, 197; car 12, 20, 42, 45, 76–78, 80, 127, 132, 133, 145, 148, 152, 155, 156, 167, 182–184, 189, 195, 196; ferry 200; motorcycles 45, 63, 145, 184; ship 42, 82, 127, 133, 134, 153, 182, 199, 200; train 42, 100–104, 114, 127
travelling 77, 78, 82, 83, 132, 145, 152, 182, 199, 200
trust 32, 35, 94, 209, 212
types: of drawing 115, 119, 124–126; of drawer 214, 215

unpredictability 22, 104, 124, 128

value(s) 2, 4, 6–8, 12, 13, 16–19, 21, 24, 25, 29, 32, 38, 72, 103, 120, 162, 169, 175, 185, 191, 193, 196, 207, 209, 211–213
variety 10, 33, 41, 77, 82, 97, 117, 118, 126, 132, 176, 189
visual: forms 50;-graphic 22; language 3, 4, 9, 20; literacy 5; media. 29; methods 39; modes 10; narrative 24, 27, 41; realism 19; representation 25, 213; meaning-making 27
*visualisers* 26, 121
vocalisation 5, 10, 15, 22, 23, 26, 98, 103, 121, 171, 213, 214
voice 2, 4, 25, 32, 33, 36, 38, 39, 42, 95, 129, 136, 159, 171, 174–177, 210, 213, 215

warfare 42, 127, 169
weapons 134, 167, 169, 171, 173
weather 34, 42, 55, 66–68, 98, 124, 126, 127, 140, 148, 151, 152, 195, 200
wind 77, 151, 152, 159, 176, 181, 194, 200, 201
wishes 2, 21, 29, 32, 37, 38, 76, 98, 142–148, 175
witches 72, 76, 121, 137–139, 206
writing 2, 3, 5, 10–12, 20, 29, 41, 42, 74, 77, 117, 127, 133, 137, 183

For Product Safety Concerns and Information please contact our EU representative GPSR@taylorandfrancis.com
Taylor & Francis Verlag GmbH, Kaufingerstraße 24, 80331 München, Germany

www.ingramcontent.com/pod-product-compliance
Lightning Source LLC
Chambersburg PA
CBHW071406300426
44114CB00016B/2200